DUEL

DUEL

A TRUE STORY OF
DEATH AND HONOUR

James Landale

CANONGATE

Edinburgh · New York · Melbourne

First published in Great Britain in 2005 by Canongate Books Ltd,
14 High Street, Edinburgh, EH1 1TE

1

Copyright © James Landale, 2005

The moral right of the author has been asserted

British Library Cataloguing-in-Publication Data
A catalogue record for this book is available on
request from the British Library

ISBN 1 84195 647 3

Typeset in Bembo by Palimpsest Book Production Limited,
Polmont, Stirlingshire
Printed and bound in Great Britain by Creative Print and Design,
Ebbw Vale, Wales

www.canongate.net

For my mother and father

Contents

Preface

This is the true story of a pistol duel, one that I have lived with for many years. When I first heard of David Landale and his quarrel with George Morgan, a tale that was handed down the family, generation to generation, the only proof was a thin scrap of paper, an all too brief transcription of an old newspaper article that begged as many questions as it answered. This book represents the fruits of more than a decade's labour to answer some of those questions, an intermittent treasure hunt that has led me from archive to library, from Scotland to the Lake District, in search of the truth. I visited the scene of the encounter, a lonely field where the local history society has marked the spot with a small cairn and plaque. I discovered, in a corner of Kirkcaldy's small museum, the pistols that my ancestral relative had used in the duel. And I dug out a sheaf of yellowing newspaper reports from the British Library that gave me a contemporary insight into the events of August 1826. The more I learned, the more I became obsessed. Yet, but for the discovery of one particular manuscript, this book would have been impossible to write. One of the lawyers involved in the trial that took place after the duel copied all the evidence for his records. For years this manuscript languished untouched in a library in Edinburgh. Yet now, unearthed and transcribed from the copperplate, this pot of historical gold dust has provided me with more than forty thousand words of first hand evidence from almost thirty witnesses describing the events surrounding what became the last recorded fatal duel in Scotland. For this, above all, is a true story. Some spellings and punctuation have been changed for clarity, and occasionally I have replaced a name with a pronoun and vice versa for easier comprehension. But I have resisted the temptation of invention and have relied entirely on the evidence available. I have not put thoughts in peoples' minds without having good documentary reason for doing so. And where there have been gaps in the story, irritating, untidy lacunae, I have left them there as shadows of ignorance.

The book also tells the story of duelling itself, how this combat emerged from the bloody affrays of the Middle Ages, how it flourished in Europe for more than 300 years, fuelled by a concept of honour we would not recognise today, and how it declined and died out at the end of the nineteenth century and the beginning of the next. It explains why men fought not only to resolve disputes but also for more subtle reasons: to demonstrate courage, to avoid shame, to emulate aristo-cracy, to enter manhood, to restore reputation and to avenge a wrong. Here, in the retelling of many duels, I have been forced to rely on many more secondary sources and that, in this most awkward of historical backwaters, can be problematic. Those who witnessed a duel tended, by definition, to be partial and it is rare when an account does not contain an inconsistency. Those who wrote about duelling tended to be just as biased either in favour or against the practice. On most occasions, I have simply omitted any detail that seemed tendentious. Where necessary, I have chosen the most plausible version of events, based on my own reading of hundreds upon hundreds of duelling stories.

This book is not, however, a celebration of duelling, nor a call to arms. What it instead seeks to do is to explain why two rational, educated men in the early nineteenth century might try to resolve a dispute by shooting at one another, and in doing so, to shed light on why duelling still grips our collective imagination. For the sporting commentator, the duel is a cliché that never strays too far from the microphone. It is a stock in trade, still, for the romantic novelist seeking to enliven a dull plot. It is the basis for many a computer game between hero and villain. And for the academic community, the duel has become the latest human activity to succumb to the scrutiny of game theory. Across the world the legacy of duelling lives on. The Queen still has an official champion, whose job, in theory at least, is to challenge anyone who disputes the right and title of the sovereign, a role that has belonged to one family, the Dymokes of Scrivelsby in Lincolnshire, since the fourteenth century. The current incumbent, Lt Col John Dymoke, who is seventy-eight, has held the office since 1946 and carried the Union Standard at the Queen's coronation. He has yet, however, to fight on Her Majesty's behalf. On the other side of the Atlantic, in the American state of Kentucky where duelling was once rife, every public official is still obliged every year to swear thus: 'I, being a citizen of this state, have not fought a duel with deadly weapons within this State, nor out of it, nor have I sent or accepted a challenge to fight a duel with deadly weapons, nor have I acted as second in carrying a challenge, nor aided or assisted any person thus offending, so help me God.'

For a very small minority, however, the duel is not an anachronistic oddity from history or a metaphor for competitive activity. It is a reality, a genuine method of conflict resolution in the twenty-first century. On the evening of March 8 2004, two elderly Mexican farmers shot each other dead in a duel over disputed water rights. Manuel and Candelario Orozco – cousins, brothers-in-law and neighbours – had argued for more than half a century over who should have access to a spring that lay on the border of their farms near Pihuamo in western Mexico. In the end, Manuel, aged seventy, and Candelario, eighty-five, decided their argument could be resolved only by a pistol duel. As dusk was falling, they walked to the centre of a field, faced each other four metres apart, and fired simultaneously. Jose Ramirez, a spokesman for the local state prosecutor's office, said that relatives had tried to prevent the duel and resolve the cousins' differences. 'But as you know,' he said, 'older people are a bit more stubborn and obstinate and they never reached an agreement.' Two years earlier and a few thousand miles to the south, the vice president of Peru, David Waisman, was challenged to a pistol duel by a congressman in a row over what role their country's first lady should play in politics. Eittel Ramos, then fifty-four years old, called Waisman out to the Conchan Sands near Lima and appointed a doctor as his second. But the sixty-five-year-old vice-president dismissed the challenge. 'We are living in the twenty-first century in a civilised world where peoples' differences are resolved according to the rule of law,' he said. 'Duelling is not a legal option.' In the same month, September 2002, on the other side of the world, an historian called Tom Reilly was challenged to a duel for suggesting that Oliver Cromwell killed fewer people than previously thought when he attacked the town of Drogheda on the east coast of Ireland in 1649. Councillor Frank Godfrey, the former mayor of Drogheda, insisted that some 2,000 women and children had been put to the sword and declared: 'I'm challenging [Reilly] to a duel for the honour of my town and the dead that Cromwell slaughtered.' Not surprisingly, Reilly demurred. A month later, Taha Yassin Ramadan, the then vice president of Iraq, proposed that President George W Bush and Saddam Hussein should resolve their differences in a duel *mano a mano*. President Bush declined and invaded instead. Peasants and politicians of doubtful sanity notwithstanding, the idea of risking life for honour is, for some, not as antediluvian as perhaps it might seem.

'Guy, what would you do if you were challenged to a duel?'

'Laugh.'

'Yes, of course.'

'What made you think of that now?'

'I was thinking about honour. It is a thing that changes, doesn't it? I mean, a hundred and fifty years ago we would have had to fight if challenged. Now we'd laugh. There must have been a time a hundred years or so ago when it was rather an awkward question.'

Evelyn Waugh, *Officers and Gentlemen*, 1955

Prologue

The loom of dawn was still rising from the eastern horizon as the four men walked up the steep track through the plantation. Panting gently from the exertion, they did not speak or look at one another. Close to the top of the rise, they climbed a fence and stepped out of the wooded lane into a dank, soggy field, still not high enough to escape the mist seeping in from the North Sea. Two of the men halted and began to talk quietly. The other two walked on a few yards, separated and stood apart, staring intently at each other. After a few minutes, one looked back at the men who were talking and shouted 'no apology', his words echoing around the field. The men fell silent, exchanged a brief glance and began their work. A coin was tossed and acknowledged. One of the men laid a mark at his feet, took twelve carefully chosen paces, and laid another. He looked up and received a nod of agreement. Both men opened their carpet bags and withdrew two pistols. These were loaded, slowly and delib-erately, one at a time, each carefully watching the other's work. The weapons, cocked and ready, were handed to the two silent, staring companions. Thus armed, they took up their positions, twelve paces apart. Neither showed any sign of nerves, each convinced they had both right and honour on their side. In a brief and unexpected inter-lude, a fifth man, a doctor, burst on the scene from the trees and breathlessly demanded to know what was going on. There was a short and fruitless conversation after which the doctor hurriedly withdrew into the wood. The two armed men handed coats, scarves and time-pieces to their companions who themselves then backed away some ten yards or so. A pause, a final check and then a question: 'Gentlemen, are you ready?' Suddenly one of the gunmen raised his pistol, earlier than had been agreed. 'That is not fair, sir!' cried one of the witnesses. 'Drop your weapon until the word fire is given.' The gunman looked up, half surprised, half irritated, still holding his pistol in the direction of his adversary. Time skipped a beat. Then slowly, reluctantly, he lowered the weapon to his side. Another pause, an agonising, nerve-tingling pause. Again the question: 'Gentlemen, are you ready?' This time there was no mistake. 'Fire!' A single report echoed off the hills as both pistols discharged simultaneously. The smoke cleared slowly in the still air. One of the gunmen groaned in disbelief. His opponent's bullet had penetrated his ribcage, ripped through his lungs, and exited under his left armpit. He stood there for a moment as if brain and body refused to accept what had happened. Then blood began pouring from his mouth, he dropped his pistol, slumped to his right and was dead before he hit the ground. His uninjured opponent did not hesitate. He fled the field, a fugitive now from the law. But he was satisfied. For not only did he have his life, more importantly, he also had his honour.

1
The origin of the dispute

In the history of duelling we read the history of mankind in the developement of our evil passions, and the occasional display of some redeeming qualities. It is a reflective mirror stained with blood, and we must wipe off the clotted gore of ages to contemplate truth in all its bearings to feel what miserable creatures we are.

John Gideon Millingen, *The History of Duelling*, 1841

Coffee for two, champagne for one.

Anon., trad., cited in *The Duel*, 1965

In the early evening of July 18 in the year 1825, fifteen men gathered upstairs at the George Inn in Kirkcaldy, a small town on the south-eastern coast of Scotland. The mood was grim. From below, a cheery hubbub filtered through the floorboards as Helen McGlashan, the plain-speaking landlady, dispensed drinks and good nature in the bar. Widowed two years earlier, Mrs McGlashan had replaced her late husband at the pumps and kept the George as it was, the heart of Kirkcaldy life. It was from this solid, granite building on the High Street that the coaches departed for Edinburgh and Dundee; it was here that people met to drink, gossip, and conduct business. On

3

another day, the men sitting round the table in the assembly room upstairs might have met as friends, enjoying a drink as the cool sea breeze blew in through the windows off the Firth of Forth. But not that evening. They sat there, unsmiling, concerned, looking to each other for solace. For their business was linen, the oldest textile in the world and Kirkcaldy's lifeblood, a stream of vitality that was rapidly draining away and threatening ruin upon them all. These men had seen their trade grind slowly to a standstill, men like Alexander Balfour and James Aytoun, whose mills spun flax – the raw material for linen – into yarn; Robert Stocks, whose factory workers wove the yarn into cloth; William Millie and his brother Thomas, merchants who sold the linen on; and William and George Oliphant, whose ships carried the cloth overseas. Even George Millar was there, the mayor and tax collector who gloried in the title of 'Provost and Admiral of Kirkcaldy', an historical hangover from the days when Charles I had declared Kirkcaldy a royal burgh. These merchants filled Millar's official – and not so official – coffers and if they were not making money, he was not collecting it.

One man looked round the room with particular satisfaction. David Landale, a flax spinner, bleacher and linen merchant, had for some months been urging his fellow traders to organise, to act collectively against their common foe, and finally they were doing something about it. By the end of the evening, the men gathered at the George Inn agreed unanimously that a 'Chamber of Commerce and Manufactures be established on the most liberal basis by admitting as members all manufacturers of linen cloth, traders in those articles made use of in that manufacture, flax spinners, bleachers and shipowners, residing in Kirkcaldy and its district'. Its purpose was clear:

'To watch over every public measure whereby the trade or manufactures in which its Members are engaged may be affected, and to lend its weight and influence for procuring relief from any general grievance.' The chamber would also pursue 'any other object which may involve the general or particular interests of those branches of trade and manufactures, where the same can be conducted with more effect by the association than by individual exertion'. Useful public documents were to be procured such as relevant 'Acts of Parliament, Customhouse and Excise Regulations, Rules and Lists of dues leviable at all the principal Sea Ports in Great Britain, and also the Laws and Regulations established in the principal Shipping Ports of Foreign nations'. Each member would pay one guinea a year subscription. And that evening, they elected David Landale their first chairman, and his close friend, William Millie, his deputy.

The linen traders of Kirkcaldy were not alone in their concern. Few trades were left untouched by the slump of 1825. It was the latest in a long line of body blows levelled at the British economy which had been ailing for a decade, weakened by the festering wounds of war. In the ten years since Napoleon had been defeated at Waterloo, Britain had been racked by economic crises which threatened to bring to a premature end the benefits of an industrial revolution begun half a century before. The war against France between 1793 and 1815 had left the country broke. Britain had bankrolled the allied armies of Prussia, Russia and Austria against Bonaparte's invading forces. A depleted standing army had been turned into the largest in British history. Numerous domestic militia regiments – whose officers were so beloved of Jane Austen's heroines – had been established as a home guard to fight an invading French force. And a huge navy of almost 1,000 ships and more than 150,000 men had been maintained to blockade the French and avert invasion. The cost was ruinous. Income tax was imposed for the first time in 1799 to cover the debts; but it failed. By the time the war ended, the government owed more than £800 million and the Bank of England had suspended all cash payments.

Although they would not admit it, Kirkcaldy's linen traders had done well out of the war. Armies needed clothing and paid well for it. Some British linen even found its way onto the backs of French infantrymen. A linen merchant like David Landale who also owned a tanning business was doubly lucky; the British redcoat not only wore David's cloth, he marched on David's leather. Linen prices were high and demand constant, both at home and abroad. With the continent cut off from trade, demand for British textiles grew overseas, seas ruled largely by Britannia's dominant navy. But the peace of 1815 brought with it swift recession. The war had put half a million British men in arms, about a sixth of the adult male population. Many thousands of those who came home were left unemployed. Those lucky enough to find work were poorly paid by employers who used the luxury of so much cheap labour to cut wages. Prices rose rapidly, in particular the price of bread, already artificially supported by the Corn Laws, a set of trade barriers introduced in 1815 to protect Britain's weakened rural economy by blocking the import of cheap foreign grain. While farmers and their workers celebrated the new tariffs, few others joined them. David Landale knew that if his employees had to pay more for their daily loaf, he would have to pay them more to afford it.

The economic crisis threatening the Kirkcaldy linen manufacturers was exacerbated by political uncertainty. The

Tory-dominated government that won the war had been in power for most of the preceding three decades. It was exhausted by conflict and ill equipped to deal with the peace. This victorious administration – led by Lord Liverpool – was later described by Winston Churchill as 'supremely unfitted' to cope with the new difficulties of the post-war settlement. These were politicians who had spent their lives fighting to protect a *status quo* threatened by France and revolution. Now they faced bewildering new challenges of economic reconstruction, social change and, above all, political reform. Such problems, Churchill said, were 'beyond the power of these men to remedy or solve'. So, like many politicians, they retrenched and protected their power base. Against all sensible advice, Lord Liverpool abolished the income tax which had fallen hard on his party's wealthy landowning supporters. To compensate for the loss of this desperately needed revenue, he put up indirect taxes across the board. Food prices rose dramatically – the extra tax on beer was particularly unpopular – and social unrest grew. This was not the kind of government that David Landale or any of the other Kirkcaldy traders was looking for.

But if they had lost faith with Westminster, the Scottish merchants were equally unimpressed by the lack of leadership from the other side of St James' Park. Since 1811 George III had been incapacitated by the mental illness that had intermittently plagued his rule since 1760. His corpulent and unpopular son, the Prince of Wales, reigned as prince regent until 1820 when, on his father's death, he finally assumed the throne as George IV. While many Britons starved, George's extravagance knew few bounds. He spent thousands turning Buckingham House into a palace, and even more on his folly,

Brighton Pavilion. As king in 1824, he put 800 men to work for almost seven years turning Windsor Castle into a monument to Gothic glory. While people marvelled at George's architectural ambition – including the eponymous Regent's Park and Regent's Street – they resented its cost to the Exchequer. The Windsor Castle rebuilding alone cost £1 million in contemporary prices – about £60 million in today's money. The sheer scale of popular hostility to monarch and ministers at the time was captured by the radical poet Percy Shelley in his sonnet 'England in 1819'.

> *An old, mad, blind, despised and dying king –*
> *Princes, the dregs of their dull race, who flow*
> *Through public scorn . . .*
> *Rulers who neither see, nor feel, nor know,*
> *But leech-like to their fainting country cling, . . .*
> *A people starved and stabbed in the untilled field.*

This was a time of riots, torched hayricks and machine breaking in factories from Kirkcaldy to Cornwall; an era awake to the potential of popular rebellion only thirty-odd years after the French Revolution of 1789. The Luddite workers, fearing the march of change, had begun smashing their new machinery in 1812, well before the war was over. At the onset of peace, educated radicals outside parliament resumed their demands for political reform, joining workers in mass demonstrations and parliamentary petitions. The government, fearing revolution, responded firmly. *Habeas Corpus* was suspended in 1817, giving the authorities the power to hold indefinitely without trial anyone suspected of radical behaviour. Two years later a large crowd of some 60,000 people gathered at St Peter's Field in Manchester to protest at low wages and to demand parliamentary reform. Local magistrates panicked and sent in mounted yeomanry with sabres drawn (it would still be another ten years before Sir Robert Peel established his civilian police force). Eleven people were killed, 400 injured, most of them women and children, in what became known as the Peterloo Massacre, a deliberate echo of the slaughter of Waterloo. The government responded with a package of repressive legislation which taxed radical newspapers, banned large political meetings, gave new search powers to magistrates, toughened libel laws, and prohibited the training of civilian militias. Such was the fire in some radical bellies that in 1820 a few even plotted to assassinate the entire Tory cabinet and take over the Bank of England. In the end, the five leaders of the Cato Street Conspiracy – named after the London street where they met to hatch their plot – were betrayed, tried and executed.

A Kirkcaldy linen merchant like David Landale had nothing to do with such radicalism. To him, unrest meant uncertainty and that was bad for business. All he and his fellow merchants wanted was to survive the down-turn. In the early 1820s, things had got marginally better. The economy stabilised, the harvests were good, and the government allowed workers to form trade unions. Merchants borrowed huge sums to get into foreign export markets, and took on enormous debts to restart work on the massive infrastructure projects which had been put on hold during the war. New canals were cut, gas lights began to illuminate the streets of the emerging industrial towns, and a nascent railway network crept across the country. All this needed money and the Bank of England provided it, adopting a reckless, expansionary monetary policy with the government's blessing. Country banks, taking a lead from Threadneedle Street, followed suit and made risky loans.

Fuelled by all this investment, stock market speculation was rife and share prices rose. It was not to last. In 1825, the bubble burst and the British economy was plunged once more into crisis when the banking sector failed. Stock prices fell, businesses collapsed and, too late, the Bank of England tried to curb the money supply. Small banks saw many of their loans defaulting and looked to the Bank of England for help. It refused. As a result, there was a run on ninety-three banks in England and Wales which were forced to shut their doors to customers seeking to withdraw their cash. In the end, the Bank of England was saved only by securing a loan of gold from, of all institutions, the Banque de France. The Victorian historian David Bremner captured the mood of despair, describing the fate of Arbroath, another textile town just up the coast from Kirkcaldy: 'The manufactures of the place were all but unsaleable, money became scarce, credit failed, and almost the whole manufacturing community, adventurer and honourable merchant alike, were engulphed [*sic*] in one common ruin. Almost every mill and factory was silent, distress prevailed throughout the town, and it was some time before Arbroath became its former self again.' So when the fifteen founder members of the Kirkcaldy Chamber of Commerce met at the George Inn in the summer of 1825, they had not only endured a decade of political uncertainty and economic downturn, they had also just seen conditions get much, much worse. They were experiencing, in the words of their new chairman, David Landale, 'the total stagnation of trade'. And for many, the future seemed bleak.

★　★　★

In 1096, a Norman knight called Godefroy Baynard accused another, William, Count d'Eu, of treason. The count, Baynard declared, had conspired against the king. Not true, said the count. The monarch in question, William Rufus, was naturally curious. He had both noblemen brought to Salisbury to find out which was telling the truth. There, in a field, before both king and court, the knights fought a bloody single combat, man against man. In the end, it was the Count d'Eu who was defeated. The king gave orders that the wounded knight should have his balls cut off and his eyes poked out. The unfortunate count's squire, William of Aldor, was whipped and hanged. Thus ended England's first trial by combat, a judicial tradition imported from the continent by William Rufus's conquering father in 1066, and a cultural forefather of the modern European duel.

The idea that men could resolve their differences through a formal, ritualised, and witnessed trial by combat originated among the ancient Germanic peoples in the centuries after Christ. It was a favourite, in particular, among the pagans of Scandinavia who developed something called 'the girdle duel'. Two combatants would be taken to a lonely island, stripped of their clothing, strapped together at the chest, given a knife each and, on command, allowed to hack at each other in a bloody frenzy until one died or gave quarter. Over the years this and other forms of monomachia developed into trial by combat – also known as judicial combat or trial by battle – a procedure established formally for the first time in AD 501 by a King of Burgundy called Gundebald. He believed that since God determined the outcome of battles, He might as well also decide lesser disputes. So Gundebald pulled together the existing Celtic, Germanic and Roman traditions into one so-called *Lex Burgundiorum* under which personal disputes between two individuals could be resolved by public combat to the death, overseen by judges and witnesses. The theory was that God would protect the innocent and condemn the guilty. St Augustine wrote: 'During the combat, God awaits, the heavens open, and He defends the party who He sees is right.' For many defendants, it was a welcome alternative to the more customary trial by ordeal where their fate was decided by how effectively God chose to heal a hand burned by a hot poker or scalded by boiling water.

There were strict rules and ritual for a trial by combat. Combatants were often shaved and oiled in a ceremony of purification. They entered a fenced-off enclosure known as the lists, the accuser coming from the south, the defendant from the north. Judges, high officials and clerics watched from specially constructed seats, the public from whatever vantage point they could find. At the eleventh hour the combatants would be urged by the clerics to resolve their dispute peacefully. If they refused, they would swear on the Bible their innocence. In a sort of voluntary form of drug testing, they would also swear they had no amulets, potions or magic charms about their person. The challenger would throw down a glove or gauntlet which his opponent would pick up to show he accepted the challenge. Then they would fight, noble combatants on horseback with swords, commoners on foot with wooden staves; this providential justice was open to all sinners, high or low. The victor had every right to kill his opponent or, if he, the crowd or the authorities were in the mood, grant mercy. A favourite method of despatch was a sword plunged firmly through the helmet visor. An alternative was to take the defeated combatant outside the lists and hang him from a gibbet. The only other way of avoiding defeat was to fight on until the stars came out, at which point the accuser was deemed vindicated.

Any man who was accused or challenged was obliged to fight. The only exceptions were women, priests, the disabled, and men under sixteen or over sixty. They and others, however, could in theory use proxy champions – the original 'freelances' – to fight their battles instead. But neither came off well in defeat. If the champion lost, he would have his right hand chopped off. His defeated principal, meantime, would be hanged, having stood throughout the combat at a gallows round the corner with a noose already hung around his neck. The crowd control was equally tough. Any of the watching public who made a noise or interrupted proceedings risked imprisonment for a year and a day, or even worse, the loss of a hand or foot.

One of the weirdest trials by combat was also one of the last to take place. In 1400, a French knight called Chevalier Maquer killed his friend Aubrey de Montdidier and secretly buried the body. There were no witnesses save the dead man's dog, a large greyhound called Verbaux. But the clever hound guided one of his late master's friends to the burial spot and scratched at the ground to uncover the body. Suspicions arose when the dog repeatedly attacked Maquer. The king was petitioned and he ruled that God would decide if Maquer was guilty in a trial by combat with the dog. So, in the shadow of Notre Dame, the knight was buried half up to his waist and armed with a stick and a shield, a procedure used occasionally for rare combats between men and women. The dog did not hesitate: he clamped his teeth around Maquer's throat and the petrified knight, screaming for his life, promised to confess the moment the hound was taken from him. Maquer's neck, thus saved from the jaws of a dog, was later stretched by the noose of a gibbet.

After the victory of Godefroy Baynard, trial by combat slowly established itself in Norman Britain and soon became common practice both in civil and criminal actions. But by the end of the Middle Ages, the custom fell out of use as the authorities slowly came round to the view that evidence-based jury trials were better than God at determining a man's innocence or guilt. There was also a growing suspicion that Providence seemed always to be on the side of the more muscular or more skilful combatant. There were one or two attempts to revive the anachronism. In 1571, a man appealed for trial by combat to resolve a dispute over manorial rights but at the last moment Queen Elizabeth ordered the suit to be settled peaceably. In 1819 a man called Abraham Thornton claimed his right to trial by combat after being accused of murdering a young girl called Mary Ashford. The Court of Appeal ruled reluctantly that, under the law, Thornton did indeed still have such a right and because there was no one to fight on the girl's behalf, he was freed. Parliament quickly closed the loophole and on March 22 that year, trial by combat in Britain was no more.

If trial by combat was the forefather of the modern European duel, then the knightly duel was a close ancestral relative. This noble combat emerged from France during the age of chivalry, a mix of sport and duel that existed concurrently with trial by battle but outlived its judicial counterpart. Early tournaments were bloody free-for-alls where teams of knights and retainers engaged in mini-battles. In one such mêlée in 1240 as many as eighty knights died in one day. Gradually these team events were trimmed down into individual combats or jousts between independent knights. These combats were very much for knights and knights alone: no commoners could take part. All those who did fight had to prove their noble heritage back at least four generations. Sometimes the jousts were more like sporting contests, others were formal duels to the death. But both variations followed similar patterns: the jousts always took place in the lists; the weapons were lance and sword; the public were allowed to watch; judges decided if the rules had been kept; a maiden's honour was often at stake. The sporting jousts were also in practice frequently as lethal as proper duels. No one could describe two men riding at one another with lances at full tilt as a safe sport. Henry II of France died after receiving a lance to the head in a sporting tournament in 1559. Yet these jousts were more than sport. They were an opportunity for knights to become familiar with combat, for retainers to be infused with martial spirit, and for kings to judge the quality of troops they might one day have to lead into battle. But perhaps most importantly, the knightly joust was used to demonstrate a newly developing concept of chivalric honour. The idea of victory and defeat began to become less central. Instead, it became just as important for a knight to behave well and show courage in the face of danger regardless of the outcome. If both winner and loser fought well, they enhanced their honour. As well as the official jousts at the public tournaments, another variation of the knightly duel developed, known as the *pas d'armes*. Here the glory-seeking knight would let it be known that for a period of time he would 'hold' a particular piece of ground – such as natural passage or a bridge – and challenge all comers to get past him. This was what the eternally optimistic knight played by John Cleese in Monty Python's film, *The Holy Grail*, was trying to do when he stood on a bridge and told King Arthur that 'None shall pass' before his limbs were hacked away from him. This introduced for the first time the idea that such encounters should take place away from the public gaze; in other words, that knights could indulge in private duels to resolve disputes.

Although the knightly duel was first introduced into England in the twelfth century, it only became firmly established in the 1300s when Edward III gave it his seal of approval by setting up a court of chivalry and by challenging King Philippe of France to a duel. The French monarch rejected the idea and allowed Edward instead to defeat him at Crécy. But by the end of the fifteenth century, these noble duels had died out as the mounted knight gave way to the unmounted archer, or as the American historian, William Stevens, put it, as 'the whole bombastic farrago of chivalry faded out before the logic of gunpowder and the laughter of Cervantes'.

There is no unbroken link between trial by combat and knightly jousts and the modern European duel. The latter emerged during the sixteenth and seventeenth centuries – first in Italy and then France – as an alternative to the murderous 'killing affrays', vendettas and assassinations which then characterised disputes between noblemen and their bands of loyal retainers. But as the old aristocratic orders and feudal baronies were threatened by the growth of centralised states ruled by absolute monarchs, nobles were no longer allowed to maintain their private armies. In the face of this loss and to preserve their status as an elite, they insisted on keeping their right to resolve disputes among themselves, outside the law, in private and to the death. They considered it an expression of their freedom and self-determination against the prohibitive laws of the monarchical state. These noblemen looked back in history and began to adopt some of the traditions of judicial and knightly combat. Above all, they seized on the often illusory concept of chivalric honour and reinvented it for a new age. Thus the modern European duel was born.

This new idea of honour is what distinguished the duel from mere single combat. The latter was simply a trial of strength and ability between two people, often carried out on someone else's behalf. David fights Goliath to save the Israelites from the Philistines and win the hand of King Saul's pretty daughter; Achilles fights Hector to avenge the death of his friend, Patroclus; Obi Wan Kenobi fights Darth Vader to give his friends time to escape on the *Millennium Falcon*. In theory, one could call these combats duels: etymologically the word means nothing more than a war between two people, an elision of the Latin words 'duo' and 'bellum'. But in fact, none of these encounters is strictly a duel because none of the combatants is fighting to resolve a dispute in which personal honour is at stake. That was the key criterion that defined a duel in the modern European era. When a man fought a duel, he fought for no one but himself and his honour. Like the knights of old, the modern European duellist did not look for victory or defeat, but simply the chance to seek redress, establish honour and show courage in the face of danger. And to do that, he had developed a bloody ritual that followed strict codes of practice, a combat that was formal, personal, consensual, cold-blooded and a privilege of aristocracy. It was a modern twist on an ancient heritage that would shortly become all too familiar to a linen merchant from Kirkcaldy.

★   ★   ★

David Landale was born on November 27 1786, the scion of a prominent Kirkcaldy merchant family. His father, grandfather and great-grandfather – all sharing the name James Landale –

ran successful businesses tanning and selling leather; all three had owned ships; and all had served as magistrates and burgesses (councillors), instilling in David an equal sense of financial probity, civic responsibility and entrepreneurial verve. 'From his youth, Mr Landale possessed a great aptitude for business,' his obituary would later record, 'and in the beginning of his career, he, along with his [elder] brother [James], assisted his father in carrying on the trade of a tanner and leather merchant in premises erected for the purpose at the Harbour Head.' This can be only partially right because David's father died when he was just twelve years old. The business was actually run by family trustees until David was nineteen and his elder brother James was twenty-one. Walter Fergus, a former provost of Kirkcaldy and friend of the brothers' late father, said that he and the other trustees 'considered them both well qualified for carrying on their business which was pretty extensive' and 'devolved the whole management upon them'. Many years later, Mr Fergus said he had 'reason to know that their exertions in business were successful'.

David had a younger brother, Alexander, but he emigrated to seek his fortune in India. His two younger sisters, Jean and Catherine, died at an early age, unmarried and childless. While James managed the old family tanning business, David swiftly 'gave his attention entirely' to the yarn trade which he considered more profitable. David Landale & Co. began to grow, focusing not only on buying and selling flax, but also spinning yarn and bleaching the finished linen. In October 1818, David established the Kirkcaldy and Leith Shipping Company and built a counting house on the east quay of the harbour. By the early 1820s, in his mid-thirties, he was one of the most prosperous men in Kirkcaldy.

As a merchant with little property, and lacking a university education, David Landale was not quite landed gentry. His family did not have a coat of arms registered with Lord Lyon, King of Arms in Edinburgh. But that did not mean he was not a gentleman. 'In England . . . blood had many shades of blue,' wrote the historian Victor Kiernan. 'Besides the time-honoured path leading a townsman to a country estate, there were many other grounds, of profession, education, property, that could warrant claim to rank, with the highest in the essentials of upper-class status.' Thus, as one of the industrial revolution's growing generation of upper middle-class businessmen, and a wealthy member of a distinguished local family who could demonstrate his forebears' eminence over several centuries, David Landale was indeed a gentleman, and in Kirkcaldy, a gentleman of rank. A surviving oil portrait shows a man with a determined air, a firm jaw, high forehead, and closed mouth with just a hint of a smile. He is stiff backed, upright and resolute. By all accounts, he was a proper and respectable character, if somewhat dour. John Lockhart, a Kirkcaldy man who knew him in later life, described David as 'naturally proud'. Another said he was an 'austere, tall figure'. One correspondent in the *Fifeshire Advertiser* wrote of his 'gentlemanly presence and sterling character'. Above all, he was a man of honour, a man for whom character and reputation was all. He had the respect of the town and his word was his bond. David was also extremely devout, a member of the Auld Licht (Old Light) Church, a conservative sect which had split from the Church of Scotland in the late eighteenth century after a row over how much of a role the state should play in the religious affairs of the community. In Kirkcaldy, the minister of the Auld Lichters was the Rev. James Black, who also attested to David's 'high character'. If David's faith played a huge role in his life, it certainly faced its toughest test in 1821. Two years before, aged thirty-three, he had met Isabella Spears, a brewer's daughter from the nearby parish of Auchtertool. They quickly fell in love and married. But suddenly, and without understood cause, she died, childless. No evidence remains of David's grief, save the suggestion that he threw himself into his work with still greater vigour.

'As his business as a yarn merchant extended, he formed the desire to combine bleaching with it,' his obituarist wrote, 'and he accordingly obtained ground and erected extensive bleach works on Lochty Water.' The bleachfield lay on the banks of Lochty Burn just a few miles north of Kirkcaldy. Here, throughout the summer, acre upon acre of meadow were covered in linen pegged out in the sun and breeze, bleaching slowly white. Sun-burned women pottered about the fields, checking pegs and hanging up more cloth. To the right stood a solid brick factory 'with red roofs and great white walls', steam belching from its tall chimney, a cluster of offices and sheds clinging to the main building like a litter to a sow. To the left ran the burn itself, running the length of David's twenty-three acres. Men, up to their chests in pools, heaved damp bundles of flax from the water. And along the periphery patrolled several guards, their flintlock muskets slung casually on their backs, watching out for local folk bent on picking up a new table cloth for free.

The linen which left David Landale's factory began its journey 1,000 miles away to the east, on the rolling Baltic seaboard. Here fields and fields of fertile coastal plain were covered in flax, its blue flowers shimmering gently like a breeze on a calm sea. Scottish farmers had tried to grow their own flax but the quality was never as good. There was, as there is today, something about the mix of the lush soil, damp climate and cool nights of the Baltic coast that produced good flax. The seeds were collected and crushed to make linseed oil; but the long, fibrous stems were perfect to make yarn. Like most linen manufacturers in Kirkcaldy, David imported his flax from Riga – now the Latvian capital, then a vital Russian sea port – with whom local merchants had traded since the early sixteenth century. The flax arrived in Kirkcaldy raw and untreated: bundles of yard-long stems roughly tied which were carried the few miles inland to the bleach works at Lochty. Here, by a process of beating and soaking, the fibres were separated from the stem and untangled with a sharp-toothed comb called a heckle. The tough men who carried out this difficult work, the hecklers, were so notoriously militant and outspoken that they bequeathed their name to the English language. The fibres were then, like any other, spun into yarn and woven into cloth.

To transform the brown linen into something which could grace a bed or a dining table – or be turned into the famous 'Kirkcaldy stripe' shirts that working men wore on their backs throughout England – it had then to be bleached white. In the early nineteenth century, this was a complicated process. The cloth was boiled in a hot alkali, washed out, dried on a bleachfield, then soaked in acid, washed out and dried again. The whole sequence was repeated until the cloth was white, something which could take several months and was utterly reliant on fresh dew, fine weather and dry wind.

Bleaching was good business in Scotland in the 1820s. More and more local manufacturers wanted to bleach their linen north of the border rather than incur the extra cost of sending it down south to be finished in England. So as the difficult autumn months of 1825 slipped into the winter of 1826, David managed to keep the business afloat. In January, the Bank of Scotland asked its Kirkcaldy agents, two brothers called David and George Morgan, to give an assessment of how some of their local merchants were faring in the slump. On the 23rd, they replied that the security of David Landale & Co. was 'quite good, and as they employ a great many people here as well as at their bleach field, they give active and great circulation to the bank's notes. Their business is all fair value accommodations and they keep steadily by the bank. They sell a great many yarns . . . they carry on a snug trade as tanners and leather merchants.' Such a favourable assessment was astonishing given the economic circumstances. It was not one which would last.

George Morgan was born on December 22 1781, the second son of a Kirkcaldy merchant after whom he was named. George Morgan senior had begun life uncertainly, a man of modest background whose eye for the ladies had more than once got him into trouble. In April 1774, he was accused of fathering an illegitimate child in St Andrews. But he settled down and married a local girl with whom he had five daughters and seven sons, three of whom died in infancy. He did well for himself and became a respectable Kirkcaldy trader, a town councillor and even, on two occasions, provost. Little is known of his son George's early life save that at the age of thirty-one, he went to war, one of the many thousands of men who went to Spain to fight Napoleon's forces. Lieutenant-General Sir Arthur Wellesley – later the Duke of Wellington – had taken his army to the Iberian Peninsula in 1808 and had slowly fought his way across the hot, dusty plains, methodically dislodging the French from city after city. Thousands died on both sides and there was a severe need for officers. Such was the slaughter that Britain's aristocracy could not produce enough young men to give up their lives and the army was forced to look for officers among the middle classes. The call went out and, in 1812, George Morgan was one of those who answered. To obtain a commission in the army, he turned to his father who knew how to pull a few strings. George Morgan senior was a friend of the Earl of Rosslyn, a leading member of Fife's aristocracy. The peer was known to have good contacts in the army so Morgan wrote to him, asking if there was anything he could do to help his son. There was. On February 1 1812, Lord Rosslyn wrote to an acquaintance, Lieutenant-Colonel Henry Torrens, who happened to be chief of staff to Frederick, Duke of York, George III's second son, who, in turn, happened to be Commander in Chief of all His Majesty's Forces. 'My dear Torrens,' Lord Rosslyn wrote, 'I shall be very much indebted to you if you will take a favourable opportunity of submitting to His Royal Highness the Duke of York my humble solicitation that he would be graciously pleased to recommend Mr George Morgan for an Ensigncy. He is the son of a friend of mine and I can affirm that he is in all respects perfectly qualified for that commission.' Thus it was that on April 2 1812, George Morgan gratefully shed his middle-class slough and slipped seamlessly into Britain's upper class. History records that on that day 'George Morgan, gentleman' was allowed to buy a commission in the 45th Regiment of Foot, one of the many small infantry regiments which formed the backbone of the new British army. It did not matter that he was an ensign, the lowest commissioned rank for an infantry officer, who would often carry the regimental ensign or colours. He was an officer in the king's army and he bore the honour that rank provided.

George was quickly shipped out to Spain to join his regiment. Throughout the next two years of Wellington's Peninsula campaign, the 45th was in the heart of the fighting and George did well to survive. Thousands of British lives were lost, many of them young officers vainly leading their men into blistering volleys of gunfire, just as another generation would in France a century later. In June 1813, George was promoted to Lieutenant. By April the following year, Wellington's victorious forces had flushed the French from Spain, invaded France and were at Toulouse. Napoleon had abdicated and was on his way to exile in Elba. The war, so everyone thought, was over. After six years in Spain, the 45th departed in June 1814 and sailed for Ireland and barracks in Cork.

There, like so many others, the regiment was forced to cut its numbers and in October 1814, George found himself out on his ear on half-pay. Although this meant he was still technically an officer in the 45th, available for recall at any moment, he could not remain with the regiment. His luck changed only when, early in 1815, Napoleon escaped from his island prison, landed in France and raised another army. The British government, forced to fight Bonaparte once more, was obliged to recall its disbanded officers. From Kirkcaldy, on May 2 1815, George Morgan wrote directly to the Duke of York, asking if the Duke could 'recommend him to His Majesty for being employed either in the 45th or any other Regiment your Royal Highness may think proper', and persuaded a friendly senior officer to write another note in his favour to Colonel Torrens. Again he was successful. On May 25, George received a commission as a lieutenant in the 77th Regiment of Foot, known as the 'pot hooks' – the letter seven reminding soldiers of the hooks which held the pots above their camp fires. In the end, however, Napoleon was defeated before the 77th had even embarked for France. Once again, George was soon asked to leave the army on half-pay. He returned home in March of 1817, perhaps suspecting that his soldiering days were over. He was thirty-six years old, unmarried and without a profession. So George was persuaded to join his elder brother, David, who worked for the Bank of Scotland. In February 1818, he started work as joint agent for the bank in Kirkcaldy at Number 1, Townsend Place. He moved in with David and his wife Margaret and children who lived not far away in the High Street. Thus the soldier became a banker.

The men of Kirkcaldy were not natural duellists. Like many other Scots, they showed less inclination towards shooting one another than their Irish counterparts, who blazed away with abandon. It had not always been thus. Sir Walter Scott wrote that in the 1730s 'duels were . . . very common in Scotland, for the gentry were at once idle, haughty, fierce, [and] divided by faction'. But Scott was exaggerating. A hundred years on, the American historian, Ben Truman, observed that 'the custom did not prevail to the same popular extent among the Scots as among their more roistering neighbours'. The exodus of nobility south since the union had left Scotland largely bereft of a gun-toting aristocracy. The remaining Scottish gentility were largely men of business and commerce, merchants and traders bent on making a good living in difficult times. But in the spring of 1826, the people of Kirkcaldy were no strangers to duelling, not least because one of Britain's most notorious encounters had taken place on their doorstep just a few years earlier. In 1821, the Christmas edition of the *Glasgow Sentinel* published an anonymous, ribald song which implied that a distinguished Tory gentleman, James Stuart of Duncarn, was a coward. Naturally he resented this and set about finding the guilty scribe. Through an informant at the newspaper he discovered that the author of these critical remarks was none other than his distant cousin, Sir Alexander Boswell, eldest son of James Boswell, the biographer of Dr Samuel Johnson. The baronet 'possessed in a very extraordinary degree the talent of irony and had taken to writing anonymous satirical squibs and articles under the title of Ignotus'. In the New Year, Stuart sent his friend, the Earl of Rosslyn, to ask Boswell if indeed he was the author of the scurrilous song. Boswell was, at the very least, evasive. He said it was 'a delicate affair' and insisted he would have to consult his friend, the Honourable John Douglas, brother of the Marquess of Queensberry. Douglas in turn told Rosslyn that Boswell would not confirm his authorship of the piece. As a result Stuart felt he had no alternative but, reluctantly, to challenge Boswell to a duel, a challenge the baronet accepted immediately. They met at dawn on March 26 on the Balmuto estate just outside Kirkcaldy, near the village of Auchtertool. Stuart, an inexperienced gunman, was at great pains to avoid a combat and repeatedly offered to accept an apology. He was, he said, quite happy to acknowledge that the song was just 'a very bad joke'. Boswell, however, had convinced himself that Stuart had no alternative but to duel and would not offer any apology. In a tragi-comedy of mistaken motives, Boswell told his second he bore no ill will against Stuart and would not aim but instead fire in the air. Stuart, meanwhile, told his friends that he too felt no malice towards Sir Alexander and that he too ought not to take an aim but, 'if he had the great misfortune to hit him, he wished it might be on the great toe, as a gentleman in England had done lately on a similar occasion'. It was not to be. At twelve paces, both men fired and Stuart's ball struck Boswell hard in the shoulder, shattering the shoulder-blade before it slid down the spine, rendering the baronet utterly paralysed. He told his second he had 'a live head on a dead body'. He was carried to Balmuto House where he lingered in great pain until 3 p.m. the next day when he died. While thousands attended Boswell's funeral, Stuart fled briefly abroad before returning to face justice. He was tried for wilful murder in the High Court of the Justiciary in a high profile trial that was the talk of Scotland. He was defended by two up-and-coming young advocates, Messrs Cockburn and Jeffery, who argued that Stuart's willingness to accept an apology, his high character, his temperate behaviour, his contrition at Boswell's death, proved unequivocally that their man had gone on the field 'without an atom of malice'. The jury agreed and, without even retiring, acquitted Stuart unanimously. It was an argument and a judgement that would be well remembered four years later by those same two advocates when they defended another Kirkcaldy duellist facing his own trial for murder.

In February 1826, the thirty-nine-year-old David Landale was beginning to feel the pinch. He had debts of several thousand pounds. He was trading little flax, he was spinning even less and although demand for bleaching was holding up, he could not take on any more business. The problem with bleaching was that once his fields were filled with staked-out cloth, he could accept no more orders. What he needed above every-thing was more land. But the prospect of securing another loan from the bank looked unlikely: not only was he already suffering from cash flow problems common to any business during recession, but the Morgans were also beginning to be more careful with the Bank's money and be less accommodating towards him and their other clients. They were, in Landale's own words, showing 'symptoms of uneasiness respecting the extent of my Discounts – a feeling which no one need be surprised at in these times'. In March their unease began to affect their decisions.

In those days, for merchants like David, the most common form of financial currency apart from cash was a bill of exchange. This was effectively a form of IOU, a written promise from one man to pay another a sum of money at a certain date. The recipient could wait until the bill became due and receive the money then. Or he could go to the bank and get the money immediately, minus a small cut – or 'discount' – which was effectively the price of the bank taking on the risk of not being paid back. The recipient could, of course, also use the bill, like any other IOU, as a form of currency in itself and pass it on as payment to someone else. But all this worked only if the credit of the man who wrote the IOU was undoubted. His financial probity, his business credibility and, above all, his personal honour had to be above question. 'Such is the origin of promissory notes,' declared *The British Code of Duel*, an anonymous handbook published in 1824. '[They] are records of promise on word of honour, whence is derivable the commercial use of the word "honoured" as relates to the payment of a promissory note, or even a bill of exchange.' Today we still talk of honouring a cheque or bill. In 1826, any man who wrote a bill of exchange he could not pay was one step from ruin. And any man whose bills of exchange were refused suffered a devastating loss of reputation. Personal honour was therefore at the heart of everyday commerce; without it, you could not trade.

That February David Landale received two bills of exchange that he wanted to pay into his accounts to clear some debt. Both were for £300, one from a client in payment for spinning some flax into yarn, the other a simple repayment of a loan. However, in such difficult times, David's bankers refused the bills and demanded hard cash instead; the Morgans effectively bounced the cheques because they did not trust the credit of the firms that had written them. This was because they, as agents, shared half the liability with the bank. If these bills were not payable, the Morgans would be out of pocket. Nevertheless, it all meant David was forced to go back to his debtors and go through the embarrassing process of asking for cash.

A few weeks later, the Morgans inadvertently made things even more difficult. Three months previously, David had bought £1,000-worth of yarn from another merchant, George Mitchell, promising to pay for it at a later date by which time he hoped to have sold some of the stock. 'But as I had not sold any of his yarns from the total stagnation of trade, I had no funds . . . to meet that Bill,' he later wrote. To resolve this cash flow problem, David suggested to George and David Morgan that they should pay Mr Mitchell's bill, give him three months to pay them back, and accept the rolls of yarn themselves as collateral. 'To this, they objected unless the goods [yarns] were entirely removed from my warehouse, which I felt reluctant to do as hazarding my respectability in the eye of the public.' In the end, David was forced to go to another bank which agreed to give him another three months to pay the bill. Soon, there were more tensions. David Landale was owed £1,000 from Messrs Ebenezer Birrell & Sons who had bought a barge of flax from him the previous September. On the day the bill fell due, Birrell offered £600 in cash and a promissory note for £400. David was quite happy with this but again the Morgans and the Bank of Scotland demanded cash alone. David was 'astonished' that his bankers could 'in such times of difficulty' cause him such 'inconvenience and embarrassment'. This time David stood his ground and, after 'a good deal of altercation', the Morgans relented and accepted the cheque.

Such was David's concern about the Morgans' increasingly inflexible position that he began to consider re-mortgaging some of his property so he would have enough cash to see him through the recession. 'This was the period when I looked to my Heritable Property for protection against such conduct in my Bankers, as I did not possess sufficient brass to ask discounts in such times from any other Bank.' Rather cannily, David approached the Bank of Scotland directors at Edinburgh directly for help. He applied for a 'cash account' – an early form of guaranteed overdraft – offering some of his property as collateral. On April 17, the bank agreed in principle that David, having put up property worth £5,000 as security, should be given a cash account with an effective overdraft limit of £3,000. The remaining £2,000 was to be held by the bank so that, if necessary, his outstanding debts could be paid off.

For David this was a huge relief, a lifeline that could see him through the worst. So it was with some confidence that a week later, at 11 a.m. on April 25, he walked into the Bank of Scotland offices in Townsend Place for a meeting with George and David Morgan. He had, he told them, a bill to be paid at Messrs Coutts & Co., the Bank of Scotland's agents in London. The bill was worth £1,000 and was due in five days' time on April 30; could they order it paid? 'They promised to do [this] by that post with the express understanding that I was to furnish them with Bills for Discount on the 1st of May (the first of each month being the only day I generally discount Bills) and to apply their proceeds in payment of the London bill.' In other words, the Morgans would pay the bill in London, David Landale would pay them back a day later. David left the bank, his business complete, and returned home, little expecting what the Morgans would do next.

James Murdoch was one of the Morgans' beleaguered employees at the bank. By trade, he was their accountant and clerk; in practice he was also their bearer of bad news and it was in this latter role that he later that day found himself traipsing up the hill to David Landale's home, a large imposing house called St Mary's which overlooked Kirkcaldy's sea-front. Mr Murdoch had a letter for the merchant from his employers; they had changed their minds.

'To my great astonishment,' David wrote later, 'while dressing that afternoon for a Dinner Party in the country, I was handed a note from [the Morgans] declining to order payment of the Bill in London which they had promised to do in the morning unless I furnished them with Bills immediately, and very officiously recommended me to apply for a renewal of the Bill to my English correspondents [i.e. to ask for an extension], which not only was impossible for want of time but which would have ruined my credit with Dealers at such a distance.' Not only were the Morgans damaging David's credit, they were challenging his honour.

The Morgans were adamant. 'It is a standing order with the Bank that moneys must be lodged with us before we order the Bank to return Bills due in London on account of individuals,' their letter stated. 'I am sure you do not wish us to depart from the Bank's rules. We must therefore decline to order paying Messrs Hitchin's Bill due the 30th inst of £1,000 until such orders are complied with . . . We doubt not but you will see in this nothing but what is fair & reasonable and the necessity we are under in keeping in strict conformity with the Bank's rules.'

David exploded and Murdoch was the recipient of his fury: 'I represented to the Accountant of the Agency here – who was the bearer of the note – how ill I was used and how unbusinesslike was the conduct of the Agents. I desired him to ask them to consider of the resolution they had expressed in their note, and to again write to me that evening whether or not they were to adhere to their promise given in the morning.' The Morgans wrote again; again their answer was no. David immediately approached other banks for help. He found it in the form of George Millar. As well as being Kirkcaldy's provost and tax collector, and a merchant in his own right, Millar also did a little banking on the side as agent of the National Bank. He immediately agreed to pay David's bill, simply on the basis of his reputation as an honourable businessman. 'I was so well satisfied of Mr Landale's stability and integrity that I instantly agreed to order payment,' he recalled. And as the last post had gone, he sent an express rider direct to Edinburgh so a message could be got to London as quickly as possible. David was so grateful that he withdrew all his accounts from the Bank of Scotland and transferred them to the National Bank. 'Having thus been forced from the Bank with whom my father and I have had an account for upwards of forty years and with no other, I contented myself that my intercourse with the Messrs Morgan was at an end.'

Yet David had underestimated the vindictiveness of George Morgan Esq., lately Lieutenant in the 77th Regiment of Foot.

2

The dispute worsens

Poulain de St Foix, a French gentleman and writer, was once challenged to a duel by a man whom he had asked to sit further away because he stank. *'I will fight you if you insist, but I don't see how that will end the matter,'* St Foix told the malodorous man. *'If you kill me, I shall smell too. If I kill you, you will smell, if possible, worse than you do at present.'*

Philip Rush, *The Book of Duels*, 1964

'A scoundrel only needs to fight a duel and he ceases to be a scoundrel.'

Jean-Jacques Rousseau, *La Nouvelle Héloïse*, 1760

Kirkcaldy in May of 1826 was a busy little port hugging the north coast of the Firth of Forth. Due south across the water stood the docks at Edinburgh, the channels between thick with shipping, plying to and from Britain's growing markets overseas. Every day some of these vessels touched at Kirkcaldy's small harbour, disembarking their cargoes of Baltic flax and English grain, before loading up with coal, nails, salt, beer and, most of all, linen. Here along the shore lived some 5,000 souls, few of whom built their homes or factories too far from the sea. '[Kirkcaldy] stretches along the foot of a bank and is properly but one street, about a mile in length, with a few narrow lanes on either side,' one contemporary commercial directory recorded. 'The town house is a plain building, with a tower and spire, situated nearly in the middle of the town; and the church, which is in the Gothic style, stands on an eminence at the back of the town. The harbour of Kirkcaldy is both safe and commodious. The trade has greatly increased of late; and several considerable manufactures are carried on, among which are extensive ones of striped Hollands, ticks, checks etc. with a considerable manufacture of stockings; there are likewise large tanneries with several breweries on an extensive scale. The harbour of Kirkcaldy has been greatly improved of late, so much so, that vessels of very considerable burden, of which class many belong to the port, may easily enter.'

Kirkcaldy thus was the model of a prosperous trading port, thriving on the back of an industrial revolution that had gathered a disparate collection of workers, spinning and weaving in their Fifeshire cottages, into a modern and mechanised textile industry whose factories and mills fed the hungry markets of the British Empire. In 1818, two million yards of linen came out of Kirkcaldy's mills. According to John Lockhart, an enthusiastic historian of the town's linen trade, 'the name and fame of "Kirkcaldy Stripes" were known in every town and village in Scotland, the North of England and Ireland. No working man would wear any other kind of shirt, for the Kirkcaldy Striped Shirting material had the hard wearing quality he desired.' It had not always been so. Samuel Johnson, passing through fifty years earlier, found Kirkcaldy to be 'not unlike the small or straggling market-towns in those parts of England where commerce and manufactures have not yet produced opulence'. But Kirkcaldy had done well out of the wars with France, the insecurity of the Channel sending the trade scurrying up the coast to the relative security of Britain's northern ports and waters. By 1826, Kirkcaldy was a town of self-confident, bourgeois merchants and tradesmen, part of the growing army of the middle class who were gradually asserting their dominance over British society. Even 100 years earlier, the author Daniel Defoe, who passed through Kirkcaldy during his grand tour of Britain, noted the town's mercantile classes: 'It has some considerable merchants in it, I mean in the true sense of the word merchant.' Pigot's commercial directory of 1826 lists bankers and bakers, bleachers and booksellers, coopers and confectioners, distillers and druggists, flax spinners and fleshers, hatters and hosiers, merchants and messengers, saddlers and ship owners, tailors and tanners, no less than twenty vintners, watchmakers and wheelwrights and even umbrella makers. To the writer Thomas Carlyle, who lived in the town between 1816 and 1818 and taught at the burgh school: 'The Kirkcaldy population were a pleasant, honest kind of fellow mortals, something of the quietly fruitful good old Scotch in their works and ways.'

A traveller arriving in Kirkcaldy in 1826, perhaps on his way to Dundee or St Andrews, might have wondered at the long High Street as his coach rattled along the thoroughfare that held the town together like a spine. Sir Walter Scott claimed the High Street was 'as long as ony toon in a' England' and Kirkcaldy was – and still is – known to many as the 'Lang Toon'. Alighting at the George Inn, right in the centre of town, the visitor would have been confronted by the hubbub of a busy, semi-industrial, market port. He might have seen William Skinner – postmaster and town chamberlain – standing outside his post office in Tolbooth Street, watching the office clerks running to catch the afternoon post. He might have caught some local burgesses scurrying into the Tolbooth or townhouse next door where they decided Kirkcaldy's business, locked up its villains, stored its weapons and collected its market dues or tolls. Keeping the less salubrious flesh market and the dung depot firmly to his back, he could stroll up the High Street, peering up the small side lanes or wynds stretching off like small tributaries down to the beach or up the hill, before stopping perhaps for a reviving hot toddy at the coffee house. Further up the street he might have encountered James Cumming, Kirkcaldy's convivial bookseller, standing outside the shop which he inherited from his cousin six years previously, trading as much in gossip as stamps, stationery and newspapers. Not far beyond, the visitor might have been directed to a small house at No. 220 where fifty years previously the economist Adam Smith had written *The Wealth of Nations*, that hand book for the industrial revolution whose lessons about free trade and the division of labour had been well learned by Kirkcaldy's merchants. If the tide were low, he might also have taken the chance to stretch his legs along the beach, amid the rock pools and salt pans where seawater was gathered and boiled for the salt that preserved meat, both at home and at sea. It was a strand that had entranced Carlyle: 'The beach of Kirkcaldy in summer twilight, a mile of the smoothest sand, with one long wave coming on, gently, steadily, and breaking into a gradual explosion, beautifully sounding, and advancing, ran from South to North, from West Burn to Kirkcaldy harbour, a favourite scene, beautiful to me still in the far away.'

At the top of the hill that finally brought the High Street to an end, the visitor could enjoy the view while catching his breath. 'The prospect from the high ground is magnificent,' wrote one visitor, 'enlivened by the constant succession of vessels sailing up and down the Forth.' To the east, he could perhaps on a clear day make out the Bass Rock just off North Berwick. To the south he might see one of the newfangled steamer ferries heading across the water towards the haze of coal-fire smoke that gave Edinburgh its nickname of Auld Reekie. At his back, up the coast to the north east, he could see the remains of Ravenscraig Castle, left in ruins since the passing of Cromwell's destructive troops. Some believe this ancient fortification had in antiquity bequeathed Kirkcaldy its name, from the Welsh *caer caled din* meaning 'fort on the hill'. Immediately below lay the harbour, its long piers stretching out into the sea like a three fingered claw. On the longest quayside stood the large counting house of the Kirkcaldy and Leith Shipping Company, a firm that David Landale set up eight years before to convey passengers to Dundee, Edinburgh, Glasgow and even London. Across the roof tops the visitor would have seen what Carlyle called 'the curious blue painted wheels with oblique vanes' that used the sea breezes to drive the flax mills below. To the right of the road, stretching away to the south, were foundries, bleach fields, spinning mills, and coal pits bordered by colliers' whitewashed cottages. Dominating the view was the church and its spire, beneath which lay the manse that two centuries later would house a young minister's son called Gordon Brown.

Opposite the church stood a solid, granite building, the only property on that side of the road, marking the outer reaches of the town. It stood alone, detached, as if aloof from the mercantile hurly-burly of the High Street below. And well it might for this was the premises of the Bank of Scotland and it was here that the recently demobilised George Morgan came to work when he returned to Kirkcaldy in 1817.

The people of Kirkcaldy knew George Morgan of old; he had grown up among them. But they had not seen him for many years and were keen to find out what kind of man he had become. What they discovered was this: George was a snob, a bore and a vindictive bully. He was, in the words of the historian Antony Simpson, a typical 'temporary gentleman', out on a limb on half-pay, one of a class of ex-soldiers 'that had absorbed aristocratic values without having been favoured by the social background or the financial wherewithal to put these to good effect'. George deliberately used his military rank to clamber up the social ladder. He was not slow to point out in conversation that he had a commission from His Majesty King George and he relished putting the letters Esq. after his name. In the social registers of the time, he is securely placed in the lists entitled 'Gentry and Clergy'. The army had declared him an officer and a gentleman and so Kirkcaldy had to accept him as one. His pride did not win him many friends. '[Morgan] seems to have been a garrulous man, impulsive and vain,' one local historian recalled. 'He loved to sun himself in the popular eye on the pavement in front of the Bank. He was . . . a jaunty, irascible, foppish Macaroni.' The description appears apt; the so-called Macaroni Club of young Englishmen who adopted flamboyant Italian fashions and behaviour of the time, were described by the lexicographer Ebenezer Brewer as 'the most exquisite fops that ever disgraced the name of man; vicious, insolent, fond of gambling, drinking and duelling.' George was also, it appears, a bit of a bore who would overuse his friends. One of his few intimates, James Fleming, an accountant, recalled that he 'frequently breakfasted as well as dined and supped with George . . . When he first took up house, he was rather stingy but latterly he became more liberal and invited me to his house oftener than I was inclined to.'

These character traits, however, might have been more easily forgiven if George were not such a bully. Morgan was quick to anger and slow to forgive, almost incapable of conversation without taking offence. He was, according to one Kirkcaldy historian, 'a touchy, fire-eating kind of man'. He carried a smart walking cane which he used to wave angrily at people and threaten them with a beating. One man who knew this better than others was Robert Kirk, a tobacconist and agent for a rival bank in Kirkcaldy, the Commercial Banking Company of Scotland. In the autumn of 1824, he sued George Morgan's brother, David, who 'had on the public street of Kirkcaldy taken liberties with his character when speaking of him to Mr Samuel Rope of the House of Roebuck, Rope and Company of London'. One morning, while the case was in court, Kirk found himself on the same Edinburgh ferry as George Morgan. 'I happened to be leaning on my walking stick,' he recalled. 'Morgan was walking near me at the time and in passing struck my stick out below me and I fell on the companion door. I said nothing but Morgan said: "Why didn't you keep your stick out of the way?"' Kirk was puzzled but said nothing. Subsequently, whenever he and Morgan passed in the street, the banker would mutter words such as 'Damned scoundrel, I'll do for you.' Eventually, a year or so later, David Morgan's lawyers were forced to settle out of court, much to the banker's expense. Soon after, one evening towards the end of August 1825, his brother, George, again tried to provoke Kirk as he was strolling outside his shop. 'The pavement here is about the broadest in Kirkcaldy and will easily admit four people when walking abreast,' Kirk recalled. 'Morgan and I were walking in opposite directions when Morgan came slap against me and almost threw me down. I said: "What do you mean, Sir?"' Morgan said: "You are a damned scoundrel", and walked on.' But he turned and deliberately bumped into Kirk a further six times until finally, Kirk responded. He grabbed Morgan by the collar of his coat and asked: 'What do you mean by this sort of conduct?' Morgan replied: 'I want you to give me a challenge. Call me out, Sir, and I will do for you.' Kirk said: 'Get along with you, you fellow. I have nothing to do with you.' Morgan left and Kirk thought that was the end of it. But five days later, Morgan again deliberately bumped into Kirk and said: 'You are a damned scoundrel. Will you go down Hatchet's Close?' The dark and narrow alleyway led down to the beach. For Kirk, this was one provocation too many. He replied: 'Yes, Sir. I will', and set off towards the close. But strangely, instead of following, George Morgan ran off in the other direction without a word or explanation. A month later, the banker apparently regained his courage and returned to Kirk's house, again as the shopkeeper was strolling outside his house while dusk fell. This time he did not hesitate and struck Kirk in the face with his stick. The tobacconist, however, grabbed the cane and held it tight. 'Damn you, Sir, let go of my stick,' cried Morgan. 'Sir, I will not let go of your stick,' Kirk replied, yanking it out of Morgan's hands. A young stone-mason called David Macrae happened to be passing and saw the whole incident. Morgan, he said, was 'evidently in a rage'. Kirk asked Macrae: 'Did you see Mr Morgan draw his stick across my face?' Macrae answered: 'Yes, I did.' Kirk threw the stick back at Morgan and said: 'Go about your business, Sir.'

After so many repeated insults and assaults, Kirk had every right to challenge Morgan to a duel. In fact he had, in theory, an obligation as a gentleman to challenge his assailant or risk accusations of cowardice and the prospect of social ostracism. Yet Kirk chose to do nothing. This would have been unthinkable even a few years previously. But by the 1820s, attitudes were changing fast. Kirk chose not to duel 'in consequence of consulting his friends and Mr Cooper, his land agent, who recommended to him that he treat it with silent contempt, as a man of Morgan's character did not deserve to be treated as a gentleman'. Kirk's friends and social circle no longer automatically expected him to duel. They were also subtly changing the definition of what it was to be a gentleman. A man in 1826 was beginning to be considered a gent not just by his social rank or even his propensity to duel, but also by his behaviour. In 1824, *The British Code of Duel* had declared that the rank of gentleman was 'the lowest distinction of civil nobility yet in character assimilates with the highest'. As a soldier, George Morgan was technically a gentleman, but in his behaviour, he was anything but.

Another Kirkcaldy man who knew of George Morgan's vengeful character was George Graham, a cloth merchant, and one of the Morgans' neighbours in the High Street. One day in September 1823, Morgan went into George Graham's shop and asked about a book Graham's son had taken from the local library. Would it, Morgan asked, be possible for him to borrow it after Graham's son had finished with it? Graham said he was sure this would be no problem as long as his son had not already passed it on. Morgan 'appeared satisfied' with this and left, remarking as he left: 'Recollect it is no favour.' Half an hour later, George Graham popped up the road to Cumming's bookshop for a paper and was greeted with some unexpected news. 'Cumming told Graham that Morgan had come into his shop in a violent rage at him for refusing to lend him a book and was abusing him very much in that way.' Graham was stunned and told Cumming it was not true. But he said he had a good mind now not to let Morgan have the book. Two days later Morgan came into Graham's shop and said he wanted to pay and close his account because of the 'misunderstanding' about the book. Graham said it was Morgan's fault for lying. Morgan flew into a rage, told Graham he would never buy anything from him again and 'would use every exertion to prevent customers coming to his shop'. When Graham again insisted that Morgan could only blame himself, the banker 'lifted up the yard[stick] from the counter and, in a threatening attitude, said he would knock Graham down, and also said: "I'll kick your arse for you," and cursed and swore and used a great deal of abusive language'. Morgan left 'in a great rage' and a few days later, took his revenge. Ruthlessly, he bought the freehold to Graham's shop and house and evicted the cloth merchant from his home of twenty years. Graham pleaded with Morgan's father to intervene, either to change George's mind or at least give him some time to find new premises. Old George Morgan senior 'expressed his sorrow at his son's conduct' but said there was nothing he could do, Graham would have to speak to George about it. Graham could not bring himself to do that so he asked the bookseller James Cumming to have a go, with equal lack of success as became clear a few days later when Morgan came across Graham in Mr Cumming's shop. 'Morgan came up to him, lifted his stick and with several oaths, threatened to knock him down and abused him in a violent manner.' Graham finally lost his temper. 'You are an insolent scoundrel, Sir,' he told Morgan, who was in such a rage that he misheard. 'What, Sir, do you call me an Irish scoundrel?' Graham replied: 'No, Sir, I know you are not an Irish scoundrel, be what you will.' Morgan advanced, raising his stick as if to strike, and said: 'Damn you, Sir. If Mr Cumming was not there, I would knock you down.' Grabbing hold of Graham's coat, he said: 'Come away with me to the sand.' Graham said: 'Let go of my coat. If you wish my coat, you shall have it, but I will go to the sands when and with whom I think proper.' With that, Morgan left and from that moment, Graham never walked the High Street again without a stick so he could 'endeavour to protect himself' against George Morgan.

George's encounters with Robert Kirk and George Graham are but two of many examples of his vile temper that have been recorded. They are one-sided stories that lack the banker's account, his explanation, his pleas in mitigation. Yet the stories appear truthful in their essence. Not only was George almost always in a rage about something or somebody, but he was also obsessed with duelling and calling people out. Whenever he got into a row, he considered his honour to be questioned. In another, similar quarrel, he told his opponent: 'I have got a pair of pistols that cost me upwards of £20 and that [is] the way to settle these matters'. But if his quarrelling was a result of bad character, his tendency towards duelling was a legacy of his days in uniform.

The armies of modern Europe were the breeding grounds in which the modern European duel flourished. Without them, duelling might have had a brief history, remembered, perhaps, as a curious phenomenon practised by a handful of Italian and

French noblemen, an anachronism that died out within a generation. Instead, duelling endured for more than 300 years across the continent. For the European army officer inherited duelling's past, he shared its values, and most importantly, he spread its practice. His forebear, the knight, bequeathed him a legacy of single combat, a tradition that warriors should test themselves against one another. The officer's peers – Europe's aristocrats and noble elites – had adopted ritualised duelling in the fifteenth and sixteenth centuries as an alternative to assassination and vendetta. And the soldier's peripatetic warmongering across the continent in the seventeenth, eighteenth and early nineteenth centuries meant that duelling's traditions and habits were scattered across Europe. The mercenary knight was duelling's most ardent evangelist. 'The prevalence of duelling must have owed much to these foot-loose adventurers,' wrote Victor Kiernan. 'A climax was reached in the Thirty Years War, from 1618 to 1648, which drew in most of Europe. It helped to spread duelling habits far and wide.' Some senior officers encouraged duelling. Like monarchs in the age of chivalry, they believed it tested a young officer's courage, fostered his warlike spirit, and gave him something to do in peacetime. It was useful to the generals that their officers feared dishonour more than death. The only check – to preserve discipline and the chain of command – was a hard and fast rule that banned officers from duelling with any rank but their own.

Some military men claimed they had to duel to confirm their courage. On April 6 1803 two high ranking officers fought on Primrose Hill in north London. Lieutenant-Colonel Montgomery of the 9th Regiment of Foot and Captain Macnamara of the Royal Navy had come across each other that morning while riding with their dogs in Hyde Park. The two beasts, as dogs do, had had a scrap. 'Whose dog is that?' cried Montgomery as he pulled the hounds apart. 'I will knock him down.' Coming round the corner at a trot, Macnamara said: 'Have you the impudence to say that you will knock my dog down? You must first knock me down.' So they met later that day. Montgomery was shot dead, Macnamara wounded and tried for murder. At the trial, he insisted he had been right to defend his honour regardless of the trivial nature of the dispute. 'I am a Captain of the British Navy,' he said. 'My character you can hear only from others. But to maintain my character in that situation, I must be respected. When called upon to lead others into honourable danger, I must not be supposed to be a man who sought safety by submitting to what custom has taught others to consider as a disgrace.' Swayed by such eloquence, the jury disregarded the judge's direction and found Macnamara not guilty. They might also have been persuaded by the evidence of one Admiral Lord Nelson who testified as to Macnamara's good character.

Senior officers also believed that duelling helped foster regimental honour at a time when hundreds of new regiments were being created; an insult to an officer became an insult to a regiment, and a regiment's honour could not go undefended. Woe betide any military men who failed to defend themselves. During the eighteenth century, a Knight of the Order of St John in Malta refused a duel: 'This meanspirited creature was sentenced to forty-five days [sitting] on a kind of stool of repentance in church, five years in an unlit dungeon, and imprisonment for life.' Likewise, the regimental colonel in Joseph Conrad's short story *The Duel* disapproved of his young Lieutenant D'Hubert's duelling but knew he could do little to stop it. 'Duelling courage, the single combat courage, is rightly or wrongly supposed to be courage of a special sort,' the colonel conceded. 'And it was eminently necessary that an officer of his regiment should possess every kind of courage – and prove it, too.' By the time of Napoleon, duelling was prevalent in most of Europe's armies, their officer castes, as ever, having this and much more in common. But it was perhaps the French who were the most obsessive duellists, and accounts of their combats have endured down the centuries.

In 1794, a young French officer called Captain Dupont received orders from his general. He was to search the streets of Strasbourg for a certain Captain Fournier of the Hussars and inform him that he was no longer invited to that night's ball. Captain Fournier had killed a local man in a duel and the general had not enjoyed having to listen to the protests of the townspeople. Dupont followed his orders but Fournier took umbrage and challenged his fellow officer to a duel. They fought there and then with swords and Fournier was laid low with a deep but less than fatal thrust. Furious, Fournier waited a month until his wound had healed and challenged Dupont again. This time it was Dupont's turn to be injured. So began a series of seventeen bloody but never lethal duels that would last for another nineteen years. As time passed, the two officers drew up a contract to regulate their duelling. If they came within 100 miles of each other, they would fight. Military duty alone would excuse an encounter. 'This contract was religiously observed in every detail and soon the state of war between the two officers became a normal condition for them. They were as eager and impatient to meet after a long separation as two lovers, and they never crossed swords without first exchanging a warm handshake.' In the end, after many years of campaigning, and promotion, by 1813, General Dupont tired of fighting General Fournier. He also wished to marry. So he arranged an unusual duel in which they stalked one another in a forest, armed with two pistols. Dupont stuck his coat on a stick and tricked his opponent into firing twice. Dupont spared Fournier's life but told him that if ever they duelled again, he reserved the right to fire two bullets first from a few yards' range. They never fought again. The story formed the basis of not only Conrad's short story, but also Ridley Scott's 1977 film, *The Duellists*.

Few duels between British officers were so notorious or so drawn out, not least because they exchanged the sword for the pistol much earlier than their continental colleagues. With a pistol, the duelling officer tended to miss or kill. With a sword, the possibility of a disarming, non-fatal wound was more likely. But the British army officer was no less a duellist. Indeed, British army regulations made it a specific offence for an officer to fail to defend the honour of his regiment, a rule which was widely interpreted as not only sanctioning duelling but insisting upon it. Officers who refused a challenge were ostracised, forced out of the regiment or at worst actually court-martialled for breaching the Articles of War. With the rapidly expanding army of the early nineteenth century, there were many new regiments, militias and yeomanry whose honour needed to be defended. And when abroad, the British officer, as a possessor of the king's commission, considered any affront to his uniform an insult to his sovereign. Thus in the years following Napoleon's defeat in 1815, many of the red-coats occupying France took part in so-called Waterloo duels with their vanquished foes. For the disbanded French officer, it provided a chance for retaliation; for the British officer, another chance to shoot a Frenchie.

But perhaps what made the British army fuel and spread duelling so much was old-fashioned class consciousness. As hundreds of middle-class men like George Morgan joined the army's officer corps to replace their aristocratic predecessors who had perished in Iberia, they began to change. 'It is true that many young men of the middle class enter the army,' wrote the historian Sir Charles Trevelyan, 'but they are incorporated at once into the upper stratum as officers. They chiefly belong to the new families created by our industrial system and their object is to take rank officially as gentlemen.' Desperate to be considered officers and gentlemen, they began to ape their aristocratic superiors. Apart from adopting swaggering, commanding airs, they found their best way up the social order was to duel. Duelling became a definition of gentlemanly rank, a gateway to bigger and better things, an instant, albeit risky, one-way ticket up the ladder. 'Middle-class officers . . . yearned for entry to the ranks of the genteel,' wrote Anthony Simpson. 'Duelling was a relatively easy avenue to this end.' Inevitably, the middle-class officers became *plus royaliste que le roi* and duelled more obsessively to establish their rank. Such were the distorted values of these middle-class officers that one, as he lay dying in a pool of blood in Hyde Park in 1803, told his second to take a ring from his finger, give it to his 'poor, dear sister and tell her this is the happiest day of my life'. Similar social forces were at work in Napoleon's army, beautifully described in Conrad's *The Duel*. The homicidal duellist, Lieutenant Feraud, the shoemaker's son, is much more desperate to establish and protect his honour than his more aristocratic opponent, Lieutenant D'Hubert, who is forced by the codes of duelling into combat after combat.

So when George Morgan arrived in Spain in 1812 as a young ensign for the 45th Regiment of Foot, he was thrown into a world where duelling was the norm, where officers called each other out on the flimsiest of pretexts, where a man was expected to die for his king in battle and for his honour in a duel. And more than that, George entered a community where hundreds of other middle-class men like him were desperate to adopt the ways of their aristocratic superiors. George loved the social cohesion, the bonding with fellow duellers, the combat; in short, the army life. But despite George Morgan's immersion in the army's duelling culture, he was at the same time remarkably reluctant to pick up his pistols. Although he did pretty much everything he could to force both Robert Kirk and George Graham into a duel, on neither occasion did he actually challenge them himself. When Kirk finally agreed to go with him 'to the sands', Morgan fled. During another of his many rows, Morgan was accused by a local magistrate, Thomas Ronald, of being 'no gentleman and never was entitled to wear a red coat'. To a soldier, there could be no greater provocation and yet again Morgan failed to issue a challenge.

It is worth stating that George could certainly not be accused of lacking courage. Anyone who survived five years on the bloody plains of Iberia had considerable reserves of fortitude. His temper was clearly powerful enough to overcome fear. He had the training, the inclination, the mettle to duel, yet he did not act. He gave every impression of a man who was constantly keeping himself in check, a man who knew he flew off the handle and threatened duels with all and sundry, but who at the eleventh hour, pulled back. For George Morgan must have known that attitudes were changing and that it was no longer so acceptable to duel. Both society and the courts were beginning to look unfavourably on any encounter unless the provocation was extreme and clear cut.

So this was the character of the man riding down Kirkcaldy High Street one day in May 1826 – an argumentative bully, a violent ex-soldier, a hesitant duellist. George was seething at David Landale's decision to withdraw his accounts from the bank and wasted no time in getting his own back. Halfway down the road, he bumped into another of Kirkcaldy's big linen merchants. Robert Stocks was one of David Landale's oldest friends. He was, in his own words, 'in habits of decided intimacy and friendship not only with Mr Landale but with all his family'. The two men were the same age, in the same trade, and sat together on the chamber of commerce. Stocks had set up his business from scratch in 1805 and flourished early, making enough money to buy one of the big local estates in nearby Abden. That morning, he and Morgan fell into conversation across their horses and the banker planted the seed of a devastating rumour. As David Landale passed by in the distance, Morgan nodded towards him and told Stocks that he had just got a cash credit from the bank for £5,000. 'That's not all,' he continued. 'I understand Mr Landale has got or is getting £1,000 on his bleach field.' This was not true – at no time did David remortgage his bleach field. But this did not trouble Morgan who saved his most dangerous remark till last. 'I wish all may go well with Landale,' he said. Brief, enigmatic, utterly lacking specifics. But Morgan knew that that was enough. He knew that in a small town like Kirkcaldy, word would get round immediately that David Landale's bankers were losing faith in him.

George Morgan did not stop there. He also gossiped about David's loans with his accountant friend, James Fleming, revealing 'that he had become uneasy about [Landale] on account of the great business he did at their office'. Although 'he believed they would ultimately be safe, [he] thought that it would be prudent to limit his accounts in the mean time and that they would require to be cautious about him.' Over a glass of hot toddy at the coffee house, Fleming passed on the news to his friend, Robert Inglis, a manufacturer based at Markinch, a small town a few miles north of Kirkcaldy. Inglis protested that he had no reason to doubt David Landale's credit and insisted that he had always done business 'on the most honourable terms'. But Fleming was adamant. On the basis of what Morgan had told him, 'Landale was not a staunch man . . . he had got a credit from the Bank of Scotland, and given a security for it over his property.' Such rumours could kill a business dead. It was one thing for a few people to share doubts about a merchant's ability to honour all his bills of exchange. It was quite another for the merchant's bankers to share that opinion. If that were the case, then anyone who was owed money by the merchant would call in their debts immediately. And that is exactly what happened. Overnight, David Landale lost his credit.

Robert Stocks was initially sceptical about George Morgan's claims. He knew the banker 'was in the habit of speaking loosely regarding people's affairs in general', and he knew that Morgan was 'acting very improperly'. But Morgan had not only alleged that David was secretly borrowing substantial sums to keep himself afloat; he had also hinted that it was not enough. In Stocks' mind, these allegations were so serious that his scepticism could not stop him protecting his own interests, even if it came at huge cost to his oldest friend. Some years earlier, Stocks' brother, John, had made David Landale a loan of £1,000 but had died shortly afterwards. Robert, as one of the guardians to his brother's children, had taken on partial responsibility for this loan. 'Although [Stocks] never doubted Mr Landale's credit, he thought it his duty – to mention to the other curator [guardian] what he had heard from Morgan.' For all the talk of trusting David's credit, they did not hesitate and called in the £1,000 loan. At a time of such financial crisis, David had no hope of raising so much cash so they agreed to accept £500 immediately with the balance to be paid by 'Martinmas next' (November 11).

Rumours of David's financial vulnerability soon reached the ears of another of his friends, Alexander Balfour, a flax spinner and wood merchant. Balfour had given his name to the Bank of Scotland as a guarantor to another loan granted to David for £1,500. On June 5, Balfour reluctantly wrote his friend a painful letter asking David to find another guarantor so that his exposure to the debt could be halved.

'I have held the pen nearly half-an-hour considering whether I should call and talk over matters with you or whether I should write you,' Balfour began. 'I have preferred the latter as it is easier to write than to speak especially upon a subject where my greatest dread is that of giving offence. I come to the point. I feel uneasy at having given my name as security to several friends. You are one that certainly, both from friendship and other ties, that I accommodated in this way with great readiness . . . From what has lately taken place in your affairs, I am sure your good sense will excuse me for mentioning this subject at present when all is anxiety and alarm. I will not by any means think of withdrawing my name from your account but think you should relieve me of the one half or, what I would prefer, to limit my individual risk by having signed your bond to the sum of two hundred pounds. I finally hope these very trying and distressing times will ere long wear over and with best wishes, I remain. My dear Sir, Sincerely Yours, Alex. Balfour.'

You can feel Balfour's great embarrassment in every sentence. But he still preferred to discomfit his friend than risk his own investment. Such was the scale of the economic crisis in the Kirkcaldy of 1826 − and the fragility of reputation − that one unfounded rumour could turn a businessman's world upside down. Simply on the word of one man − a distrusted man at that − two of David Landale's best and oldest friends were prepared to call in their loans, knowing that by doing so they were making his circumstances even more perilous. At a time when his cash flow had dwindled to a trickle, David was having to give up his last reserves of credit. Not only that, his honour as a merchant had been challenged.

David was furious. His situation before had been bad; now it was on the brink of disaster. He immediately set about discovering who was behind these rumours. He began with Alexander Balfour who told him he had heard it from William Russell, another manufacturer. Russell said he had heard it in his counting house, possibly from his partner, Michael Barker. David confronted Barker and asked where he had got the information. Deeply embarrassed, Barker said he had heard it from Alexander Beveridge, the teller at a local bank. Its name? The Bank of Scotland. David could not believe it. His own bankers were the source of the rumours against him. Only, they no longer were his bankers. Piqued at losing his account, the Morgans of the Bank of Scotland were wreaking their revenge by casting aspersions on his credit.

David stormed up the hill to the bank and confronted George. How, he asked, did 'the particulars of the new bank account ... come to the knowledge of the public in so circumstantial and correct a manner?' George pleaded ignorance and said he presumed Robert Stocks had told Alexander Balfour. David went back to Stocks. Who was his informant? 'He replied most solemnly that it was Mr George Morgan.'

For David, this was too much. Morgan's behaviour was beyond the pale. He sat down immediately and wrote the draft of a letter of protest to the directors of the Bank of Scotland in Edinburgh. Landale did not have to respond like this. He knew George Morgan's reputation and knew that it was not the first time he had threatened someone's credit. George had once put around a rumour that a Kirkcaldy merchant and magistrate, Thomas Ronald, was closely tied up with another merchant who had just gone bankrupt. Ronald said the rumour 'had a tendency to hurt his credit' and tracked down its origin to George. But he took no action, 'his friends advising him to take no further notice of it, the impression being that Morgan was such a man that no good would likely result from pushing the matter further'. David's friends offered different advice. He showed the draft letter to his friend, the mill owner, James Aytoun who said it looked fine, remarking that George's conduct was no surprise to him for 'he had made free with my credit in a transaction from which he had no reason to take such a liberty'. David asked William Millie, his friend and deputy at the chamber of commerce, if the letter was not a bit strong. 'I approved the letter entirely,' Millie recalled, 'and thought that no language too strong could be used.'

So it was that on June 23 1826, David despatched a fiery, 2,500-word polemic of complaint to the Bank of Scotland head office in Edinburgh. He began gently, thanking the bankers for their courtesy and liberality in granting him the cash credit earlier in the year. It was this that obliged him now to explain why he had withdrawn from the bank. He came straight to the point. Their agents, the Morgans, he wrote, had showed 'so much silly ignorance and then conduct latterly so base and ungenerous a spirit that I must crave your indulgence till I repeat the whole'. And the whole is what the bank directors got. David took them through all the events that had taken place, transaction by transaction, how the Morgans had refused him credit, how they had demanded cash, how they had failed to pay a bill as instructed:

> I make every allowance for a Banker protecting himself but surely a customer like me who has passed every Bill through your office which he has discounted for ten years back, has a considerable claim to the character of a prudent Merchant from the unusually small number of returned Bills that have appeared from his customers and amongst whose transactions he will defy the Agents to pick out one the least ambiguous in its character. Surely, I say, that such a customer of the Bank should have been treated with more respect and confidence, more especially as I had put one part of my property into their hands worth at least £8,000 and assured them upon my honour that besides my stock in trade, I had expended upon my bleachfield upwards of £5,000, upon which I had not borrowed a farthing.

David focused his attack on George Morgan personally. The banker, David said, had often sought to undermine his debtors, 'hinting his alarms that these people would be bankrupt before my Bill was paid (which by the bye is a very usual practice with that Gentleman both in public and in private)'. When David protested at the damage caused to his reputation by the bank's refusal to pay the £1,000 bill, 'the younger Morgan replied that he cared not who might be embarrassed, they must look out for themselves, and added that his Brother might take the responsibility of discounting the Bill but for his part, he would have nothing to do with it.' But David Landale saved his strongest criticism for George's rumour-mongering, his aspersions against David's credit, and his disclosure of David's transactions.

> Before this occurred, you will please keep in mind that I had entirely withdrawn my business from your office in consequence of the agents having refused to do my business, and they finding that other Banks were ready to accommodate me, had the baseness and ill nature to circulate reports prejudicial to my credit, and to divulge transactions which in their official situation should have remained only with themselves. Whatever taint these rumours circulated from such a quarter, and in such times, may have upon my credit with strangers, I know not; but it has given me no uneasiness as respects the opinion of my fellow citizens – the character of the parties can easily be contrasted by them; and should the Directors think it due to an honourable but much aggrieved individual to employ any confidential person from the Head office to enquire into the circumstances I have just related, I doubt not they will obtain information from almost every Merchant in Town respecting the character of their Agents, that will disclose to them the reason why an

agency which ought to be and might have been most extensive in its transactions, has dwindled to nothing in their hands. I request the favour of you to lay this letter before the Directors and I remain with much respect, Sir, Your very humble servant, David Landale

It was a powerful, heartfelt letter. And from someone as measured as David Landale it was little short of a rant. It ended with David's strongest card. The Morgans' behaviour might have damaged him, but it was also damaging the Bank of Scotland whose business in Kirkcaldy 'had dwindled to nothing'. If he was appealing to the bankers' sense of propriety, he was also appealing to their pockets. There was, he was suggesting, a serious problem for the bank in Kirkcaldy and the directors had a duty to investigate. David signed the letter, sealed it up and had it taken to the post, little anticipating what a dramatic impact it would have.

3

From dispute to duel

Thou wilt quarrel with another man that hath a hair more or a hair less in his beard than thou hast. Thou wilt quarrel with a man for cracking nuts, having no other reason but because thou hast hazel eyes. Thou hast quarrelled with a man for coughing in the street.

William Shakespeare, *Romeo and Juliet*, Act III Scene i

How can such miserable worms, as we are, entertain so much pride as to conceit that every offence against our imagined honour merits death?

Benjamin Franklin, cited in *The Art of Duelling*, 1836

Early in the morning on Tuesday June 27 1826, a postman made the long tramp up the hill to David Landale's home. St Mary's stood quietly in several acres of woodland away up the slope from Kirkcaldy's high street and harbour. It was, at two storeys high, more a good sized town house than a mansion. But with nineteen windows registered for tax purposes, it was still one of Kirkcaldy's largest dwellings, and a suitable home for an established local family and prominent businessman.

It was now four days since David Landale had written to the Bank of Scotland directors in Edinburgh. He was convinced of his own rectitude and propriety but knew, nonetheless, that there would be consequences. He expected a row. What he did not expect was an olive branch, contained in the letter delivered by the postman that morning:

Dear Sir,

I will be glad if you will dine with me tomorrow at five o'clock. Mr Campbell from the Bank is to dine with me,

Yours etc,

Da Morgan, Esq.

David must have been stunned. He had just accused David Morgan and his brother of gross professional impropriety and here they were inviting him to supper with Charles Campbell, one of the bank's chief inspectors who happened to be passing through Kirkcaldy on his way back to Edinburgh from Inverness. There was only one possible explanation. David and George Morgan had not yet been told about David Landale's letter and wished to mend fences. David believed that 'the Morgans, seeing that they had lost by far their best customer, began to regret that they should have done or said anything to have hurt either his feelings or his credit'. The invitation was 'with a view no doubt of bringing about a reconciliation'. Yet there was no way David could have gone to dinner with the Morgans at such a time; it would have been highly improper. 'After the manner in which Mr Landale had been treated by these gentlemen, he could not possibly think of accepting of Mr David Morgan's invitation,' his lawyers said later. So David replied by return:

Dear Morgan,

Under the circumstances in which I am placed by your late conduct as agent of the Bank of Scotland to me, I don't feel that it would be consistent with my own dignity to accept of your kind invitation and, more especially where I am to meet a confidential servant of the Bank. But altho' I consider it due to myself to decline this invitation, I beg to assure you that my feelings towards you as an acquaintance and townsman are not in any degree altered.

I am, Dear Sir,

Your Obt Servant,

D Landale.

It is a letter that would have puzzled David Morgan. He knew David Landale was upset by the way he had been treated but he would not have expected such a direct refusal of an offer of bridge-building hospitality. The protestation of continued respect was also curious. Why did Landale need to say that? All he had done was reject an invitation to supper. It was a slight, but only a modest one. Only when David Morgan learned of Landale's letter to the bank would he have understood. And that would take another ten days. For back in Edinburgh, David's letter had dismayed the bank's directors. They met several times in the boardroom of their imposing four-storey headquarters on the Mound at the foot of Edinburgh Castle. How should they respond to this? A valued client had pulled out of the bank while casting grave aspersions on their Kirkcaldy agents. The directors needed more information and on July 11,

Archibald Bennet, the Joint Secretary to the bank, wrote to David and George Morgan demanding an explanation.

> Sirs,
>
> Receive herewith letter dated 23 June 1826, account David Landale to the Treasurers of the Bank complaining of the conduct of you and Mr Geo Morgan Jnr as the Bank's agents at Kirkcaldy. Which letter you will peruse and return hither with your special report for the consideration of the directors, with your earliest convenience. The Directors wish particularly to be informed whether any disclosure of the Bank's affairs or the affairs of its customers, such as suspected by Mr Landale, has been made.
>
> I am, Sirs,
>
> Archibald Bennet Esq.

The letter was straightforward and direct, and David Morgan was left with no doubt as to its meaning: his job was on the line. Fortunately, George had left the day before to go to Ireland and David was able to consider his response without having a furious and impetuous brother getting in the way. David Morgan was much more the banker than his brother – he was careful and methodical, a legacy if nothing else from his previous career as a magistrate, councillor and stentmaster. He mulled long and hard and it was almost two weeks before he replied. His letter was substantial and detailed, a point by point rejection of David Landale's complaints; the tone defiant, that of a disappointed man who has been unjustly criticised. He had, he said, been 'in some measure prepared' for David Landale's criticism. 'This I had no objection to, had he done it in a candid manner, but I must say that I did not expect from him such abuse, nor did I think he could have had the effrontery to lay such a document before the Directors of the Bank of Scotland.' He painted a picture of an honest banker who had become concerned about the scale of a client's debts and lack of income during an economic crisis. David Landale, he implied, was backing himself into a cash flow crisis by being too kind to his customers, allowing them too much time to pay their debts:

I wished quietly and in a becoming manner to reduce Mr L's discounts within bounds, and I did think by doing so in these disastrous times, I was doing justice both to Mr L and to myself. I wished to check a little his wish to speculate and to try to induce him to lessen his credits with those I considered not worthy of them.

I resolved therefore, when a proper opportunity occurred to mention to Mr Landale that his discounts were high, and that he should endeavour to reduce them . . . As I really was anxious for his welfare, I pointed out to him two or three of his customers, with whom I thought he had gone far enough. Mr L did not take the hint as I wished he should. He replied that he knew best whom to trust, it was my province to judge of the Bills, and that I might reject what I pleased, it would give him no offence. Mr Landale had been renewing his customers Bills to a great extent without our knowledge and he well knew that if any things untoward had happened to him, that many of these never would have been paid.

David Morgan's message was simple: his hesitation over paying David Landale's bills was not a deliberate attempt to damage a valued client at a time of need, but a genuine desire to protect the bank from potentially unrecoverable losses. He knew how to appeal to the bank directors' innate conservatism and played it for all it was worth. While he, David Morgan, was being sensible, Mr Landale 'was rather too free with his name to assure to himself the character of a prudent merchant'. He accused Landale of lying over the £5,000 bank loan, claiming he had initially sought the cash 'for a speculation in flax'. This, he said, was merely 'a blind' to cover the fact that he needed the cash to protect himself against bad debts. As for telling David Landale while he was dressing for dinner that the bank would not pay the £1,000 bill in London, David was unapologetic.

> Mr L sent us a note on the 25th April desiring us to write to the Bank by that evening's post to order the Bill to be paid, but sent us no funds for that purpose, nor mentioned a word to how the Bill was to be provided for. This we considered as acting very irregularly and carelessly in such times. When he afterwards called on the same day, I naturally asked him how the Bill was to be paid. He replied by Bills to be discounted next month. This placed us in a very awkward situation: no money in his account, no Bills to show, no time to lose . . . If Mr L was pushed for time, that was his fault, not ours. He should have looked into the matter sooner.

Finally, after much circumlocution, David Morgan touched on the central charge of whether his brother George had broken client confidentiality rules and spread rumours damaging to David Landale's credit. David Morgan was defiant as he protested both his and his brother's innocence: 'There never was circulated by us a word to Mr Landale's prejudice that I know of. With regard to any disclosure of the Bank's affairs or the affairs of its customers, this never happens. I consider secrecy in Banking establishments as the very life of Banking. I am always careful to prevent disclosures, even in the most trifling matters.' If there was any disclosure, it had not come from the Bank. 'When the Bank's negotiations were at a certain stage and of cause necessity known to several persons not connected with this office, it was almost impossible in a small town like this to prevent such a matter from getting out.' He ended with a passionate defence of his and his brother's record as Bank agents: 'I have always endeavoured to manage the Bank's affairs here to the best of my abilities and my anxious wishes are that while I give every fair and reasonable accommodation to the Bank's customers, I may avoid going to imprudent lengths, in order to prevent loss or trouble to the Bank, to our sureties or to ourselves. As the Bank's agent, I have neither friend nor foe, and I can with truth affirm that I never refused to discount a Bill through prejudice.'

It was an effective letter – the best arguments available, to the point, tailored to its readers. David Morgan can only have prayed that it was enough to save his job. A few days later, George Morgan returned from Ireland. He was naturally furious at David Landale's letter – 'a more unmeaning and uncalled for complaint was perhaps never before made' – but his brother managed to calm him enough to write a response to Edinburgh that was reasonably measured. In his letter of August 3, George admitted that he had indeed had a conversation with Robert

Stocks in the High Street about David Landale. But he insisted that it had been Stocks and not him who had raised the subject of David's debts.

> Mr Landale passed on horseback and Mr Stocks on this occasion said to me that he understood or had heard that Mr Landale had obtained a loan of a large sum over his property from the Bank. I replied he had. By this time, it was well known in the town and the publicity originated with Mr Landale himself, and it reached my ears long before this that Mr Landale had said that he got the loan in spite of us. No particulars were mentioned as to the nature or terms of the Bond.

So concerned was George about bolstering his account of events that he even got his lawyer to try to establish the facts.

> I sent my law agent to wait on Mr Stocks and the only difference he gives of the above is that he is not sure whether it was himself or me that first mentioned the subject. But he added at all events, it was not news to him and that not a word was said [that day] to leave any bad impression on Mr Stocks mind with regards to Mr Landale.

For six more days the Morgans anxiously awaited their fate. Throughout this time, Mr Bennet and his fellow bank secretary, George Sandy, pestered them for more information. On July 31, they wrote to find out how much money David Landale had drawn on his £5,000 overdraft and how many outstanding bills he had to pay. Two days later they asked if David had paid the premiums on his insurance policies. And then on August 8, they wrote asking for a full statement of all obligations to the bank by David personally and David Landale & Co. as a company. One can only imagine how both Morgans felt each time they opened a letter with an Edinburgh postmark. Finally, on August 9, in a letter from Mr Sandy, they learned the directors' judgement. The brothers were to be admonished but unpunished. They should not discuss bank matters in public but were right to protect the bank's business:

> It is new and painful to receive so long a statement in the nature of a complaint against agents of the Bank in the conduct of the Trust committed by the Bank to them. But this trust includes, particularly the selection of Bills for Discount, and your bounden duty to the Bank, to your sureties and to yourselves is to conduct the Bank's business with regularity and safety, a duty however by no means inconsistent with reserve and forbearance of personal altercation or offence. Generally agents of the Bank ought to abstain as much as possible from speaking of the Bank's concerns – or those of parties' concerns with the Bank – unless on the proper occasions and points of official duty. With these general remarks, the Directors signify to you the full continuance of their reliance on your prudence as well as zeal in the conduct of the official Trust committed by the Bank to you.

For David Morgan, this was a huge relief. For his brother, it was a green light. From the moment George first read David Landale's critical letter, he had been living under an intolerable burden of self-restraint. His brother had, quite sensibly, told him to keep his head down until the bank decided what to do. Now, in his eyes, he had been cleared by his employers and felt free to pursue his dispute as he wished. And the following Saturday, August 12, in a letter to David Landale, he made his wishes very clear.

Sometimes people kill out of revenge, passion or rage. It is more difficult to understand why people kill for seemingly trivial reasons. And yet many duels were caused by quarrels and disputes of absurd triviality. Men challenged each other over a rude remark, a gossipy aside, an accidental jolt in a pub, an irreverent word about religion or politics. The historian John Atkinson blamed: 'ructions at elections, tiffs at the theatre, gambling debts and army jobs, sackings and promotions, cynical words in Parliament, bluster on the quarter deck, a sister, a daughter, an obstinate horse and a London parson's shilling pamphlets on chastity, adultery and rape'. The nineteenth-century historian Andrew Steinmetz spoke of the 'misapprehended joke, an adverse criticism, a collision in a waltz' that 'led men, professing to be gentlemen and Christians, to hack and hew at one another as though they were wild Indians'. The list of trivialities goes on: men fought because one looked impertinently at another, because one chose the same dish as another in a restaurant, because one used the familiar French *tu* instead of *vous*, because one used an over-familiar nickname, because one believed Dante a greater poet than Ariosto, because one disagreed with another's claim that anchovies grew on trees, because one walked out of a room while another was speaking. In 1816, a French admiral challenged a German man for 'waltzing against him' at a ball. In August 1882, a young Englishman visiting Heidelberg fought a duel over a German student's lack of table manners. After watching the student repeatedly lap up gravy and apple sauce with his knife at the hotel dining table, the Englishman told him: 'You will cut your mouth open if you don't leave off eating gravy with your knife.' The student stormed out, his seconds returned with a challenge, and, despite all attempts to resolve the dispute peacefully, the next day the Englishman found himself standing reluctantly opposite the German student, pistol in hand. 'It is a dreadful shame that I should have to kill this young man because he does not know the proper use of his knife and fork,' he told his seconds. 'Still, it would be just as unfair to let him kill me.' So he shot the young German dead. A few years earlier on the other side of the Atlantic, an American diner almost came a cropper for having equal scruples about table manners. When the fearsome Kentucky duellist Alexander McClung used his bowie-knife in a restaurant butter plate, the diner said: 'Waiter, remove the butter. That man has stuck his knife in it.' McClung seized the butter plate, shoved it in the man's face and said: 'Waiter, remove the butter. This man has stuck his nose in it.' The furious diner exchanged cards with McClung but instantly withdrew the challenge the moment he learned the identity of his much feared opponent.

There were clearly differing grades of insult. An ill judged remark could provoke a duel but could equally be resolved peacefully with a better judged apology, depending on the sensitivity of the recipient. A deliberate libel, however, such as calling a man a liar, a coward, rascal or blackguard, was a one way ticket to the duelling field. Calling a man a liar – or 'giving him the lie' – was considered a very serious allegation because it supposed a man lacked the courage to tell the truth. A refusal to duel in this circumstance implied the man was either indeed a liar or instead a coward who feared combat. The only surer way of provoking a challenge would be to assault an opponent physically, either with the full force of a horsewhip or the gentle slap of a glove. Either way, a duel would follow. To the modern mind, these duels appear absurd, their causes ridiculous and the corresponding reactions disproportionate. But to the eighteenth- and nineteenth-century gentleman it did not matter if the cause were trivial if his honour was questioned. This is the paradox. Men held an unwavering concept of personal honour – which few hold today – and were prepared to risk their lives to defend it. But at the same time, that honour was a fragile creature that was easily compromised. And it was compromised above all by the simple act of a challenge. However absurd the cause, the rules of duelling declared if a gentleman were challenged, he must fight, just as his forebear, if accused, was obliged to fight a trial by combat. There were, of course, exceptions to the rule. Some accusations were so serious that by definition they could not be resolved by a duel. If the accusation were true, the accused could not be a gentleman and thus was ineligible to fight a duel. But if the charges were false and the accuser thus a liar, it was he who lost himself the right to duel. Some men were such large characters that they could get away with not fighting. Sir Walter Raleigh told a young upstart who spat in his face: 'Young man, if I could as easily wipe from my conscience the stain of killing you as I can this spittle from my face, you should not live another minute.' But for most men, rules were rules. *The British Code of Duel* declared: 'If . . . a gentleman evade a justifiable call, he thus necessarily puts himself without the pale of honour.'

One of the greatest threats to a man's honour was his relationship with the opposite sex. Men duelled obsessively over women, to possess them, to impress them, and to protect them. Just as the knight errant had defended damsels in distress, the duellist fought to avenge dishonoured women, whether they be wives, daughters or mistresses. 'Men of honour perceived the duel as a most efficacious device by which to redeem a woman's honour,' wrote the American historian Kevin McAleer. 'The sigh of Cupid's bow could portend a screaming bullet.' Some women must have privately resented the idea that their honour was dependent on the behaviour of their men folk rather than their own actions. But others were not too unhappy with this arrangement. Like Helen, many women found the idea of being fought over attractive, and those who did the fighting even more so. The nineteenth-century duelling expert, James Pemberton-Grund, wrote: 'By one of those curious contradictions peculiar to the sex, [women] turn faint at the sight of blood but welcome with a ready smile the duel-list who sheds it.' Some women were so intoxicated by the idea that they actually encouraged duels, shamelessly luring impressionable young men into risking their lives to defend female honour, an honour that seemed even less robust than its male counterpart. Many a young man was sent to his death in defence of a girl's reputation that had suffered only the most spurious of slights. Many a father died in the attempt to restore a wayward daughter's reputation. One woman even provoked a duel to avenge her husband. Mrs Symons was furious with a certain Captain Best who had beaten up her husband for cheating at cards. So she wrote to Best's close friend, her former lover, Lord Camelford, and alleged that the Captain 'speaks of your lordship in disrespectful and disdainful terms, especially when he is beside himself with wine'. Camelford, an impetuous duellist, immediately challenged his friend without asking for an explanation or confirmation of the false allegations. Refusing all attempts at reconciliation, even though he had learned that Mrs Symons was lying, Camelford stood up against Best on March 10 1804 and was fatally wounded. 'He died as he had lived, a blood-thirsty monster,' wrote one historian, 'solely because he wished to display his superiority as a shot and endeavoured to sacrifice a companion whom he esteemed for a miserable woman whom he despised.' Duelling historians of the nineteenth century were most disapproving of women's involvement. Abraham Bosquett, the author of a guide to duelling known as *The Young Man of Honour's Vade-Mecum*, was scathing: 'There can be no doubt that among the most potent causes of duels were the insinuations of artful, dangerous and vicious females, and inflammatory mistresses, who prided themselves much in being the object of a duel, and frequently insinuated that dishonourable overtures had been made to them by the nearest connections or intimate friends of their keepers, with a view to enhance the idea of their pretended chastity.' The more sedate *British Code of Duel* was no less robust: 'The female who could willingly and thoughtlessly become the cause of excitement to quarrel between gentlemen must resign the character of lady.' That said, both authors still believed that the gravest offence a man could make was to insult a woman. The *Code of Duel* declared that for 'the positive seduction of a female of an honourable family', there could be no apology; a duel was unavoidable.

The most famous duel over a woman resulted in the death of the Russian poet, Alexander Pushkin. The author of *Eugene Onegin* – a story with a duel at its heart – was an inveterate duellist known for his courage under fire and when he suspected that his beautiful wife, Natalya, was having an affair, he did not hesitate. He sought out her admirer, the Baron Georges d'Anthes, a French-born diplomat, and wrote him a deliberately insulting letter. D'Anthes issued a challenge by return of post. On the way to the duel just outside St Petersburg, Pushkin's sled passed close to that of his wife, who was ignorant of the imminent combat, and the poet covered his face so she would not recognise him and try to stop the duel. Later, standing knee-deep in the snow, D'Anthes fired first, his bullet striking Pushkin's thigh bone and deflecting into the lower abdomen. Pushkin fell and lay in the snow face down, motionless for a few minutes, after which he got up, declared he was strong enough to fire a shot, and discharged his pistol at D'Anthes who was lightly injured in the arm and chest. Pushkin, however, was more gravely wounded. He was carried home where he lingered for a day in such pain that at one moment he considered shooting himself. Outside his house a crowd gathered to mourn his imminent loss. On the afternoon of January 29 1837, the day after the duel, Pushkin died, aged just thirty-seven. He was not the only author for whom the duel was a practical as well as a literary art form. Joseph Conrad, however, was more fortunate than Pushkin. While living in Marseilles in 1878, Conrad fought an American called Captain JK Blunt for the love of a Polish beauty called Paula de Somogyi. They fought with pistols and Conrad was lightly injured in the chest, apparently proudly bearing the scar for the rest of his life. He got his own back on his opponent not by killing him but by sketching an unflattering portrait of him in his novel, *The Arrow of Gold*, which included an American duellist called Blunt. Not all men, however, were willing to duel over a woman. In 1823, the future Lord Cardigan stole and subsequently married the wife of his best friend, Captain Frederick Johnstone. He sent a message to the now divorced Johnstone: 'Sir, Having done you the greatest injury that one man can do another, I think it incumbent upon me to offer you the satisfaction which one gentleman owes another in such circumstances.' Johnstone told the messenger: 'Tell [Lord Cardigan] that he has already given me satisfaction: the satisfaction of having removed the most damned bad-tempered and extravagant bitch in the kingdom.'

Some women were not above a little duelling themselves. At first they followed literature's noble tradition of the cross-dressing heroine who adopted male attire to avenge a wrong. As early as 1390 a young girl called Agnes Hotot took part in a duel in Northamptonshire after her father was laid up with gout on the day of the combat. He had had a dispute with a man called Ringsdale over the ownership of a strip of land. Agnes dressed up as a man, tucked her hair 'cap-a-pie', mounted her father's steed and met Ringsdale on the field. 'After a stubborn fight, she dismounted her adversary and when she was on the ground, she loosened her throat-latch, lifted up her helmet and let down her hair upon her shoulders.' She later married into the Dudley family who, in honour of her courage, adopted a crest of a helmet and a woman's head with dishevelled hair. In later times, some women disguised themselves so they could fight their own battles. In the early eighteenth century, a Madame de St Belmont was insulted by a French cavalry officer, but because her husband was in prison for fighting Louis XIV, she was forced to seek satisfaction herself. She sent her adversary a challenge signed 'Chevalier de St Belmont' and he accepted. On the field, dressed as a man, she disarmed him and then revealed her identity. 'You thought,

Sir, that you were fighting the Chevalier de St Belmont, but you were mistaken,' she said. 'I return you your sword, sir, and politely beg you to pay proper respect to the request of a lady in future.' The humiliated officer's shame must have been great. On other occasions, women did not even bother to dress up as men. On August 21 1777, Mademoiselle Leverrier went out onto the streets of Paris to find her former lover, a naval officer called Duprez, who had jilted her for another girl. 'Instead of shooting the man down, as she could have done, she generously handed him a pistol and told him to defend himself. There, however, her consideration for him stopped for while he chivalrously fired his pistol into the air, she shot him full in the face.'

And, of course, on a few occasions women fought among themselves. In 1721, the Comtesse de Polignac and the Marquise de Nesle fought over their right to the Duc de Richelieu's bed. It began with an undignified scrap at a party in the Palace of Versailles, all scratches, torn clothes and scattered jewels. And it ended the next morning at 6 a.m. with a duel. The first exchange of shots was ineffective, but in the second round the Comtesse was hit in the ear, the Marquise rather more seriously on the left shoulder. But women did not always fight over men. In 1792, a certain Mrs Elphinstone paid a visit to Lady Almeria Braddock and was rude to her hostess. 'You have been a very beautiful woman,' declared Mrs Elphinstone in the somewhat unflattering past tense. 'You have a very good autumnal face even now, but you must acknowledge that the lilies and roses are somewhat faded. Forty years ago, I am told, a young fellow could hardly gaze upon you with impunity.' Lady Almeria, not surprisingly, was furious and demanded satisfaction in Hyde Park in central London. They began with pistols at ten yards, Mrs Elphinstone putting a bullet through Lady Almeria's hat. They then set to with swords, and Mrs Elphinstone was lightly injured. Lady Almeria declared herself satisfied, Mrs Elphinstone agreed, and both women curtsied to each other before departing the field.

Yet these and other so-called 'petticoat duels' were exceptions. They were encounters largely between women of low repute such as courtesans and dancers, rare aberrations to what was chiefly a male affair. Historians down the ages have suggested a variety of unacceptable reasons for this – women's 'natural timidity', their preference for a sharp tongue rather than a sharp blade and so on. The historian Robert Baldick said: 'A kinder and no less plausible explanation would surely be that they have more sense than the opposite sex.' Perhaps the real reason is that women throughout history have been burdened with a different concept of honour from men. 'A woman's honour was defined in terms of chastity, fidelity and modesty rather than physical courage, so it could not be enhanced through a duel,' wrote the duelling expert Paul Kirchner. Here again is an indication of how central honour was to duelling. If a duel was simply a single combat to resolve a dispute between two people, women would surely have been involved in more encounters. A woman can hold a pistol just as easily as a man. But women did not get involved because a duel, at its heart, was the defence of a very specific and very male conception of honour.

Compared to the many trivial reasons for a duel, David Landale's assault on his banker's reputation was a devastating calumny that more than justified a challenge. He had not looked at George Morgan the wrong way or jostled him accidentally in a pub. He had denounced Morgan to his employers, behind his back, in the frankest of terms, accusing him of silly ignorance, and base and ungenerous conduct. He had accused George of breaking that most sacred of covenants, a banker's promise of confidentiality. This was all more than enough justification for George to call David out. Yet the former soldier and serial seeker of duels chose on this occasion not to issue a challenge. Instead, on Saturday August 12 1826, a few days after he'd been cleared by his employers, George simply asked David Landale for an apology:

Sir,

I purposely refrained from taking any notice of your letter to the Bank dated 23rd June last till the Directors should come to a determination thereon. That being now done, the cause of silence no longer exists. You must be perfectly aware that your letter contains falsehood and calumny which it is your duty if possessed of honour to apologise for, and retract. I have therefore to request you will immediately send me a written apology for your conduct in using such false unfounded and ungentlemanlike expressions with regard to me.

I am Sir,

Your Ob Svt,

Geo. Morgan

Lieutenant, Half Pay 77th Regt of Foot

This was a curious response. Not many years before, an officer and a gentleman would have acted differently. He would not have waited until an employer or senior officer had ruled on his guilt or innocence. He would not have demanded an apology. He would simply have issued a challenge, immediately. Yet George Morgan, as he had been in all his previous disputes, was more tentative about reaching for his pistols. He would never have admitted it but he had clearly decided that in the short term, his job was more important than his honour. He did not want to upset his employers further by taking part in a hasty duel. And even once cleared by Edinburgh, he was persuaded by his brother, David, not to issue a direct challenge himself. David Morgan wrote: 'George had made up his mind to challenge Mr Landale if he should refuse to apologise for the expressions contained in his letter to the Directors of the Bank, but I advised him not to do so, and this advice . . . George followed.'

George was also wary of challenging because of a mistaken belief about how the law applied to duelling. He told his friend, James Fleming, that he had 'intended to challenge Landale immediately after he knew what the letter to the Bank contained, but that he was dissuaded from doing so for this reason that a person giving a challenge was liable to be sent out of this country by transportation for doing so, and that as Landale had tried to oust him from the Bank, he supposed that he was determined to get him sent out of the country'. As it happened, George was wrong. The law had indeed once threatened duellists with 'banishment'. But not only did the statute consider the sender and the receiver of challenges as equally culpable, it had been repealed in 1819. The reality is that George just wanted to see if he could tempt David Landale into issuing the challenge himself. The clue lies in his decision to sign the letter with his military rank. Some have suggested George was just signalling that he was writing in a private capacity, not as a banker. Others, like David's lawyers, have claimed the signature 'showed a determination on the part of Mr George Morgan to challenge Mr Landale in the event of no apology being given'. Neither explanation seems right. What this showed was that George wanted to fight David in a duel but only if David was prepared to issue the challenge. James Aytoun, a Kirkcaldy merchant and one of David's close friends, said the use of rank 'evidently showed that [Morgan] meant to take up the matter not as a banker but as a soldier'.

George's response does not seem to have surprised David. He immediately wrote back, refusing to retract a word. But on Aytoun's advice, he did ask George to be more specific about his complaint:

> In reply to your letter of this day's date, I am not aware of having stated anything in mine to the Bank Directors respecting you but what I can substantiate by the most respectable evidence. But should you be pleased to point out to me those passages to which you allude as being false and calumnious, I shall then consider what reply to make.

This was not the response that George had expected. He wanted an apology or a challenge, not an exchange of correspondence. He dashed off a reply immediately.

> I have just received your letter of this date which is altogether evasive. You must have been perfectly aware without reference to me that your letter to the Bank was false in most of the particulars and that it was also calumnious and injurious to me, but as you affect ignorance I shall point out one or two very injurious passages. You say in

reference to me that it is a very usual practice with that gentleman both in public and private to hint people would become bankrupt and that we had shewn so much silly ignorance and latterly so base a spirit. Again speaking of the agents, you say a letter you received from Mr Balfour awakened me to see the baseness of their conduct, and again after pressing the Directors of the Bank to make certain enquiries, you say I doubt not but they will obtain information respecting the character of their agents that will disclose to them the reason why an agency which ought to have been most extensive in its transactions has dwindled to nothing in their hands. These, Sir, are statements and expressions which no Gentleman would allow to pass without apology. I must decline entering into any correspondence with you because nothing can possibly satisfy me but an ample apology for the very injurious, unhandsome and ungentlemanlike manner in which you have treated me in the letter to the Bank.

The next morning, a Sunday, David consulted James Aytoun again before going to church. 'We agreed that in replying to this letter, Mr Landale should state that no evasion was intended by him. As he held himself answerable to the memorial, the leading facts contained within being true, no apology could be given as he, Mr Landale, considered himself as the party aggrieved.' David, however, had a problem. He knew that his further refusal to apologise might finally trigger a challenge from George Morgan. But over the next few days, David had long-standing plans to be away from Kirkcaldy. He feared that his absence would be seen as a dishonourable attempt to escape the duel. James Aytoun was clear what David should do.

Mr Landale mentioned to me at the same time that he was engaged on the Tuesday following [August 15] to attend as a sponsor at the Baptism of a friends' child in [Angusshire] and whether, under the circumstances, he should go. I advised his going, because I thought it might tend to cool irritation on either side (though I did not give this as a reason) but agreed that it was necessary he should state the cause of his absence to Mr Morgan lest any improper handle should be made of it at such a crisis. He was therefore to mention to Mr Morgan that until Saturday the 19th he could not have it in his power to receive such communication as Mr Morgan might be pleased to make him, that being the earliest day he could return consistent with arrangements previously made.

It was sound advice and David took it readily, replying to George early on Monday morning.

Sir,

I received your letter of the 12th inst on Sunday morning. You little know me to suppose that my last letter to you was evasive or that I will retract one word from the letter I addressed to the Treasurer of the Bank of Scotland on the 22nd June last. I consider myself warranted in what I stated in that letter by your and your brother's conduct towards me, whose credit at a time of unprecedented difficulty it was your duty to have supported in place of attempting to undermine by expressing yourselves 'that things would not go right with me' and making my transactions, which came to your knowledge in your official capacity, the topic of ordinary conversation, to the material facts of which I hold the testimony of Mr Stocks. I still consider myself the aggrieved individual and therefore there can be no apology due to you. I feel it due to myself to inform you that I am engaged to stand Godfather for the child of a friend in Angusshire tomorrow and from other engagements in the north, it will be out of my power to return to Kirkcaldy till Saturday when I shall reply to any communication you may think proper to make me.

A few hours later, at 11 a.m., to David's bewilderment, the postman brought back the letter with no reply. 'To Mr Landale's surprise, his letter was merely returned under a blank cover from Mr Morgan,' David's lawyers recalled later. 'Altho' this of itself did surprise him, he thought it still more extraordinary that Mr Morgan should not have followed up his own threats by a challenge. If Mr Morgan had not intended to surely he should never have written the two letters as he did?'

David's legal team again misunderstood George Morgan's motives. His letters were designed not to signal a challenge from him but to provoke a challenge from David. But they had failed. It was now clear that David was prepared neither to apologise nor to issue a challenge. This was exactly the kind of behaviour that infuriated George. One Kirkcaldy historian, Jessie Findlay, concluded: 'I can well understand that . . . Landale's correct and lofty attitude would prove a profound irritation' to a man who was so 'hasty, irascible and hopelessly in the wrong'. George decided he was left with no alternative but to escalate the dispute. There was one course of action which would provoke a challenge without fail. He would horsewhip David in the street. And what's more, he would tell everyone that he was going to do so. That Monday afternoon, George informed his friend James Fleming that if he did not get an immediate apology from David, he would 'lay a cane across his shoulders'. The intention was clear: 'I will assault him publicly for the purpose of forcing him to challenge me.' Fleming 'strongly advised him against [this]' and said he should take 'Counsel's advice' instead. 'Morgan's answer was that . . . he being a military man could neither live in this country nor join his regiment if called upon without doing what he proposed.' In fact, George was wrong. His friend Henry Wood, captain and adjutant of the local Fifeshire Militia in which George himself served, believed that in such circumstances a military man should have issued the challenge himself. He said later that in response to David's letter, 'Morgan as a gentleman ought then to have given the challenge to Mr Landale in place of horsewhipping him.' In his opinion, 'Mr Morgan did wrong in not doing so in place of what he did.'

Later that day, Alexander Balfour, the wood merchant and friend of David Landale, was walking up from the harbour where he had just seen the arrival of one of his ships laden with timber from the Americas, when he bumped into George Morgan. 'Mr Morgan mentioned that both he and his brother had been very ill used by Mr Landale and that he was just on his way to horsewhip him,' Balfour said. Like Fleming, Balfour advised Morgan against this but '[he] appeared determined and went away'. Half an hour later Balfour came across Morgan again who was now rather frustrated. Morgan told him that 'he had not seen Landale, he had not come out'. George demanded to see the letter which Balfour had written to Landale back in June, asking for greater security for a loan because of the doubts about David's credit. Morgan believed – incorrectly – that it was from this letter that David had first learned of the banker's allegations about him. Balfour told Morgan he was 'sure he had not mentioned either his or his brother's name in any letter to Mr Landale' but even if he had, he would not show the letter to Morgan. The banker went on his way, Balfour says with some understatement 'apparently rather dissatisfied'.

At 9.30 that Monday evening, William Tod was getting ready for bed when there was a call at his door. It was George Morgan's servant maid, saying that her master wished to see him immediately, despite the hour. Tod, a blacksmith by trade, was foreman to Alexander Russell, one of Kirkcaldy's five iron-mongers. As such, he had 'known George Morgan for many years and occasionally did little jobs for him on his Master's account'. This did not normally involve being summoned in the middle of the night. However, he knew what kind of man George Morgan was so he sighed, excused himself from his wife, and, being 'partly undressed', pulled his trousers back on before hastening into the night. He found George upstairs in his dining room, wearing his dressing gown and in a state. Tod wrote: 'Morgan was standing at a table with a pistol in his hand, which he held out to me and said, "Tod, take out this ramrod" for he could not do it himself. I took the pistol and with great ease pulled out the ramrod.' Morgan handed him a second pistol and again asked him to remove an apparently jammed ramrod, which he did. 'Morgan then asked me what I thought of the pistols and I said I thought they were very handsome.' Morgan proudly told him they had cost him twenty guineas. 'He then gave me a ball and desired me to see how it fitted. I put it into the pistols and as it shook a little, I said I thought it was too small. Morgan said that wouldn't do and desired me to cast two or three dozen for him and gave the mould for that purpose.' Morgan asked how long this would take and Tod told him the bullets could be ready in a day or two. If the blacksmith thought this was all a little odd, he did not say so. But that night, when he returned home, he told his wife that 'Mr Morgan looked a little queerish' and 'appeared to look serious and different from what he commonly did'.

On August 22 1838, a duel took place between two men on Wimbledon Common. Charles Mirfin and Francis Eliot had been driving home from the Epsom races when their phaeton and gig had crashed. In the heated argument that followed, blows were struck which could not be ignored. Attended by their seconds, they met at dusk, fired at twelve paces and Mirfin fell. So far, so lethal. According to a later judgement, 'the affair appeared to have been managed with a strict regard to the practice usually followed on such occasions'. When these codes of duelling were followed, the law tended to be tolerant, juries either acquitting defendants or convicting them of manslaughter, a crime punishable with a modest fine. Yet on this occasion, Francis Eliot and the two seconds were charged with wilful murder. Eliot fled the country but the two seconds were caught, convicted and ordered to be hanged at Newgate prison, a sentence commuted at the last minute to twelve months' solitary confinement. Such punishment was exceptional, yet in the eyes of society fully justified. For these men were guilty of a far greater crime than duelling; they were guilty of being common, or as the court records put it, 'of doubtful gentility'. Mirfin was a linen draper from the Tottenham Court Road, the son of a mercer from Doncaster; Eliot was an innkeeper's nephew from Taunton; the seconds, for heaven's sake, were bricklayers. They had all broken the one cardinal, unbending rule of duelling, namely that it was a privilege of gentlemen and gentlemen alone.

The duel's forebear, trial by combat, had been class blind, open to high and low, peer and peasant. But its successor, the chivalric combat of tournaments, jousts and pas d'armes, was something for knights alone. According to one contemporary code, 'whosoever cannot prove his nobility for four generations and another shall not have the honour of being admitted into the tournament.' This restricted practice endured for half a millennium, as *The British Code of Duel*, drawn up two years before George Morgan picked a fight with David Landale, makes clear. 'If a gentleman detracted from another, the combat should be allowed. But if a clown, he was to take the remedy of legal action. A clown might not challenge a gentleman to combat because of the inequality of their condition.' According to the duelling expert John Atkinson: 'No matter how angry an offended party might be, he would issue a challenge only if the offender were a man of his own social standing. An insult offered by a person of inferior status was punishable there and then by horsewhipping the rascal, but never by inviting him to meet you on the duelling ground.' The flip side of the rule was that if a gentleman was challenged by another, he had no alternative but to fight or risk public humiliation and social exclusion. Men who declined to duel risked being 'posted' by the challenger, a socially embarrassing process by which posters informing the world of his refusal were pinned up around town. Yet the code restricting duelling to gentlemen alone was more than just a rule, it was in fact the quintessence of the institution. Duelling was a badge of rank. Those who had 'smelt powder' were by definition part of the gentlemanly class. Only gentlemen possessed the sort of honour that could be defended in a duel. The historian Donna Andrews wrote: 'The willingness to fight a duel, as well as the recognition of being a person who was "challenge-able" defined, in great part, what it meant to be a gentleman.' But who exactly was a gentleman? 'What a gentleman is 'tis hard with us to define,' wrote the diarist John Selden in 1689. The gentlemanly class was broad, wide and porous; it included the rich aristocrat, the poor squire, the landed gent, and the military man. In Jane Austen's *Pride and Prejudice*, Elizabeth Bennett, a poor squire's daughter, compares herself thus to the aristocratic and wealthy Mr Darcy: 'He is a gentleman; I am a gentleman's daughter: so far we are equal.' In this way, the duel was a leveller, something that bound together the upper echelons of society, what one historian somewhat grandiloquently called 'the sign and seal of a mystic equality between higher and lower, a fraternal bond uniting the whole multifarious class'. Another historian, Anthony Simpson, was more prosaic: '[Duelling] compelled the rich aristocrat to treat the poor scion of the landed gentry as a social equal, much as social custom came to require that a challenge originating in the manor house had to be taken seriously in the castle.' In practice, it was never that simple. In some cases, it was not clear who qualified as a gent and who did not. So horrified was the *Daily Telegraph* in October 1862 at the prevalence of lower-class duelling in Ireland that the paper said a gentleman there was defined as anyone 'who puts on a clean shirt once a week'. *The British Code of Duel* suggested somewhat impractically that if a duellist's opponent were a stranger, and his background uncertain, 'he may be fairly expected to produce his armorial bearings'.

The problem for David Landale in 1826 was that these feudal

definitions were breaking down in the face of a new, growing and more powerful middle class, riding high on the back of the industrial revolution. The gentlemanly class began to include businessmen, industrialists, merchants, surveyors, engineers, lawyers, doctors, journalists even. As such, confusion set in and in response, attitudes changed. A gentleman began to be defined a little more by his behaviour and a little less by his rank. David Landale had no doubts about his own position. He was not technically gentry – he held no substantial landownings – yet he was a merchant, a ship owner and a man of some means, with respectable family lineage back several generations. That made him a gentleman. He was also a prominent member of the community, elected to represent Kirkcaldy businessmen, a God-fearing, law-abiding employer who was known for his good character. That too made him a gentleman. His problem was George Morgan. The banker was technically a gentleman, the proof being that he was an officer commissioned into George III's army. Yet he was not behaving as a gentleman, breaking confidences and issuing threats of violence. The question for David was this: had George given up his right to be treated as a gentleman within the codes of duelling?

After William Tod's unusual summons to George Morgan's home on Monday evening, there was a brief stand off. David left for Angusshire to attend his godson's baptism and George waited for Tod's apprentice to cast some new bullets for his pistols. But at the weekend David returned to Kirkcaldy and immediately began to take soundings from his friends. He was still expecting a challenge from George and he wanted advice on what he should do if it came. Should George Morgan be treated as a gentleman and fought? Or should he be ignored as a loose-lipped rogue?

David Landale turned first to his friend and fellow linen merchant Robert Stocks, the man who had been the first recipient of George Morgan's malicious gossip. He said David would be under no obligation to fight. 'I told Mr Landale . . . that in my opinion he was not bound to fight Mr Morgan if challenged by him upon the ground first, that I conceived Mr Landale to be the party aggrieved, and second that I conceived that Mr Morgan was a man of such a character that Mr Landale would lose nothing in the estimation of the public by refusing to meet him. [My] opinion of Mr Morgan's character was founded from the circumstance of his having been engaged in so many previous quarrels and ill-natured broils with a number of the respectable inhabitants of Kirkcaldy.' Robert Stocks clearly believed that George Morgan, through his boorish behaviour, had ceded the right to be treated as a gentleman and therefore his challenge could be ignored. Another of David's friends, William Millie, his deputy on the chamber of commerce, made the same point: 'I said [that] if Morgan gave a challenge, I did not think that Landale should accept of it from such a character as George Morgan.'

Certainly there was evidence that Kirkcaldy society did not expect a duel from anyone who argued with Morgan. In 1822, Morgan and the merchant Thomas Ronald had a furious argument on the steam ferry back to Newhaven about the right way to steer the boat. 'Both got warm and high words passed,' but both men were pulled apart by witnesses. Ronald told Morgan he 'would fight him in any way he chooses' but was persuaded not to by watching friends. 'They almost all said that Morgan was such a meddling sort of character that Ronald should have nothing further to do with him.' But David Landale would have none of this. He believed he could not use

Morgan's character as an excuse. Morgan might be a rogue but he was still a gentleman. He told Millie that 'Morgan held a commission from His Majesty, was received in the company of gentlemen, and that if he gave him a challenge, he thought he would accept of it.' He told Stocks that 'he considered Morgan his equal because Morgan was an officer, joint manager of the Bank, was received in the same society and frequently sat at table with him.'

David then consulted another friend, the merchant, James Aytoun, who again urged caution, but from a different tack. He argued that men should duel only over matters of honour, not disputes of business. He also suggested that David would have better recourse through the courts. 'As it now appeared probable that Mr Morgan was meditating a Challenge, and anticipation of this formed subject of our conversation, and Mr Landale asked me in the event of his receiving such a communication . . . what I thought he should do,' Aytoun wrote. 'I told him, I did not think that he was under any obli-gation to fight Mr Morgan on account of a quarrel origi-nating in matters of business, that the jury court was open to him if he had been wronged, and was a more reasonable appeal in such a case than to single combat.' By the 1820s, the civil courts were growing in power and were now a place where redress for personal injury could be sought. '[David] then asked what answer I would advise if he received a challenge,' Aytoun continued. 'I proposed that he should . . . immediately lay Mr Morgan's letter before a few friends and would be entirely guided by the advice he might receive from them. Mr Landale acquiesced in this idea and I then asked him who the friends would be that he would call together for that purpose. And after some discussion as to who they were to be and the number of them, three were fixed upon.'

This was fair enough but David also wanted to know what he should do if George decided instead to assault him in the street as apparently everybody in Kirkcaldy expected him to do. James Aytoun told David 'that it was whispered through the town that Mr Morgan had been looking out for him and was telling different individuals that he was to horsewhip him, Mr Landale, as soon as he could fall in with him.' Aytoun advised David that this would change everything:

> I said I was amongst the last men who would countenance a Duel, particularly arising from matters of business, but that in my view of it, its character would be altogether changed if Mr Morgan should in any manner of way publicly assault him, and that in such an event, I could see no alternative but by giving Mr Morgan an immediate challenge. For though [Morgan] might not stand high in public intimation, he bore a Commission from His Majesty and was received into the society of those who considered themselves as gentlemen. He could not therefore on that account refuse to fight with him or receive from him such an insult without calling him to account for it.

Robert Stocks was still far from convinced. He and James Aytoun, knowing that they had both been advising David, met one evening for 'a long conversation . . . on the whole matter from beginning to end'. But in the end, even Stocks was persuaded. He told David that 'if Morgan proceeded to strike [him], he was warranted in challenging him'. With this unanimity of advice, David's mind was settled. He told Aytoun:

'I have now completely made up my mind both as a Christian and as a man to the consequences, and if I shall receive a stroke, I cannot avoid giving Morgan a challenge.' David even asked how he should behave at the very moment he was attacked by Morgan. Aytoun replied that 'he should carefully avoid having any words with him, and that he should merely turn round to any person passing at the time, and ask them if they had seen the occurrence'. All that David had to do now was decide who should act as his second. He summoned his old friend William Millie. 'Landale said, if [Morgan] put his threat into execution, then he had no alternative but to challenge him, and said that if he was obliged to, he hoped I would second him.' Millie clearly had not been expecting this onerous duty and was taken aback. He 'neither said that he would or would not, and thereupon left Landale'.

By now, after all the hypothetical speculation, the reality of the situation was beginning to sink in and David's friends began to be concerned for his safety. His doctor, Alexander Smith, wrote telling him to 'be on his guard not to run the risk of being exposed'. James Aytoun, in particular, began to fret and went to see David on Sunday morning.

> As matters were now verging to extremity, I felt considerable anxiety from the forenoon of Saturday and I ruminated in my mind if there could be no means to prevent the necessary consequence of a blow. It occurred to me that a man going about to tell what he intended to do was not a common proceeding, and I thought there was a chance that if [Morgan] should see Mr Landale prepared to meet his assault by having a good whip or other weapon of defence in his hand, that it might not be

proceeded in. I – next forenoon betwixt church services – waited on Mr Landale and stated to him what had occurred to me since I had seen him the day before, but that I did not offer it as an advice as my own mind was not made up as to its propriety, but merely proposed it to him for consideration. Mr Landale disapproved of it as not likely to put an end to the matter, and might produce a scuffle in the public street which we both deprecated.

As David agonised, George Morgan, according to some reports, practised. The experienced soldier had seen much action in Spain but it had been a long time since he had fired a weapon in anger. Since William Tod had been true to his word and delivered thirty freshly cast bullets to his house the previous Friday, George had risen at dawn to get his eye back in. According to evidence given later in court: 'About that time, for about two or three mornings early, the reports of a pistol were heard not far from Mr Geo Morgan's house from which it may be inferred that he was practising shooting. He must have intended so – otherwise he surely would not have ordered so many bullets.' A correspondent with the *Kirkcaldy Advertiser* later reported: 'Mr Morgan had been for some time preparing for the duel as the back of his house was completely riddled with bullet holes.'

4

The day before the duel

There can be nothing more contrary to good discipline in a wel-ordered commonweale, than this wicked and unjust kind of fight, which destroyed so farre foorth as it beareth sway, all civill societie. For it breedeth the contempt of God and his commandments, of Religion, of lawes, constitutions, and civill government, of Princes, of magistrates, and finally of countrey, parents, friends and kindred.

Lodowick Bryskett, *A Discourse of Civill Life*, 1606

If an oppressed nation has a right to appeal to arms in defence of its liberty and the happiness of its people, there can be no argument used in support of such appeal which will not apply with equal force to individuals. How many cases are there . . . where there is no tribunal to do justice to an oppressed and deeply wronged individual?

John Lyde Wilson, *The Code of Honor*, 1838

The morning of Tuesday August 22 1826 broke cold and damp, rain coursing down on Kirkcaldy's townsfolk as they scurried to work. It was, James Aytoun later recalled, 'a very wet day'. So when George Morgan strolled down the High Street at 10 o'clock for his morning newspaper, he for once was carrying an umbrella rather than his usual cane. He

95

entered James Cumming's shop, selected a paper and engaged 'in a little conversation' as he rummaged in his pocket for a coin. But as he turned to leave, he spotted David Landale passing by outside. He did not hesitate. He rushed out of the door and struck David violently across the shoulders with his umbrella.

'Take you that, Sir!' he cried.

David staggered back in shock. He had not seen George coming and took the full force of the blow on his shoulders. But, gathering his wits about him, he ran quickly into the shop before Morgan could get in another blow.

'Mr Cumming, I hope you observed what passed?' he asked the bookseller. Cumming said he had indeed seen it all. But George Morgan was not yet done. He followed David inside. 'By God, Sir, you shall have more of this yet!' he yelled and moved forward to strike David again.

Furious at the indignity of this sordid fracas, David exclaimed: 'I have never got such treatment in my life!' and ran out before the banker could assault him again. George Morgan made chase but returned to the shop a few minutes later. He was, Cumming said, 'much agitated'. Between breaths, he said to the bookseller: 'By God, James, I have never told you a word about the shocking usage that my brother David and I have got from Landale.' He pulled David's letter to the Bank of Scotland from his pocket and began to read a few sentences. But Cumming was having none of it. Although the shopkeeper knew George Morgan well, and was even a trustee of one of the Morgan family trust funds, he refused to take his side. 'George, I don't care what that letter contains, nor what usage Landale had given either you or your brother,' Cumming said. 'Your conduct in striking

Mr Landale was very improper on your part.' George insisted on reading out more of the letter but, according to Cumming, 'was unable to do so from the state of agitation he was then in'.

Then, unexpectedly, David appeared back at the door of the bookshop. He had assumed that George Morgan would have left by now and wanted to make sure Cumming would bear witness to what had taken place. Seeing David again gave George fresh heart, and after folding up the letter, he cried: 'By God, Sir, you shall have more of this.' But David had had enough. With all the dignity he could muster, he told George Morgan: 'You are a poor, silly creature. You are a coward, Sir, a poor, silly coward.' And with that he walked out into the rain, followed a few moments later by his adversary.

A duel was now unavoidable. One gentleman had struck another and both were locked into a sequence of events from which neither could escape. David and George's actions would in the next few hours be guided by codes of honour laid down over hundreds of years. Of course, the rules changed in detail from year to year and country to country. Duellists across Europe found many different ways and means of shooting one another. All that mattered was that this body of self-regulation existed; without it, a duel could not be distinguished from common murder. The swordsmen had drawn up a huge literature of fencing custom and practice – one of the earliest being the *Flos duellatorum* published in Italy in 1420. So when the sabre was eventually exchanged for the pistol as the duelling weapon of choice, the gunmen drafted their own codes. A large number were published, particularly in Italy, and many were confusing, inconsistent and contradictory. In France, the most famous was the Comte de Chatauvillard's *Essai sur le duel* published in 1836. Two years later American duellists could consult John Lyde Wilson's *The Code of Honor; or rules for the government of principals and seconds in duelling*. But in 1826, the most widely accepted English language *code duello* – as they were known from their Italian origin – was the so-called 'Thirty six Commandments' drawn up in Ireland in 1777. A group of duellists from counties Tipperary, Galway, Mayo, Sligo and Roscommon had met at the Clonmel summer assizes and agreed the rules to curb the excesses of an increasingly bellicose but confused Irish gentry. The authors tightened up the existing rules, added a few of their own for good measure and set the tone for duelling mores for the next half century. They set out precisely how a duel should take place, who should be involved, what everyone should do, how they should start, how they should end.

Yet this code, like many others, had gaps. While they set out in detail how two men should shoot at each other, they tended to be vague about why they should do so in the first place. Few defined what exact behaviour could be deemed to undermine a gentleman's honour. Some attempted to place different types of insulting behaviour on a scale and match them to corresponding rules for the resulting duel. Thus, according to some codes, it was worse to accuse a man of lying than to accuse him of cheating; not for nothing does the word challenge share the same etymology as the word calumny. According to other codes, the worst accusation that could be made against a man was to say he had insulted a lady. Yet few of these scales were meaningful. This left wide discretion for men to duel for absurdly trivial reasons if they considered their honour challenged, or to ignore greater slights without fear of losing face. Yet George Morgan had chosen one of the few insults that all the codes agreed could not be ignored. 'As a blow is strictly prohibited under any circumstances among gentlemen, no verbal apology can be received for such an insult,' the Irish code declared. A man like George Morgan, it decreed, had only three options, none of which was appealing: 'the offender handing a cane to the injured party to be used on his own back at the same time begging pardon; firing on until one or both are disabled; or exchanging three shots and then asking pardon without proffer of the cane.'

The Irish gentlemen were particular about how a challenge should be made. 'Challenges are never to be delivered at night, unless the party to be challenged intend leaving the place of offence before morning; for it is desirable to avoid all hot-headed proceedings.' This was crucial – there had to be a delay between the challenge and the duel to ensure that it took place in cold blood. Yet the Irish code and others were remarkably imprecise about how a challenge should be written, the result of which was that many added insult to injury and precluded any possibility of an amicable solution. Few duellists would have done well to follow Sir Toby Belch's advice: 'Go, write in a martial hand; be curst and brief; it is no matter how witty, so it be eloquent and full of invention . . . and as many lies as will lie in thy sheet of paper.' Brevity does not always lend itself to good manners, as one Italian nobleman showed when he wrote: 'Sir, if your courage is equal to your impudence, will you meet me tonight in the wood?' A high-spirited young witness who considered himself unjustly cross-examined by a barrister sent this challenge to the lawyer: 'Sir, you are renowned for great activity with your tongue, and justly, as circumstances that have occurred today render evident. I am celebrated for my activity with another weapon, equally annoying and destructive; and if you would oblige me by appointing a time and place, it would afford me the greatest gratification to give you a specimen of my proficiency.'

It was not until 1836 that a duelling code set out in terms exactly how a challenge should be written. *The Art of Duelling*, written anonymously by a man who gave himself the nom de plume Traveller, said it was 'ungentlemanly' to write mocking challenges. 'A man,' he said, 'should conduct himself (however grievous the offence he has received) during the whole affair with the greatest possible politeness.' His challenge, therefore, should be written 'carefully and expressed clearly; avoiding all strong language: simply stating, – first, the cause of the offence; secondly, the reason why he considers it his duty to notice the affair; thirdly, the name of his friend; and lastly, requesting a time and place may be appointed.' This is exactly what David Landale did.

There was now no doubt that David Landale should challenge George Morgan. He could do so with absolute propriety and duty, at least according to the duelling codes. He no longer needed to worry about whether he should duel over a business dispute or whether he was partly in the wrong because of the strong language he had used against Morgan. It was now all much simpler. A gentleman had been assaulted in the public street by another and was obliged to defend his honour. So David swiftly scribbled out his challenge to Morgan:

Kirkcaldy 22 August 1826
Tuesday [1 o'clock]

Sir,

In consequence of the ungentlemanlike insult you gave me this morning when passing Mr Cumming's shop, I must request you will meet me tomorrow morning at 7 o'clock precisely at the first cross road that sets off on the right in going from Torbain to Carden Mill with pistols, and give me that satisfaction which as a gentleman I am entitled to.

I am, Sir,

Your most obedient servant,

D Landale

As challenges go, it is precise and detailed, albeit in David's barely legible scrawl and covered in ink blots. It is the letter of a gentleman seeking redress for his questioned honour, not an angry man bent on revenge. Again, quite correctly, David did not deliver the challenge himself but asked his friend, William Millie, to do so for him:

Tuesday morning, 1 o'clock

My Dear Sir,

Morgan has just struck me with his umbrella in passing Cumming's shop. I immediately called him a cowardly rascal and left him. There is no alternative left me but to challenge him which I have long made up my mind to and enclose one that you may deliver it immediately with

all secrecy for my honour. If you hesitate, give it to Thos
Spears,

Yours,

D Landale

PS. I go to Edinburgh by the 2 o'clock coach to purchase
a pair of detonating pistols. Keep all quiet and meet me
if you are to second me, at Mr Ferguson's gate tomorrow
morning at a quarter past six o'clock. If you cannot, 10
o'clock this evening.

D Landale

PPS. Secure Thos Spears or your brother John, if you
have any doubts. Some of you must meet me tonight
twixt 9 & 10 o'clock.

William Millie received the letter an hour later at his factory
up the road in Pathhead and he opened it with a heavy heart.
Its contents did not surprise him. But he still cursed his luck.
He did not want to have anything to do with a duel. Millie
had only a passing concept of what a second did, and did not
want to be involved in a scandal. He had made his reluctance
known at the weekend when David had asked him if he were
prepared, in theory at least, to be his second. Yet when the
moment came, David had asked him anyway, despite acknowledging Millie's reluctance in the letter. He asked Millie no less
than twice to find an alternative second if he decided ultimately
he was not up to the job, suggesting either Thomas Spears or
his brother John Millie as possible alternatives. It was a clever
point to make, insinuating that if Millie did not agree to be
second, then the task would fall on someone else's shoulders.

Yet Millie was right to be cautious. For the role of second in a duel was not only onerous, it could also be lethal.

In the late Middle Ages, the codes of chivalry withered in the face of social change. Where once European noblemen resolved their disputes by combats or jousts, they now assassinated one another in what became known as killing affrays. Throughout the fifteenth and sixteenth centuries, backed by groups of retainers, these gentlemen frequently ambushed one another and engaged in private war, war that was always dangerous, and almost always lethal. Slowly, as these unregulated affrays were replaced by more ritualised duelling, the retainers began to take a lesser part in the fighting and a greater role in organising the encounter. These men became known as seconds.

Initially, at least, the seconds continued to take part in the fighting. 'They were not passive witnesses: they fought each other,' observed the French historian François Billaçois. 'Moreover, once a second had killed his man, or put him out of action, he would go to the aid of the duellist he was seconding.' Many principals welcomed this; many knew they stood a better chance with an expert fighter alongside. One can hear the dismay in Lear's voice when he is about to be captured: 'No seconds, all myself?' One early French historian of duelling said many seconds could not help themselves but join in, through the sheer joy of the fight. Yet, in 1712, there was huge public outrage at a terrible and bloody duel in Hyde Park between a violent drunk, Lord Mohun, and the Duke of Hamilton. Both men hacked at each other with savage abandon. 'The Duke of Hamilton received a wound on the right side of the leg about seven inches long, another in the right arm, a third in the upper part of the right breast, running downwards towards the body, a fourth on the outside of the left leg. Lord Mohun received a large wound in the groin, another in the right side through the body and up to the hilt of the sword and a third in the arm.' Not surprisingly both men died. The seconds – Colonel Hamilton of the Foot Guards, and Lieutenant-General MacCartney – fought one another as well 'according to the old custom' and both were subsequently found guilty of manslaughter. But what prompted the wave of popular opprobrium were the claims that the Duke had actually been killed by Mohun's second and a footman who had joined in after their master was struck down. Colonel Hamilton and one of the surgeons insisted after the duel that Mohun did not make the fatal blow that finally killed the Duke.

By the late eighteenth century, it was rare for seconds to take part. The Irish code still accepted the principle that seconds could fire at each other: 'When seconds disagree and resolve to exchange shots themselves, it must be at the same time and at right angles.' But few went this far. Occasionally, a second would challenge a duellist who had just defeated his principal but this was frowned upon. By 1824, *The British Code of Duel* was quite clear about this: 'It has happened that from some dispute in regard to arrangements, which are in themselves very simple, or on the conduct of a dissenting principal, seconds have become principals to each other. Nothing can be decidedly more wrong.'

It was not, however, just the possible danger that made William Millie a reluctant second. He also knew what a burden the job could be. To be a second was, according to *The British Code of Duel*, 'the most awful responsibility that perhaps can fall to any gentleman'. The role was part best man, part umpire.

The primary responsibility was to represent the principal. It was the second who would try to negotiate an amicable resolution – in fact, this was a very solemn duty upon which almost all the codes agreed. Some disputes were substantial, and nothing could be done to avoid a duel. But many were absurd, drunken misunderstandings that two effective seconds could easily resolve without either party reaching for their pistols. 'They are bound to sift thoroughly the matter of dispute,' *The British Code of Duel* declared, 'to ascertain whether it be a question for duel, whether the challenger is entitled to call on the challenged, whether the latter is not so decidedly in the wrong . . . or whether there be any mode of honourable arrangement without the last resource'. But if the second failed to secure a peaceful resolution, then it was he who would organise the subsequent duel. He would represent his friend and, by his decisions and judgement, hold his friend's honour in his hands. It was a job that descended directly from a knight's need to be attended by a faithful squire. 'He should be in close attendance upon his friend and support him if his spirits flag.'

Yet the second had another responsibility, and that was to ensure that the rules were followed and honour was satisfied. He had, in fact, two masters – his principal and the codes of honour. He was one of the two crucial witnesses whose testimony would determine whether or not the rules had been followed. At one extreme, the seconds were there to distinguish a duel from murder; at the other, they were there to tell the world that the two men had behaved with honour. 'Though on opposite sides, they were in a real sense colleagues,' wrote the historian Victor Kiernan. 'They were assisting the combatants but they were also delegates of the class to which all concerned belonged and whose standards of conduct all of them were taking the field to vindicate. It was part of the institution that seconds should be guided by a gentlemanly sense of fitness, rather than by narrow partisanship.' On occasion, if the seconds could not persuade their principals to see sense and resolve their dispute amicably, they might collude to prevent injury. Many duels were resolved without bloodshed because the seconds deliberately under charged the pistols. Others took more drastic action: 'When two foreign officers taking part in the Carlist war in Spain in the 1830s were bent on fighting, their seconds set them to fight on the beach at San Sebastian, on sand too loose to enable either of them to shoot straight.' And if all that were not burden enough, the second also had to contend with the law. This was quite clear. In the eyes of many courts, if anyone were killed in a duel, the seconds were as culpable as the man who pulled the trigger. They were technically accessories to murder and could be punished as such.

The duelling experts were full of advice about who would make a good second. The Irish code stipulated very clearly that seconds must always be 'of equal rank in society with the principals they attend'. They should also be men of character. The historian Robert Baldick concluded: 'All authorities were agreed that seconds should be men of experience and moral courage, justice and urbanity.' The experienced duellist Abraham Bosquett wrote in 1817 that a second should be 'a man of honour and a man of sense, cool but determined that you shall acquit yourself honourably. If he is, besides, a man of experience and conciliating and persuasive address, then so much the better.' Others recommended men who have 'seen some shots exchanged', who were not married, who held no official position. All agreed it was important to choose a second who would do everything they could to stop a duel. Many seconds were in practice more aggressive than their principals and exacerbated rather than calmed disputes. From his description of two seconds in *Nicholas Nickleby*, Charles Dickens knew their kind well: 'Both utterly heartless, both men upon town, both thoroughly initiated in its worst vices, both deeply in debt, both fallen from some higher estate, both addicted to every depravity for which society can find some genteel name and plead its most depraving conventionalities as an excuse, they were naturally gentlemen of unblemished honour themselves, and of great nicety concerning the honour of other people.'

Some duellists had other, more particular advice about who was eligible to be a second. The seventeenth-century French author, Pierre de Bourdeille Brantôme declared that Muslims and other 'infidels' could not be seconds: 'It is not proper that an unbeliever should witness the shedding of Christian blood, which would delight him.' And Traveller, in *The Art of Duelling*, believed that a duellist would do well to avoid an Irish second. 'I should advise his never choosing an Irishman on any account, as nine out of ten of those I have had the pleasure of forming an acquaintance with, both abroad and in this country, have such an innate love of fighting, they cannot bring an affair to an amicable adjustment.' But the choice was crucial. Lieutenant Stanton of the 97th Regiment of Foot, wrote in *The Principles of Duelling* that: 'The second is like the pilot on board a ship on whom your safety depends. The grand object is to procure a second whose honour, integrity, friendship and judgement may be relied upon.'

William Millie may have been honoured by the trust his friend David Landale was placing upon him. But he knew little about duelling and was nervous about the challenge for he knew it to be great. 'A man who accepts the office of second to a friend undertakes a most important charge,' Traveller wrote. 'Unfortunately, few are aware of the great responsibility that devolves upon them, and from ignorance, inexperience and want of presence of mind, often commit serious mistakes.' Then again, it might still have been the sheer danger that gave Millie pause for thought. The historian Andrew Steinmetz described a 'celebrated duel' between two men called Pierrot and Arlequin. 'They fired together and each of them killed his adversary's second.'

In the end, William Millie decided that his loyalty to his friend outweighed his reservations about being a second. So, with his brother John as moral support, he set off to Kirkcaldy where followed an absurd sequence of events for a matter so grave. Millie knew no more of the umbrella assault than the brief description in David's letter so he headed first to James Cumming's shop to find out what had happened. Cumming, inevitably, was not there. So Millie had no choice but to deliver the challenge without knowing the full circumstances of what happened. He went to what he thought was George Morgan's house only to be told by the maid that he no longer lived there. Feeling a little foolish, Millie asked her where he now lived and was directed to his house in Kirk Wynd just off the High Street. There he rang the bell and was told by a servant that yes, this was the right house, but no, Mr Morgan was not at home and was not expected until dinner time. So Millie and his brother headed off towards the bank when suddenly they came upon Morgan walking down the street accompanied by his accountant, James Murdoch. This presented Millie with a dilemma prescribed by the social and duelling niceties of the time. He had found the man he was looking for, but it would have been quite improper for him to deliver a challenge in the public street. So Millie simply bowed to Morgan – who bowed back – and walked past him ten yards or so, desperately hoping that the banker would stop and enter his front door. Yet Morgan did not do so – he too walked on by. At this, Millie lost patience and told his brother John to run after Morgan. Millie told Morgan he had a communication to make to him from David Landale. Unsurprised, Morgan asked Millie to walk into his home.

Inside, they walked upstairs to George's office. Without saying a word, Millie handed him David Landale's challenge. George read it hastily and said: 'Certainly, by all means.' But according to Millie, he 'appeared flurried a little', as if the reality of what he had set in train was suddenly dawning upon him. He asked Millie to clarify the location – David Landale's handwriting was appalling and the word 'Torbain' was hardly decipherable. Millie confirmed the name and asked Morgan to let him know if any unforeseen circumstance would delay the meeting. Morgan insisted there would be no delay because he had his pistols ready. 'He immediately took up a case which he said contained the pistols and clapped the case down on the table in a rather bravado manner,' Millie later recalled. All he had to do, George said, was find a friend to act as a second.

This is puzzling. George Morgan had sought this duel and yet had not prepared for it by arranging a second. On one level, it is possible that George was still in denial about the possibility of a duel. As his past encounters showed, for all the bluster and bombast, he tended to run whenever a duel became a real possibility. George might still have believed that David would not go through with it. But there is also some evidence that George struggled to find anyone to agree to the role. George was clearly not a man who made friends easily and those that there were might not have been suitable. They might also have refused because George was the aggressor or because they just did not want to be part of something they considered a bloody anachronism. According to the bookseller James Cumming, George saw two local men immediately after he had received the challenge, a Mr Hugh Aitken and a Captain Henry McMillan. There is no hard evidence that George asked either to be his second but it is a reasonable supposition that he did. Either way, even if they were asked, neither did act as his second. In the end, George was forced to trick 'a slight acquaintance' – not even an old friend – into helping out. Lieutenant William Milne of the Royal Navy, one of many hundreds of naval officers in the 1820s stranded on half-pay without ship or enemy, lived a few miles south of Kirkcaldy in the small village of Burntisland. At around four o'clock, George took a chaise down the coast and explained the situation to Milne, this time deliberately failing to mention that he had assaulted Landale. He just needed a second, he told Milne disingenuously, to help 'get the affair adjusted' peaceably. Milne wanted to hear more about what had happened but George refused. He was in a rush and would tell Milne all about it on the trip back up the road. Eventually, Milne agreed, 'without imagining that the quarrel was of so serious a nature, for Morgan did not mention to him that he had struck Landale'. Thus in ignorance Milne travelled back to Kirkcaldy with Morgan to meet his counterpart, William Millie, and agree the terms of the duel.

★

On October 30 1824, two old friends bumped into each other in the Black Bull Inn on Leith Street in Edinburgh. Captain Gourlay and Mr Westall, we are told, 'recognised each other in friendship'. They had last seen one another a month before at Doncaster races where Mr Westall had lost a bet of seventy guineas to the captain. After a few drinks and a little conversation, Captain Gourlay gently reminded his friend of the debt. At this, Westall wondered if he could do a deal. Captain Gourlay had himself lost a similar bet to one of Westall's friends. Would it be possible to set the debts off against each other? His friend, Westall said, had already agreed that this arrangement would be acceptable to him.

It was not acceptable, however, to Captain Gourlay. He flew into a rage and 'an altercation ensued' during which he accused Westall of being a swindler. He in turn called Gourlay a liar. 'On this, the Captain, snatching up the poker, made a blow at Mr Westall's head: the poker missed its aim, but descending on his shoulder, was snapped in two by the force of the blow; which for some minutes, rendered him insensible.' When Westall recovered, he went back into the coffee room, and after 'much warm language', a duel was arranged. The following morning, both men, accompanied by their seconds and surgeons, met at South Queensferry, a spot west of Edinburgh where the Forth Bridge now spans the firth. They took a boat over to the north bank where, after due process, 'Captain Gourlay, receiving Mr Westall's ball, fell dead upon the spot.' Westall returned to Edinburgh where he later sold his pistols to a gunsmith called John Thompson who had a shop on Princes Street. And it was here two years later, on the afternoon of Tuesday August 22 1826, that David Landale found himself staring at a bewildering variety of weapons in the display cabinets.

For while George Morgan had struggled to find a second, David Landale had spent several hours attempting to find something equally important for a duel – a set of pistols. He had none of his own and it had simply not crossed his mind that he should get some, an indication both of his unfamiliarity with firearms and his previous hopes of achieving a peaceful reconciliation. According to one account of the duel, 'Landale had not fired a shot in his life before.' So, as he said in his letter to William Millie, he had taken the two o'clock coach to Edinburgh to buy some. He had little idea of what he wanted so he wandered down Princes Street and ended up browsing in John Thompson's shop. 'He went by mere chance into a shop and asked for a pair,' his lawyer, Henry Cockburn later recalled. 'Knowing nothing about such engines, he asked if he could depend on them. "You may depend on thae pistols," said the lad. "Thae's the pistols that shot the man at the ferry last year." ' Which is how David Landale returned to Kirkcaldy that evening in possession of two duelling pistols that had already proved themselves to be true and lethal having successfully shot dead the late lamented Captain Gourlay.

In 1826, it would have been unthinkable for David Landale to have reached for anything but a pistol to fight a duel. Until the 1770s, the duellist's weapon of choice had tended to be the sword. But by the late eighteenth century, new technology had finally produced pistols that were moderately accurate and reliable and they became the duellist's preferred weapon. The swordsmen, particularly on the continent, put up a stout, rear-guard defence. The blade, they argued, required years of training to master, a discipline that ensured that duelling was practised only by well-born aristocrats who had been suitably instructed since their school days. It required more courage, they said, to slide cold steel into a man's belly than to fire an impersonal bullet at his chest from a distance. Above all, the traditionalists claimed that pistols were less dangerous because in practice they were less reliable and accurate than their supporters claimed. It was quite common for a pistol duel to end with neither bullet 'taking effect'; but a swordfight could end only when blood was shed.

But over time, the pistols prevailed, particularly in Britain and Ireland. Pistols were possessed as lovingly as swords, and specialised duelling weapons became family heirlooms, handed down from father to son, along with the skills to use them. The great Irish duelling judge, Sir Jonah Barrington, was given two pistols by his father, one called 'Sweet-lips', the other 'The Darling'. But pistols popularised duelling, making it accessible to more than just the upper classes. David Landale owned no firearms, nor is there any evidence he had any experience of using them, but he was able to buy a pair of pistols in Edinburgh one day and use them in a duel the next. The pistol users believed their weapon sat more easily in duelling's tradition of honour, where the outcome was determined more by luck or providence than by skill. *The British Code of Duel* declared that: 'Projectile weapons are consonant to the principle of duel, as relates to guarding against the false pride of strength or agility, since the most delicate sense of honour, and the utmost rectitude of mind may be found often unaccompanied by these qualities.' Duellists put their lives in the hands of fate, or more prosaically, they put crude pistols in their own unfamiliar hands and hoped for the best. Nor were they expected to aim properly; that was considered bad form (except in Germany where the opposite was true). Instead, duellists were expected to raise their pistol, point and fire immediately. By contrast, the pistol users considered a swordfight to be a straightforward competition of skill and strength, more single combat than a duel. Size mattered hugely in a sword fight, but in a pistol duel it was relevant only if one of the participants was so fat that he presented a significantly larger target. And above all, the pistol duellers insisted that theirs was the more dangerous combat. A pistol duel often ended when a man was down whereas a sword fight was frequently halted after an arm was scratched.

The golden era of the duelling pistol lasted from the 1770s to 1850, when duels were so prevalent that gun makers made weapons specifically for the task in hand. Early duelling pistols were crude affairs, adaptations from army pistols or the short weapons riders kept on their saddles for protection on the road. But by the early nineteenth century, duelling pistols were so sensitive and refined that they were of little use for anything else. They could certainly not have been used for battle or day-to-day protection. The archetypical duelling pistol tended to be about 16 to 18 inches long, weigh about 2 pounds, and could fire a lead ball 250 yards, kill at 40 yards and be accurate at 20. Many had hair-triggers to minimise hand movement. The barrels were deliberately smooth bored. Rifled barrels were considered ungentlemanly because the spiralled grooves increased the gyroscopic speed and accuracy of the bullet and thus made the pistol more lethal. Initially, at least, the duelling pistol would have been what was known as a flintlock. By the early nineteenth century this used quite old fashioned but well tested technology. When the trigger was pulled, a hammer containing a small bit of flint scraped down a strip of metal creating sparks. These ignited the gunpowder sitting in a small priming pan fixed to the side of the pistol. This then ignited the powder in the touch hole leading into the barrel which in turn set off the main charge behind the bullet. This was the classic firearm of the time – the weapon of Waterloo and all the wars against Napoleonic France, a gun that had been around since the 1650s. This was the weapon chosen by George Morgan to fight his duel, the weapon that he showed off with such bravura to William Millie when he delivered David Landale's challenge. This flintlock had served George well in Spain where he saw how lethal the firearm could be. In just one battle to seize control of Salamanca in July 1812, Ensign Morgan would have seen more than 7,000 allied soldiers shot dead or wounded. In Bernard Cornwell's books, Captain Sharpe and his 'chosen men' often survive a hail of musket balls. In reality, the flintlock, despite its age, could kill effectively and George Morgan was aware of this.

But by now, a new type of weapon was emerging to challenge the flintlock. In 1805 a craggy-faced Scottish clergyman called Alexander Forsyth had come up with a new way of igniting the gunpowder. He was an inveterate wildfowler who spent hours on the Aberdeenshire foreshore shooting curlew and golden plover. Yet he was unsatisfied with his old flintlock. There was always a momentary delay between pulling the trigger and the shot firing because of the time it took for the gunpowder in the pan to ignite, travel down the touch hole and set off the main charge. The flash of the gunpowder in the priming pan alerted the birds to his shot and they had time to take evasive action. And he was often frustrated by damp gunpowder which failed to go off. A damp touch hole often produced the proverbial flash in the pan. So in a garden shed at the back of the manse, the Rev. Alexander Forsyth set about inventing a new way of igniting the gunpowder in his musket. Eventually he discovered that a particular mixture of sulphur, powdered charcoal and potassium chlorate exploded when it was struck with force. So instead of using flints to make sparks, he could now ignite the main charge of gunpowder simply by hitting a small plug of the explosive compound. He quickly engineered a new firing mechanism and thus was born the technology which is used in modern shotguns today. Forsyth soon discovered the benefits of his so-called percussion or detonation gun. It was more reliable because more of the firing mechanism was internalised and less open to the weather. Moreover, controversially, the sporting clergyman also believed his gun shot harder and faster.

According to the weapons historian, John Atkinson, not everyone agreed. 'Arguments raged among duellists and other sporting gentlemen on the rival merits of the flintlock and its successor. Diehard flintlock men admitted that the percussion weapons fired faster but claimed that the flintlock fired farther and they would not be shaken from this belief. Their argument was answered by champions of the new lock who pointed out that it not only fired faster but enabled the pistol or gun to shoot harder because there was no longer a touch hole through which part of the explosive force could escape.' Eventually, it was the army that settled the argument. In 1834, two platoons took part in a musketry contest at the Woolwich Arsenal. One was armed with flintlocks, the other with percussion muskets. They each fired 6,000 rounds. The flintlocks misfired two times out of every thirteen shots. The failure rate for the percussion muskets, however, was only one in 166. The percussion bullets were also shot more quickly, more accurately, and with greater force, punching

their way further into the green elm targets than their flintlock counterparts.

The pistols David Landale chose in John Thompson's shop
on Princes Street are beautiful. The stocks are fashioned out
of patterned walnut which has been ribbed for a firmer grip.
The hexagonal steel barrels are 340 mm long and house a ram
rod underneath. The box, in which they still sit today, contains
a powder flask, lead bullets and mould, and, of course, a pile
of old percussion caps. For the pair of pistols that David chose
had not only proved themselves in shooting dead the unfortunate Captain Gourlay, they also happened to be the most
up-to-date percussion duelling pistols that money could buy
and probably the best thing he could have in his hand when
he faced George Morgan's flintlocks in the morning.

It was only when Lieutenant Milne was sat firmly in the chaise
and well on the way to Kirkcaldy that George Morgan told
him what had really happened that morning on the High
Street. The sailor was furious. He 'objected strongly to be a
second for this, as it was the last thing one gentleman should
do to another, that of horsewhipping'. But Morgan was insis-
tent, pleading even. It was, he said, 'a hard case to find a second
and Milne was the only officer among his friends he could
apply to'. Against his better judgement, Milne agreed to remain
George's second, 'principally that he might affect an amicable
arrangement'. So when Milne arrived at William Millie's home
a little while later, at about six o'clock, he was a second who
was far from committed to fighting his man's corner.

William and John Millie were walking off their dinner in
the park behind their house. 'You will no doubt be aware, Mr
Millie, of the errand I have come on,' Lieutenant Milne

declared. A reconciliation is what he wanted, anything to prevent a meeting. He admitted that his acquaintance with George Morgan was 'slight, but from what he had seen of him, he was very much a gentleman'. He had met Landale, too, a few times and considered him also 'a gentlemanly man'. But he said that David's letter to the bank was 'rather undermining conduct' and read out a few sentences. By sending the letter to the bank and not to the Morgans, David had clearly endeavoured to undermine their character.

Millie disagreed and insisted that David was the aggrieved party. He also described in more detail what had happened that morning. He agreed that it would be good to see if any arrangement could be fixed upon 'but I am afraid that nothing short of a written apology by Mr Morgan to Mr Landale would suffice,' he said. They talked some more before Milne said it was clear that he was not 'yet significantly acquainted with all the circumstances and business of the case' and needed more time to think about it. They agreed to meet later that evening at the George Inn. In what appears to have been an attempt to save face, Lieutenant Milne then began what William Millie called 'a long dissertation' on the role of seconds. He asked Millie if he had been a second before. Millie said, no, he hadn't, he 'was little acquainted with the etiquette of duelling but he thought he knew all that was requisite'. Milne, however, retorted that he had been engaged in several duels 'both as principal and as second'.

Both men returned to their principals. Millie told David what had taken place and he confirmed that David was indeed prepared to accept a written apology from Morgan. But when Lieutenant Milne returned to the George Inn, where Morgan was waiting, he let rip. Now that he knew the facts, he knew that Morgan was utterly in the wrong. The basic rules of duelling had been breached. He told Morgan that in his opinion 'he was quite wrong in not having sent Mr Landale a challenge after he [David] had refused to apologise for the terms in the letter to the Bank in place of horsewhipping him'. He said that as Morgan had struck David, the merchant had no alternative as a gentleman but to issue a challenge. If he, Milne, had been 'placed in the same situation . . . by being struck, he would most certainly have acted as Mr Landale had done, and considered that there was no way of avoiding it'. He added that 'in similar circumstances, whatever his previous conduct had been, he would have listened to nothing short of an ample apology'. And while Landale had been wrong to write the letter, he 'considered Morgan's conduct in striking him much worse'. It was a devastating critique of his behaviour by a fellow officer.

Nevertheless, despite all this, Milne said he would still stand as Morgan's second. He proposed a deal to end the dispute amicably. Both sides would admit that they were wrong: 'Mr Landale in having written to the Bank in so strong terms without sending a copy of his letter to Messrs Morgan, and Mr Morgan in having struck Mr Landale, that both parties ought therefore to meet half-way and shake hands.' Milne drew this up as a written proposal and Morgan accepted it. He was in no position to disagree.

Before Milne and Millie met in the inn to make a final attempt at a peaceful resolution, there was one further task for both sides. Both had to engage surgeons to attend the duel, something all the codes insisted upon. *The British Code of Duel* said it was 'expedient that a surgeon should attend each of the parties [and], whenever possible, a gentleman should be selected who has had some practice in gun-shot wounds'. *The Art of Duelling* said a duellist 'should have been careful to secure the services of his medical attendant who will provide himself with all the necessary apparatus for tying up wounds or arteries and extracting balls.' For that was the key task of the doctor, to remove the bullet which rarely had enough force to pass straight through the body, something one surgeon complained bitterly about. In May 1833, a Mr Guthrie gave a clinical lecture on duelling wounds at Westminster Hospital. 'There is neither charity nor humanity in the manner of choosing pistols at present adopted,' he said. 'The balls are so small that the holes they make are always a source of inconvenience in the cure, and the quantity of powder is also so small that it will not send a ball through a moderately thick gentleman. It therefore sticks in some place where it should not – to the extreme disadvantage to the patient, and to the great annoyance of the surgeon.'

But few doctors in 1820s Fife would have had even Guthrie's expertise in gunshot wounds so, like most duellists, David Landale and George Morgan simply called upon their general practitioners. David asked Dr Alexander Smith to 'accompany him to the country' the following morning at six o'clock 'in the direction of Lochgelly'. George called on Dr James Johnston and 'wished him to be in the neighbourhood of Torbain in his professional character' about half past six the next morning. The nature of their summons was deliberately vague. Few doctors would misinterpret the meaning – who else but a duellist would require the assistance of a medical man in an isolated field at dawn? Yet doctors were kept intentionally at arms length in a duel, and told few details of the dispute. This was to give them some protection from the law if the case ever went to trial. 'To guard themselves from being charged as accessories, under the municipal law, surgeons should remain out of sight, though at but small distance, till called upon by the seconds.' Others suggested that surgeons 'should turn their backs to the combatants so as not to see the firing; but as soon as they hear the report they should turn, and run to the spot as speedily as possible.' This allowed them to claim that they were not technically present at the encounter. It also stopped some doctors unwittingly winding up two already nervous duellists by ghoulishly preparing their instruments for the future patient. This role, which one historian described as being 'auxiliary to the duel but not its accomplice', also gave the doctor a degree of impartiality which allowed him to carry out his second key task. 'The role of the doctor at duels was a delicate one,' wrote the American historian Kevin McAleer. 'His purpose was not only to extract balls, if not too deeply embedded in tissue . . . but he was also consulted to see if a bout should continue.' The doctors were expected to establish the gravity of any wound, regardless of whether it was his principal or the opponent, and judge whether a duel should continue. This was indeed a delicate role, one that balanced the often conflicting demands of medical necessity, the wishes of a patient and the codes of honour. Some duellists insisted on continuing despite their wounds and protested furiously if a duel were stopped. Others were secretly delighted at the intervention of a physician.

There are only a few examples of doctors taking part in duels. In one, two doctors called Woodward and Mead fought over a point of medicine outside the gates of Gresham College in London. During the combat, Woodward slipped, fell under the mercy of Mead's blade and cracked a typically medical joke. 'Take your life,' cried Mead. 'Anything but your physic,' Woodward replied dryly. In one duel the attending surgeon actually joined in. Lord Bruce and Sir Edward Sackville had hacked and slashed themselves into a bloody impasse in a duel in 1613 in the Netherlands when suddenly, as Sackville later recalled, 'my Lord's surgeon, when nobody dreamt of it, came full at me with his Lord's sword, and had not mine with my sword interposed himself, I had been slain by those base hands'. In July 1844, an American doctor called Marsteller was shot in a duel and showed extraordinary courage in extracting the bullet from his hip by himself. But perhaps the most extraordinary story of a duelling medic was that of Humphrey Howarth, the MP for Evesham who as a young man had served as an army surgeon for the East India Company. In 1806, he attended the races at Brighton and dined one night at the Castle Inn. There he fell into discussion with the Earl of Barrymore, an Irish peer. Discussion turned into quarrel and they arranged to meet on the race course early next morning. Both men were eccentric rogues but even Barrymore was astonished when his opponent appeared on the ground armed solely with pistol and pants. 'The seconds and a few friends who went to see the show were soon convulsed with laughter when they saw Howarth, who was a fat old man, deliberately take off his clothes and present himself naked (except his drawers) to the murderous weapon of his adversary.' Barrymore thought Howarth was larking about but in truth the MP was deadly serious. From his earlier, medical life on the sub-continent, he knew all too well that men who had been shot were more likely to die from an infected wound than the loss of a major organ. 'I know that if any part of the clothing is carried into the body by a gunshot wound, festering ensues,' Howarth told his opponent. 'And therefore I have met you thus.' The historical novelist, Patrick O'Brian, makes Stephen Maturin, his doctor/spy, fight a duel in a similar state of undress. 'I always fight in my breeches,' he tells his friend Captain Aubrey. 'Cloth carried into a wound makes sad work.' Traveller, the anonymous duelling expert, would never have consented to naked duelling but agreed wholeheartedly with Howarth's analysis. He advised the duellist: 'If in the habit of wearing flannel next to the skin, he should omit putting it on. Wounds, comparatively trifling, have often become dangerous from parts of the flannel clothing being carried into them, particularly in warm climates.' By the same token, some doctors would use freshly laundered silk handkerchiefs to clean wounds, pulling them through bullet holes to draw out any dirt. In the end, however, in Howarth's duel, his unlikely precautions were redundant. Both he and his opponent missed each other and resolved their dispute without bloodshed.

The George Inn was packed when William Millie walked through the door at 10 o'clock that night. Mrs McGlashan and her children, Elizabeth and John, bustled about collecting tankards as Kirkcaldy's menfolk huddled round the fires, their damp clothes steaming into the fug. Lieutenant Milne was already there waiting for him in a quiet room upstairs.

Milne explained his plan. Both men would accept they were equally wrong and would meet halfway and shake hands. He handed Millie the paper he and Morgan had drawn up setting out the detail. Yet Millie would have none of it. 'I told him that such an arrangement was totally out of the question, as it concerned Landale, a deeply injured party, and that nothing short of a written apology from Morgan would satisfy me, as to be consistent with the honour of my friend Landale.' Lieutenant Milne shook his head and said that Morgan would never agree to that. Neither second appeared to know that most codes of duelling ruled out any kind of apology in such circumstances, that it was impossible to draw back from a duel once a blow had been struck.

Recognising that a peaceful resolution was now unlikely, Milne began to cover his back. He knew he was backing the wrong horse, that his principal was the clear aggressor, so he needed to have proof that he had at least attempted an amicable solution in case the worst happened. 'As we did not seem likely to agree and as the matter was likely to become serious, I took down a memorandum in pencil of what had passed and signed it in my name,' Milne recalled. He passed it to Millie who agreed it was a fair account of what had been said and signed his own name.

Now that any pretence of avoiding the duel was over, Millie and Milne began to squabble over the details, above all where it should take place. There was, Millie said, 'a warm argument on the right of choosing the ground'. David had already chosen to duel a few miles out of Kirkcaldy in a suitably isolated spot near Torbain. This agreed with the rules of the day: 'The place should be away from the haunts of men, and also from any quarter that has been recently often used as a resort for this purpose.' Yet Milne insisted it was his right, as second to the man who had been challenged, to choose the ground. Some duelling codes agreed with Milne, others disagreed; by the 1820s there had been such a profusion of rule books that many were contradictory. Millie asked what was wrong with Torbain, and Milne said it was 'too great a distance from Kirkcaldy'. Millie said that David had 'no predilection for the ground mentioned in the challenge except its privacy' and asked what alternative ground Milne would propose. The lieutenant 'wished the meeting nearer Kirkcaldy for his own convenience' and suggested Mr Douglas's park at the back of the town as 'more appropriate'.

This was too much for William Millie. 'Good God, Milne,' he cried. 'Are you aware of the situation of the park? It is within pistol shot of a public washing green where there are constantly washerwomen from sunrise to sunset. They might as well fight in front of the George Inn!' Millie had had enough. He told Lieutenant Milne that if he did not agree to the ground mentioned in the challenge he would consider his objections 'frivolous and evasive'. This 'irritated Milne in some degree' and in an ominous warning, he warned Millie to 'take care what he said'. The last thing Millie wanted was to provoke Milne himself into a duel so he got up, told Milne he would see him on the appointed ground at the appointed time the following morning, grabbed his coat and hat, and left, deeply 'irritated by Milne's trifling objections'. A rather perplexed Lieutenant Milne ran after him down the stairs. 'Mr Millie, I want to speak to you,' he cried. Millie said over his shoulder that he had nothing further to say. But Milne continued to the door of the inn. Millie told him this was not the place to talk upon such a subject and begged him to desist, but Milne asked the waiter to fetch his hat and followed Millie out into the street. 'He walked along the street with me for a short distance,' Millie recalled, 'and was going on with some trifling objections, all tending to delay as I thought. I told him to put up the papers he had in his hand unless he wished all the parish to know of it, and again requested him to meet at the hour and place mentioned in the challenge.' Milne nodded silently. Millie said: 'Good night, I shall expect to see you again' and walked off into the night.

The seconds' confusion over the rules of duelling and their uncertainty about the propriety of their actions offer another, small signal that by the 1820s the age of duelling was reaching its twilight years. In previous days, the two principals had unwittingly done the same. David Landale's doubts, his need to consult friends constantly about his decisions, his lack of pistols, all pointed to a man who did not consider a duel to be the automatic consequence of a dispute. Despite the bluster, George Morgan's refusal to challenge David after a clear-cut insult, and his ignorance of the law, betrayed a reluctance to duel when twenty years previously it would have been inevitable. And on this day, the day before the duel, William Millie had shown himself a reluctant second who too was unfamiliar with the duelling codes. And while Lieutenant Milne undoubtedly had experience of duelling, he was so aware of the impropriety of the encounter that he had everything written down to protect him once the smoke had cleared. The duel, which once had been widely accepted, was no longer so welcome. Its social legitimacy was beginning to fade and that trend was on show with every doubt expressed.

There was, however, one man who appeared content that a duel should take place, and curiously, it was George Morgan's brother. David Morgan knew George was furious with David Landale for what he had said in the letter to the Bank of Scotland directors in Edinburgh. He knew that George wanted to fight David Landale and had in fact persuaded him not to issue a challenge immediately after they learned of the letter. Yet when a duel appeared imminent, David did nothing to prevent it. On the morning before the duel, shortly after George assaulted David Landale outside the bookshop, David Morgan came to see James Cumming to find out what had happened. Cumming had already written out a brief note of the events both outside and inside his shop which he intended to send to David Morgan. But as he was about to send out the letter with one of his boys, the banker himself came through his door. Cumming gave him the letter to read. David shook his head and said: 'James, you have no idea of the usage we have got from Landale. If you heard all the outs and ins of it, you would almost excuse George for doing what he did.' Then he paused and said ominously: 'I cannot help it, George has taken it up as a military man.' Later in the day, David caught up with his brother. As he recalled later: 'I was aware that my brother George had received and accepted of a challenge sent him by Mr Landale, indeed the challenge was shown to me.' But crucially, George told him about the challenge on the 'express promise that he would not in any event divulge the matter'. So David Morgan 'accordingly gave no information to prevent the duel'. He claimed later that he had always imagined that 'an arrangement would be effected'. And 'even when he knew that the parties were going to the ground, he still imagined that matters would be made up without having recourse to extremities'. However strange it might seem today it appears that David Morgan knew his brother George was determined to resolve this dispute as 'a military man' and did nothing to prevent his brother risking his life fighting David Landale.

For some, the night before a duel was one of slow fear. Duellists feared death or injury certainly, but above all they feared failure:

failure to show courage, failure to act honourably, failure to behave properly. James Boswell, Johnson's biographer, wrote the following before a duel in 1776: 'My greatest uneasiness was the fear of fear, an apprehension that my nerves, or whatever else it is, should yield to impressions of danger, though my soul was brave.' The duelling codes acknowledged this and suggested various remedies. The anonymous author of *The Art of Duelling* believed the would-be duellist should deal with his fear head on. He should treat the duel 'jocosely' and 'summon all his energy and declare war against nervous apprehension'. To that end, Traveller provided some detailed advice:

> That his mind may not dwell upon the affair, he ought to invite a few friends to dinner and laugh away the evening over a bottle of port; or, if fond of cards, play a rubber of whist. He should, however, carefully avoid drinking to excess, or taking any food that tends to create bile. The man who makes too free with the bottle over night seldom rises with a very steady hand in the morning: and many poor fellows have suffered through intemperance and want of care previous to fighting. If a man leeches [walks onto the duelling ground] boldly, and as a lion, it always checks the ardour of his antagonist. But if he crawls out like a poor ragamuffin going to be shot, it in some degree raises the courage of the opposite party, and renders his aim, of course, more steady.
>
> Should he feel inclined to sleep when he retires to rest, and troubled images disturb his imagination, let him take some amusing book – one of Sir Walter [Scott]'s novels, if a lover of the romantic; or Byron's Childe Harold, if he delights in the sublime, and read until he

drops asleep, leaving word with a trusty servant to call him at five, and provide a strong cup of coffee, to be taken immediately on rising.

The historian Kevin McAleer believed the reality was more mundane. 'The ever-dwindling hours would ordinarily be spent in the lugubrious business of writing letters of farewell to loved ones, communicating last wishes to friends, drawing up a will, and generally ordering one's affairs so that no one could be compromised by posthumous papers and documents.'

Yet some would-be duellists could not face it. One of the most convincing fictional descriptions of how a man felt the night before a duel was written by the French writer and frequent duellist, Guy de Maupassant. In his short story *The Coward*, he tells the story of a young nobleman sitting alone at home the night before a duel, racked with the fear that he might show fear in the face of death. 'His agitation, which had becalmed for a moment, was now growing every minute. Along his arms, along his legs, and in his chest, he could feel a sort of quivering, a continuous vibration. He could not remain sitting or standing. There was not a trace of saliva left in his mouth, and every few minutes he made a noisy move-ment with his tongue, as if he were detaching it from his palate.' He tried to write letters, he tried to read, he tried drinking a bottle of rum – nothing helped. And when he practised holding his pistol, his hand wobbled uncontrollably:

> He looked at the end of the barrel, at that little deep black hole which spits death and he thought about dishonour, about the whispers in the clubs, about the laughter in the drawing rooms, about the women's contempt, about the allusions in the papers, about the

insults cowards would throw in his face. He was still looking at the weapon, and, lifting the hammer, he suddenly saw a cartridge-cap shining underneath like a little red flame. The pistol had been left loaded by chance, out of forgetfulness. And he felt a vague inexplicable joy at the discovery. If, facing the other man, he did not have the calm, noble bearing that was required, he would be ruined forever. He would be stained, marked with an infamous sign, expelled from society! And that calm, bold bearing was something he would not have – he knew it, he felt it. Yet he was not a coward, since . . . The thought which occurred to him did not even take shape in his mind; but, opening his mouth wide, he suddenly thrust the barrel of his pistol down into his throat, and pressed the trigger . . . When his valet came running in, attracted by the noise of the shot, he found him dead, lying on his back. A jet of blood had splashed the white paper on the table and made a big red stain below these five words: 'This is my last will'.

George Morgan was not so fearful. But he was undoubtedly nervous. While the two seconds argued at the inn, George paced up and down the street outside his home. He was, according to Captain Henry Brown Wood, 'much agitated'. Wood – a friend of George's and a fellow officer in the Fifeshire Militia – came across the banker as he was on his way home from Edinburgh to Cupar, a town some miles north-west of Kirkcaldy. George told Wood all about the imminent duel – which he described as 'an unpleasant business' – and the captain was sympathetic until he heard how his friend had horsewhipped David Landale. 'Good God, I am sorry for it,' he exclaimed, much to George's discomfort. 'What could I do?' George asked pleadingly. 'I could not help it, after his having written such an infamous letter.' Despite disapproving so much of George's behaviour, Wood agreed to stay with his friend until Lieutenant Milne returned. Perhaps it was the night air, perhaps it was the familiar, military company, but by the time Milne came back from the inn, George felt more himself. He bade Captain Wood goodbye and boldly invited him to dinner the next day. The captain thought this meant George still expected the dispute could be resolved peacefully. But George clearly meant it to show that it would be he who would survive the duel.

David Landale, if he felt any fear, kept it closely to himself. He spent the evening before the duel sitting in his study at St Mary's 'calmly arranging all his books and papers, and putting his affairs in order for the fearful chances of the morrow'. His friend, Robert Stocks, popped round for a drink but extraordinarily David did not tell him either about the assault or the duel planned for the next morning. 'He told me he had been in Edinburgh on business but did not mention what the business was, nor did he mention a single word about being struck or having sent a challenge and from his manner, I could not have discovered that matters had gone that length.' Nor did he tell his other close friend, James Aytoun, who only learned of the duel once it had taken place. Late in the evening, William Millie dropped in briefly to tell him what Lieutenant Milne had had to say in the George Inn. David told his second that he had been right to turn down Milne's offer of a joint apology. Left alone again, David continued with his letters.

His most detailed instructions were to his friend and land agent, John Anderson. It was a letter that was calm, poised

and utterly self-possessed, a letter that prepared for all even-
tualities. 'My dear John,' he wrote. 'I meet George Morgan
tomorrow upon an affair of honour as it is usually called
. . . The keys of my private box, where are all my valuable
papers, will be found in my pocket. You must for your own
sake deposit them with Mr Aytoun, who is an executor and
who knows well what to do. My Will is there deposited, and
also a letter addressed by me to my trustees recommending
some things to them in the event that I fall.' He regretted
that the titles of his property were 'lying in some disorder
but they can be easily put to rights. My private ledger will
require to be written up for last balance of the Company's
ledger. I have every confidence that you will conduct things
prudently under my trustees until my brother's arrival from
India.' His younger brother Alexander was still living in
Bengal.

David was also prepared, however, for another outcome.
'In the event I kill Morgan, I shall immediately proceed to
Glasgow. You will pack up my portmanteau with my long
black coat, vest, trousers, with a few long shirts, neck clothes,
stocks [cravats] and black silk stockings and dressing gowns,
boots, shoes etc and address them to Messrs John Strang &
Co, wine merchants, Glasgow.' To minimise the risk of being
found, David suggested that the portmanteau should be
disguised in a pack sheet and the address should only be
attached the moment it was placed on the post wagon at
Leith. The key to the portmanteau, he wrote, should be sent
separately in a small sealed parcel. He asked Anderson to
write to him, informing him of 'what has occurred but take
care who delivers the parcel'. As if that were not enough,
David also found time for a few last-minute business instruc-

tions. 'Buy or order no Antwerp bark till September and if Mr Kay will not draw direct let him value on Kinloch & Sons, with whom I have a credit for 500 pounds. Pay no more than six shillings a hide except J. H & Sons should fix the price for himself.'

It is a remarkable letter. David Landale prepared for death or escape with equal equanimity. There is no fear in his tone, just an acceptance that what he is doing is right, regardless of the outcome. Duelling may have passed its apogee but David felt exactly the same as hundreds of other men who had followed similar paths over previous centuries. Above all, he felt that what he was doing was right both in the eyes of society and of God. To some Christians, this might be puzzling. The duellist by definition breached Moses' commandment not to kill. He ignored Christ's teaching on suffering, humility and turning the other cheek. And he undoubtedly did not believe that vengeance was the business of the Almighty alone. Some duellists recognised this apparent paradox. In 1783, the night before a duel, a British officer called Lieutenant-General Thomas, wrote in his will: 'Almighty God, I commit to you my soul in hopes of mercy and pardon for the irreligious step I now (in compliance with the unwarranted customs of this wicked world) put myself under the necessity of taking.' He was right to take such precautions for the following morning he was dealt a mortal wound. Yet most duelling Christians had no such scruple. They believed that a duel was not murder, that the Bible permitted self-defence, that, in the words of *The British Code of Duel*, 'the qualities of a true Christian are the same as those essential to form the character of a gentleman'. On the night before his duel, David

Landale shared these beliefs. 'In the event of my falling,' he wrote to John Anderson, 'I beg of you to make no foolish lamentation, as I feel confident before God that I am doing my duty as a Christian and as a respectable member of society.'

5

The duel

*Ten paces — of not less than 30 inches each — is always the minimum
. . . and the second is not allowed to deliver the pistol cocked into his
principal's hand without using his utmost endeavour once again to obtain
a reconciliation. If this is not forthcoming and a wound appears to be
mortal, the parties should not separate without expressing forgiveness.*

Anon., *The British Code of Duel*, 1824

*'It has a strange, quick jar upon the ear,
That cocking of a pistol, when you know
A moment more will bring the sight to bear
Upon your person, twelve yards off or so.'*

Lord Byron, *Don Juan*, Canto IV

The road north-west out of Kirkcaldy winds gently up the
hill through a suburban clutter of housing estates, petrol stations
and one-stop shops. It is a road of commuter traffic jams by
day and boy racers by night, typical of the edge of an expanding
Scottish town, stretching through semi-rural, semi-urban
communities struggling to find identity where there is none.
If you drive to its end, you reach the fast A-road that links
Fife with the Forth Bridge and the rest of the world. But a

motorist with less global ambition, leaving Kirkcaldy at a more leisurely pace, may notice a small lane off to the left. On this, the road to Torbain, he leaves behind the town more suddenly than he expects. The countryside soon takes over and he may be forced to stop as sheep are hustled by man and dog to fresh pasture. The road curls westwards along the valley, creeping steadily higher into the folds of the hills. After a few miles, there is a dark track to the right that disappears into Torbain wood. The way is blocked by a sturdy steel gate but the determined explorer can continue on foot. Thick Fife mud sticks to his boots as he walks between the tall birches and swaying spruce firs. Rainwater gurgles persistently along a ditch so swollen that it threatens to become a burn. It is a shadowy, sodden spot where local people feel they can dump rubbish and set fire to cars without risk of discovery. Walk on, however, and the traveller is rewarded, for suddenly the rutted track rises, the deep, impenetrable plantation stops and the horizon returns once more as two fields stretch out to the north. To the left is soggy barley stubble picked over by hungry crows, to the right open, fallow grass, damp with cowpats and surface water. In the distance, he can see the Ochil hills. What he cannot see is a single human dwelling. There is a farmstead up ahead but it is hidden from view by the lip of the rise. It is utterly isolated. The traveller may be only a few miles from Kirkcaldy but he could be a hundred. Something then catches his eye. To the right is a small cairn, a pile of rocks cemented roughly together, about a foot high, hidden amid the grass and nettles at the side of the track. Fixed firmly in its centre is a simple plaque: 'Near this site the last duel in Scotland was fought on 23rd August 1826.'

★

The purpose of a duel was to shoot one's opponent while avoiding being shot oneself. This vital truism underlay every technique, every trick of the trade the duelling experts advised. Rule number one, above all else, was to present the smallest target possible, as Traveller explained in *The Art of Duelling*: 'The risk in duelling may be considerably lessened by care in the matter of turning the body towards the adversary,' he wrote. 'I have often seen a raw, inexperienced fellow expose his person most unnecessarily, standing with a full front towards his antagonist . . . he offered the other party a much larger surface to fire at than the laws of duelling require, rendering, of course, the danger to himself greater.' So, naturally, he explained how it should be done:

> To be in position, a person should stand with his right and left shoulder in a line with the object he wishes to hit; his head bent to the right, and his eyes fixed on the object. His feet should be almost close together; his left arm hanging down, and his right holding the pistol, with the muzzle pointing to the ground close to his feet. He should keep his shoulders well back, and his stomach rather drawn in: then, stamping his feet twice or thrice on the ground to feel that he stands firmly, let him raise his right arm steadily, bending it at the elbow, and, drawing the pistol into a line with the object, bring that part of the arm between the shoulder and elbow close to the side – throw out the muscles strongly and let it cover the breast as much as possible.

Abraham Bosquett even had discreet advice for how a gentleman should protect his nether regions: 'the right hip must be twisted a little, so as merely to cover or guard the lower extremities of the belly'. The pistol itself should be used as a guard against a bullet. A broken stock and a sprained hand were better than a mortal wound. In 1837, in Brownville, Pennsylvania, a man called Banner Anderson survived a duel at close quarters because of his pistol. In 'one of the most extraordinary freaks of fire-arms, [his opponent's] ball lodged right in the muzzle of Anderson's pistol, whilst the contents of Anderson's pistol lodged in [his opponent's] breast. He expired in three hours.' At the same time, the duellist had to be careful; many died not from bullet wounds but injuries suffered from the splinters of their shattered pistol.

The contrast with the open-legged, front-facing, two-handed, arm-locked stance favoured by policemen in modern television drama could not be greater. The duellist stood sideways to present as small a target as possible and held his pistol in a bent arm that covered as many vital organs as possible. The only disadvantage of standing sideways was that if you were hit, the bullet was likely to pass through more than one organ. For some, like the Whig politician, Charles James Fox, there was no option. In 1779, he fought a duel with an MP called William Adam after a row about a speech in the House of Commons. Fox, who was 'remarkable for his portly figure and rotundity', was urged by his second: 'You must stand sideways.' To which Fox replied: 'Why? I am as thick one way as the other.' That 'thickness', however, was to Fox's disadvantage and he was wounded in the chest, fortunately only lightly.

Size was crucial in a duel. The small duellist had a clear advantage, as evidenced by perhaps the most surreal duel that ever took place, between a fat soldier and a dwarf. Jeffery Hudson had entered royal service by emerging from a large pie at a party for Charles I. He belonged at the time to the

Duke of Buckingham but Charles's 15-year-old queen, Henrietta Maria, was so enchanted by the little man that she insisted he join the court. She called him Lord Minimus, Charles made him a captain in the Royal Army and he had his portrait painted by Van Dyck. But while Hudson was naturally the butt of many jokes, he was also a proud man and one day a young officer called Charles Crofts went too far. He teased Hudson for coming off worst in a fight with a turkey cock. For Hudson, this was too much and he challenged Crofts to a duel. The soldier thought he was joking and turned up armed with a water pistol. But the dwarf was in earnest and demanded a real duel with real pistols on horseback. This was a shrewd move. Not only did this even out the height difference in Hudson's favour, it also consigned his fat opponent to a slow-moving, overburdened horse. By contrast, the 18-inch dwarf presented a much tougher, smaller moving target. So it was no surprise that Hudson shot his opponent dead through the heart. Unfortunately, this was the last of Hudson's luck. He incurred royal disfavour, was exiled, captured by Barbary pirates and spent the next twenty-five years in prison in North Africa. In the end, he escaped and retired to his native Rutland where they still drink a beer named in his honour.

If being small, or standing sideways and aiming with a bent arm, were the best ways of protecting his person, what was the best way for the duellist to hit his target? The answer, according to Traveller, was all in the aim: he should point not at the man in general but at a fixed point on his body. 'If aiming at a man, for instance, mark well one of the gilt buttons upon his coat,' he wrote. 'A person can never fire with accuracy unless he aims at some small object. Were he to endeavour to hit a man, he would very probably miss him: but if he aimed at one of the buttons of his coat, the ball is almost certain, provided he is a passable shot, to strike within a circle of two or three inches round it.' For the duellist to protect himself from such a technique, Traveller recommended that he should 'wear a black coat on these occasions' so that his opponent has nothing specific to aim at.

When the moment came to pull the trigger: 'Be cool, collected and firm, and think of nothing but placing the ball on the proper spot. When the word is given, pull the trigger carefully and endeavour to avoid moving a muscle in the arm or hand — move only the forefinger and that with just suffi- cient force to discharge the pistol.' Above all, a duellist needed focus, as Joseph Conrad pointed out. 'A duel, whether regarded as a ceremony in the cult of honour, or even when reduced in its moral essence to a form of manly sport, demands a perfect singleness of intention, a homicidal austerity of mood.'

Gilbert Garner was not happy. He was tired, his horses were tired, they could all have used a lie-in. Yet here he was stum- bling down to the stables at 5 a.m., rubbing his eyes and shaking the sleep from his head. The 28-year-old chaise driver had arrived back at the George Inn in Kirkcaldy in the early hours of the morning of Wednesday August 23 after a long journey from Largs almost 100 miles away on the other side of Scotland. He was shattered and had hoped that Helen McGlashan, his employer of the last seven years, might have given him a little time off to recover. But as he drove his carriage into the courtyard round the back of the inn, those hopes were quickly dashed. 'I was told by John McKelvie, the waiter, that Mr [William] Milne had ordered a chaise to be ready for him that morning at six o'clock,' Garner later recalled. 'At first I refused to go because my horses were worn out. [But when I] went to the stable ground at 5 a.m. . . . to assist in getting a chaise ready, the other post boys' horses having cut, I was obliged to get ready myself.' Reluctantly, he prepared his horses. Had he known his destination that morning, he would have been even more reluctant.

Across town, another coachman lay snoring in his bed. John Mason knew he had to get up early but was still fast asleep in his room at the Cross Keys pub where he worked as the personal driver for the innkeeper, James Tait. At 5.40 a.m., he was shaken roughly awake, and told that Doctor Alexander Smith had arrived and was looking for his chaise. The 19-year-old driver gruffly pulled on his clothes and roused his horses. He too had no idea what his task was that morning. Had he known he also might have preferred to stay in bed.

David Landale had no trouble waking up. We do not know if he spent a sleepless night awake with his conscience and his nerves or if he slept through, at peace with himself and his fate. What we do know is that when his friend and second, William Millie, arrived to pick him up from St Mary's at 6 a.m. 'he found him ready'. There is no record of what, if anything, David did to prepare for his encounter. Perhaps he prayed, ate a little, and finished sorting his papers. Naturally Traveller had firm views about how a duellist like David should prepare for an encounter: 'Let him drink . . . coffee, and take a biscuit with it, directly he rises,' *The Art of Duelling* advised. 'Then, in washing his face, attend to bathing his eyes well with cold water . . . I do not advise his taking more than a biscuit and cup of coffee. To eat a hearty breakfast is wrong; I am not one of those who subscribe to the Italian opinion that nothing can be well done by an Englishman unless his stomach is full of roast beef. The digestive organs are seldom prepared for the reception of food at such an unnatural hour as six or seven, and the brain would consequently be oppressed with the fumes proceeding from an unhealthy digestive process.' Some duellists believed, perhaps a little optimistically, that fasting before an encounter could even protect life. In 1852, an American newspaper editor called Harry De Courcey was shot in the stomach during a duel and yet to everyone's amazement, he made a full recovery. The apparent miracle was later explained by his second, another newspaperman called Ed Kemble, who had, 'during the two days' negotiations [over the duel's terms], kept his man closely locked in his room and had only allowed him a little tea and toast at very long intervals. The result was that he went on the field with an empty stomach, and the bullet passed through between the intestines without cutting any of them. Kemble's care saved Harry's life for he soon recovered and lived for years afterwards in excellent health.'

In the absence of food, Traveller suggested that the duellist smoked a cigar and 'if a married man, avoid disturbing his wife or children.' Certainly David Landale did everything not to wake his family. When Doctor Smith arrived at St Mary's to tell David the chaise was being prepared, he found both duellist and second ready to go, standing quietly outside the front door. David told the doctor to return to the inn and get the chaise to pick them up in Coal Wynd, a street about ten minutes' walk away where the clatter of the carriage and the horses' hooves would not disturb the house. In the meantime, David and Millie crept stealthily away from the house via the back, garden door. This allowed not only for a secret departure from St Mary's but it also meant they could avoid walking on the High Street, where they might have met someone and had to explain their presence at such an early hour. Instead, they could pass discreetly along the back streets, past the colliers' cottages, the glebe land and the new quarry. As it happened, they did not evade all notice. 'A miner living in Collier Row . . . was on his way to the well to get his stoups filled when he met Mr Landale and Mr Millie coming from the house,' a correspondent recalled in the *Fifeshire Advertiser* many years later (May 11 1907). 'Seeing them leave the garden door open, he entered and instead of water filled his stoups with Mr Landale's apples.' Ignorant of his stolen fruit, David crept through the still streets of Kirkcaldy with William Millie. Doctor Smith returned to the Cross Keys to find John Mason awake, his horses and chaise waiting and ready. They drove up the road to the agreed rendezvous at the top of Coal Wynd and found David and Millie waiting, the second holding what appeared to be a travelling carpet bag. Mason 'held up his hands' and brought the chaise to a stop. The two men got in and they were off.

George Morgan was already on his way to the ground. His second, Lieutenant William Milne, had arrived at the banker's house around 6 a.m. to find George up and ready. Without further ado, both men had walked down to the George Inn to find a sleepy Gilbert Garner ready with his chaise and tired horses. Milne carried with him a solid mahogany box containing George's flintlocks. Both men got in and headed up the hill on the road to Torbain. George had been up for some time. So concerned was he about his doctor, James Johnston, over-sleeping that he had gone to see him at 5 a.m. to make sure he was awake. Quite what the doctor thought of this we do not know. Nor do we know how he felt when

George called on him again at 6 a.m. to make sure he had not gone back to sleep. George told him that the chaise was ready. With all the restrained fury of a man taken unjustly from his bed, Dr Johnston replied that 'he wouldn't go in the chaise but would be at the place appointed at the stipulated time.' As it was, George's concern was partially justified for in the end Johnston struggled to attend the duel on time. Yet the doctor was not late because he had over-slept. He was late because he apparently found himself a prisoner in his own house. For according to another recollection of the duel, recorded in the *Fifeshire Advertiser* years later on May 25 1907, the doctor's wife did not want him to attend the duel.

'His family naturally objected, locked the door and hid his boots so that he could not get away,' the anonymous corre-spondent wrote. 'But with the aid of a faithful domestic, he slipped through a back window in his slippers, ran up through the garden and emerged on the highway at the corner where Mrs Methven's gate now stands. Here a carriage was waiting for him and he was able to keep his appointment.' There is no way of knowing how true this story is. It contains one certain inaccuracy – Dr Johnston did not take a carriage to the duel, he rode a horse. But his family would certainly have known that he was about to attend a duel – how could they not when George had woken them all up twice that morning already? There is every reason they would have objected, knowing that doctors were often found guilty by association if a duellist died. And Dr Johnston was undoubtedly late and only just made the duel in time.

For the apprehensive duellist on his way to meet his fate, Traveller inevitably had yet more advice: 'While proceeding to

David Landale, steely-eyed, resolute, the model of a respectable nineteenth-century Scottish merchant. Date of portrait unknown, possibly 1849, but most likely 1835 to mark his election as provost of Kirkcaldy. Courtesy of the Viscount Ingleby. Photographed by Harry Middleton.

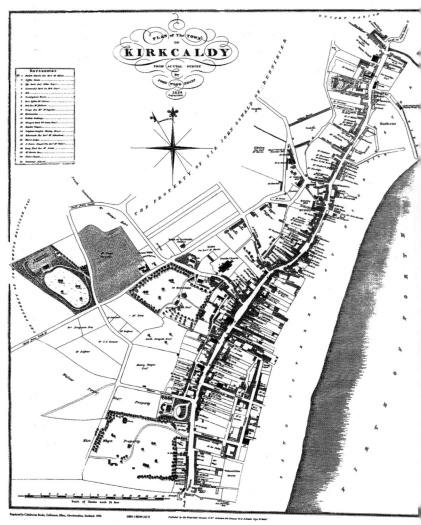

John Wood's map of the 'lang toon' of Kirkcaldy, drawn up in 1824, two years before the duel. Courtesy of Caledonian Maps, www.caledonianmaps.co.uk 01599 566751.

Kirkcaldy, 12th Augt 1826

Sir

I purposely refrained from taking any notice of your letter to the Bank dated 23d June last till the Directors should come to a determination thereon, that being now done the cause of silence no longer exists. — You must be perfectly aware that your letter contains falsehood & calumny, which it is your duty if possessed of honor to apologize for, and retract I have therefore to request you will immediately send me a written apology for your conduct in using such false un-founded & ungentlemanlike expressions with regard to me

I am
Sir
Your Mo Serv
Geo Morgan.
Lieutenant
Half Pay 77th Regt
of Foot

To/
David Landale
Kirkcaldy

George Morgan's letter to David Landale, dated 12 August 1826, urging the merchant to apologise for the critical remarks he had made about the banker. The use of his old regimental rank was seen as deliberately provocative. Courtesy of the National Archives of Scotland.

David Landale's barely legible letter, dated 22 August 1826, to his friend William Millie, informing him of George Morgan's assault and asking him to act as his second. Courtesy of the National Archives of Scotland.

David Landale's pistols. While George Morgan trusted to his old-fashioned but reliable flintlocks, David bought these newfangled percussion pistols the day before the duel. The case (below) still contains David's powder flask, bullet mould and spare ramrod. Credit: Fife Council Museums, Kirkcaldy Museum & Art Gallery.

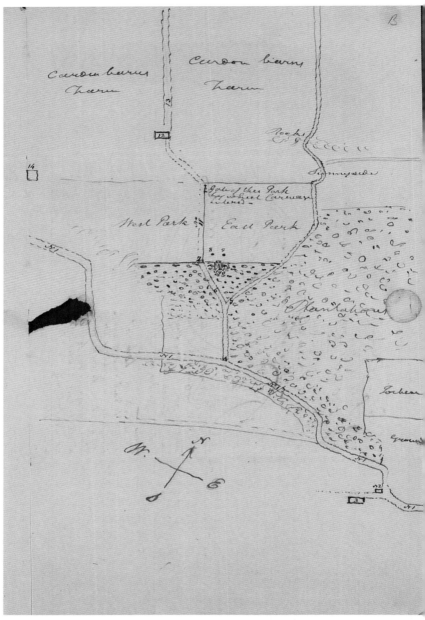

Birds' eye sketch of the duel scene, drawn by Will Douglas, Kirkcaldy magistrates' clerk, as evidence for the trial. George Morgan's position is marked by the number eight in the bottom left-hand corner of East Park field, David Landale's position by the number nine. Courtesy of the National Archives of Scotland.

David Landale, photographed in his declining years, probably in the 1850s. Courtesy of the Viscount Ingleby. Photographed by Harry Middleton.

Probable photograph of Mary Russell, who married David Landale two years after the duel. He was forty-two, she was twenty-three. They had eleven children. Courtesy of the Viscount Ingleby. Photographed by Harry Middleton.

the scene of action, if he feels himself nervous, or imagines he is not sufficiently braced up for the encounter, he should stop and take a bottle of soda-water, flavoured with a small wine-glass of brandy: this will be found an excellent remedy, and from experience, I can strongly recommend it as a most grateful stimulant and corrective.' David Landale took no such Dutch courage but clearly could have used a little. He by turn doubted the propriety of his behaviour, he feared the lethal consequences of the duel, and yet he still made clear his determination to act with honour. David 'expressed his anxiety that the affair should be settled without fighting' and he asked Dr Smith 'whether, if he accepted an ample written apology from Morgan on the ground, he would be exonerated as having acted as a man of honour'. Dr Smith, quite properly, kept his counsel. 'I said I had only a professional duty to discharge,' the doctor later recalled 'and therefore would not interfere, or give any opinion, or be present at any conference on the subject.' He knew only how easy it was for a medical man to become embroiled in the murky intricacies of a dispute and was determined to stay out of it.

William Millie answered David's question instead. '[He] remarked that there would be no materials on the ground to enable them to make out a written apology, and from his conversation last evening with Mr Milne, he had no idea that any apology such as Mr Landale had in view would be made.' And he had this warning for David: 'He should take care that if accepting [an apology], it should be such as would not compromise Mr Landale's honour.' David acknowledged his second's warning but nevertheless 'said that if Mr Morgan offered an apology for his conduct in striking him, Mr Millie should accept it.' He told his second that a verbal apology would 'by all means' be enough. 'I don't wish for Morgan's life,' he said. 'I merely wish reparation of the injuries done me.' The old school would have disapproved of this. The Irish rule book of 1777 was quite clear. While 'seconds are bound to attempt a reconciliation before the meeting takes place . . . no apology can be received . . . after the parties have actually taken the ground, without exchange of fires.' Yet by 1824, according to *The British Code of Duel*, attitudes had changed: 'Having with all due precaution arrived at the field, it still remains the duty of the seconds to attempt reconciliation by every honourable means in their power.'

By now, David was clearly nervous. According to his doctor, he 'seemed rather anxious that an arrangement should take place'. One local historian said David was 'not a blood-thirsty man' and was thus naturally afraid. This is not surprising because David thought that Morgan was much more likely to get the better of him. He told his friends that 'from Morgan being a military man and likely to have more experience, he was afraid that he might be the sufferer.' Dr Smith later confirmed this, saying that David had 'said that he expected to be shot by Morgan'. Nonetheless, David knew he could not back out. He said he was 'determined however to risk the meeting and take the chance rather than live dishonoured . . . Whatever might happen, he went to the ground with the approbation of his best friends and his own conscience and did not go to the meeting with any feeling of personal hostility towards Morgan but to vindicate his own honour, and that unless something was given to Morgan's conduct, neither he nor any of his neighbours could live in peace.' With that, David handed Dr Smith two letters, one to his brother Alexander Landale in India and the other to his clerk in Kirkcaldy. David said that 'in the event of his falling', he hoped Dr Smith would 'do his duty to him both as a friend and a medical man' and ensure these letters were safely posted.

Suddenly, the chaise pulled up. William Millie poked his head out of the window and saw another chaise stopped up ahead. Beside it stood George Morgan and Lieutenant Milne. They were lost. Gilbert Garner had driven to Torbain as instructed. But he had got into difficulties finding Cardenbarns Farm. Neither he nor George nor Lieutenant Milne knew where exactly it was. So, minutes before something so serious as a duel, they had been forced to stop and ask for directions. It was all rather undignified. Gilbert had spoken to a couple of women in Torbain Farm and was just coming back when David Landale's chaise pulled up. Millie told them they had 'mistaken the ground' and urged them to 'drive a little further on'. The convoy proceeded another mile or so up the 'rutty and umbrageous' road to Lochgelly before turning off up a track to the right, deep into Torbain wood. Some 500 yards in, the track forked and the chaises stopped and everyone stepped down into the gloom. William Millie bade Lieutenant Milne good morning and told him they would find 'the first suitable field clear of the wood'. David Landale and George Morgan exchanged not a word. Both parties then walked silently up the track together, each 'on a different side of the road', according to Gilbert Garner, 'without taking notice' of each other. Dr Smith, meanwhile, waited a little until the others were almost out of sight. 'He then left the chaise, strode in through a plantation till he came in sight of the parties, but still in the wood, and about 40 yards from them.' There, hidden from sight, he waited as the four men reached the edge of the wood. Several fields of pasture opened up before them. The way, however, was blocked by a firmly tied gate so they all 'leaped the wall' into the field. Today the field is known as Sandy Faulds. But in 1826 it was known rather less imaginatively as East Park and it was there that David Landale and George Morgan prepared to meet their fate. As they walked onto the field, William Millie asked Lieutenant Milne formally 'if he had any communication to make to him', to which the naval officer replied he had none. George Morgan, seeing the two seconds conversing, made his views perfectly clear, crying out 'No apology' with a loud finality that echoed off the trees in the morning air.

It is possible for two men to duel with almost anything that could constitute a weapon. And in the history of single combat, almost anything has been used: swords, slings, spears, clubs, maces, knives and, of course, fists. In parts of Wales and the United States, men would kick each others' shins in combat known as 'purring'. The duellists would put on special shoes toed with copper, grab each other's collar and kick their shins into a bloody mush. In parts of Turkey and central Asia, men fought with their foreheads: 'At a given signal, they rush at one another, butting forehead against forehead like two goats. The remainder of the duel is fought wholly with the forehead; neither blows nor kicks are permitted as the man who uses any weapon apart from his forehead is disgraced.' The defeated duellist was expected to use his last remaining energy to cut his own throat. Duellists, on occasion, had to make do with what came to hand. On April 14 1813, two French prisoners of war being held on a prison-ship in east London fought with scissors tied to the ends of broom handles. One died, the survivor was cut in forty places. On some occasions, duellists had to use weapons chosen for them. A sixteenth-century Habsburg monarch, Maximilian II, who still bore the title of Holy Roman Emperor, could not decide between two suitors competing for the hand of his daughter, Helene, so he 'ordered a large bag to be produced, and . . . decreed that whichever succeeded in putting his rival into this bag should obtain the hand of his daughter.' Despite the absurdity of the combat, the two men fought for more than an hour in front of the whole court and the winner was indeed married the following day. In France, two Spaniards, a tobacconist and a barber, once duelled with razors: 'The barber, having naturally the advantage, sent his adversary to the hospital with a horrible gash in the face.' In 1843, in the same duelling-obsessed country, men even fought with billiard balls. 'Two gentlemen, named Lenfant and Mellant, having quarrelled over a game of billiards, drew lots who should first throw the red ball at his adversary's head,' Andrew Steinmetz recalled. 'Chance favoured the latter, who threw the ball with such force and correct aim at the forehead of the other as to kill him on the spot.' And in later years, duellists were on occasion quite imaginative in finding ways of killing one another when the pistol or the sword were denied them. In 1894, two British officers stationed in India duelled by sharing a darkened room with a lethal snake. After ten minutes, the snake bit one of the officers who died a few hours later in venomous agony. The survivor reputedly fled the room in fear, his hair turned instantly white from the shock.

Some duels – if one stretches the definition a little – were even resolved by the humble spoken or sung word. The African bushmen, the Australian aborigines and the Inuit tribesmen of the Arctic all have traditions of resolving conflict through a verbal battle of wits. Thus, as Richard Cohen described, a duellist in Greenland would challenge his opponent to a duel of satirical songs: 'One after the other the two disputants sing at each other their wisdom, wit and satire, supported by their partisans, until at last one is at his wits' end, when the audience, who are the jury, make known their decision.' Perhaps, as one historian noted dryly, one must be half-frozen to enjoy such good sense. Yet such traditions of verbal jousting do have surviving echoes today in the modern, oral combat between rival rap stars. In 1826, however, there were only two ways for a rational, sensible, educated European gentleman to resolve a dispute and that was either to stab his antagonist with a sword or shoot him with a pistol. And David Landale and George Morgan had chosen the latter.

There are many ways that men can shoot each other and there was never one agreed set format for pistol duelling. The traditional duel, where both sides stood twelve or so paces apart and fired once together, had many advantages. It was over quickly; either you were hit or not. Once both men had fired, the seconds were more than likely to intervene and insist that honour had been satisfied. Unless your opponent was particularly belligerent or foolhardy, he was as likely as you to be content with a shot a piece. Both men had showed their courage and defended their honour. Even if the duel did continue, they rarely lasted beyond three exchanges. 'Three fires should be the ultimatum in any case,' *The British Code of Duel* declared. 'Any further reduces duel to a conflict for blood, or must subject it to the ridicule of incapacity in arms.' Many duellists, however, objected to simultaneous firing because it gave them less time to demonstrate their courage. There was no way better of showing your mettle than by remaining calm as your opponent pointed a pistol at you and fired. But by the 1820s, this had fallen out of favour, most duellists still thinking it arduous enough to face a simultaneous fire. 'It requires some nerve to elevate the hand, and keep the pistol perfectly steady, when the muzzle of an adversary's weapon is directed upon you, and when aware that a very few moments will bring its contents much closer than is agreeable,' Traveller noted.

The famous back-to-back duel, in which participants walked away from each other and turned and fired on command, was deliberately designed to foster reactive rather than aimed shooting. Yet although it is perhaps the image that most people have of a duel, it was actually less common than might have been imagined. It had the undoubted advantage of being safer because it was harder for the duellist to aim as he whirled around to fire. 'This is perhaps, the most humane sort of duel,' Andrew Steinmetz wrote, 'as there are many chances that the parties will miss each other.' Except the English whom he thought were better trained for this kind of manoeuvre. 'Your Englishman, who has graduated on the bogs and moors, will have a fatal advantage in this flurried style of shooting.' There was always, however, the added risk of cheating – duellists would often be tempted to turn a fraction early to get their shot in first.

On the continent, one of the most common variations was known as the duel *à la barrière* or the 'barrier duel'. Some form of barrier was marked out between the duellists over which neither could cross. Sometimes this came in the form of a single rope, other times a gap of several yards, a no mans' land marked out with stakes or handkerchiefs. The duellists took their marks some distance from the barrier and on command, walked towards each other. They could fire, once, at will. If a duellist fired and missed, he had to remain absolutely still while his opponent continued walking up to the barrier, normally within a certain time limit. The opponent was then obliged to fire the moment he reached the barrier. It was this kind of duel that Alexander Pushkin described so accurately in *Eugene Onegin*, when the eponymous aristocrat shoots the poet Vladimir Lensky dead.

> 'Approach at will!' Advancing coldly,
> With quiet, firm, and measured tread,
> Not aiming yet, the foes took boldly
> The first four steps that lay ahead –
> Four fateful steps. The space decreasing,
> Onegin then, while still not ceasing
> His slow advance, was first to raise
> His pistol with a level gaze.
> Five paces more, while Lensky waited
> To close one eye and, only then,
> To take his aim . . . And that was when
> Onegin fired! The hour fated
> Has struck at last: the poet stops
> And silently his pistol drops.

Onegin was lucky. The historian Kevin McAleer considered that it was almost always better to wait and fire second. 'The major benefit of firing second was the complimentary sashay to the barrier. And in my reading of hundreds of duelling accounts, it was not necessarily desirable to get the drop on an opponent. The second shot was more than likely to be the telling one.' Would that a young English officer had known this before he agreed to take part in a barrier duel with a Frenchman in the 1850s that was witnessed by Sir Algernon

West, one of Gladstone's private secretaries. In the version of the barrier duel they adopted, if either fired first but missed, they were expected not to stay still but to continue walking towards the barrier, getting even closer to their opponent. 'At the given signal, the two combatants started to walk to the rope, with the liberty of firing whenever it so suited them,' West recalled in his memoirs. 'The young officer, with the impetuosity of youth, at once fired his pistol, and having missed his man, continued to walk up to the barrier, when he became face to face with his opponent, who had reserved his fire. The Frenchman put his hand on the young man's heart, and said, with a sickening familiarity: "Brave jeune homme, ton coeur ne palpite pas," and stepping back, he continued: "Pauvre jeune homme, je plains ta mère," and shot him through the heart.'

The barrier duel had several variations. In one, the duel *à marche interrompue*, the combatants were not allowed to walk straight towards each other and the barrier. Instead they would walk in a zig-zag line, taking just two paces before changing direction, 'halting and advancing like Indian skirmishers, with power to fire the moment either halts'. Crucially, the duellist who fired second was not allowed to move any closer to his opponent. Steinmetz recommended this as a good duel for novices, 'who might be naturally agitated by their debut', because the movement was good for settling the nerves. In a duel *à ligne parallèle*, the combatants were separated by two parallel lines which lay about fifteen paces apart. The two men took up their positions at either end of the lines about thirty-five paces from each other. They then walked along the lines, the gap between them narrowing all the time. If one fired first and missed, he had to remain stationary while the other had thirty seconds to continue closing the gap before firing himself. In the duel *au signal*, the seconds would control the encounter with a clap of the hands: one clap for the duellists to start walking towards each other, a second to level their pistols and a third to fire them. A tough duel; the temptation to fire early must have been huge, but the consequences were dreadful – 'If one fires before or after the signal, by so much as half a second, he shall be considered a dishonourable man; and if by the disgraceful manoeuvre he shall have killed his adversary, he is looked upon as an assassin.'

Perhaps the most lunatic was the duel *au mouchoir*, an early form of Russian roulette. The duellists would choose between two identical pistols, only one of which had been loaded. They would then each hold the corner of a handkerchief and fire at each other, effectively at point-blank range, not knowing if they held the loaded weapon. The result was almost always fatal. Andrew Steinmetz was most disapproving: 'These extravagances – outpourings of an indecent and ungentlemanly animosity – receive but little toleration, and the genteel code . . . takes no cognizance of its incidents.' He described one such duel between two Frenchmen fighting over a woman: 'The seconds prepared the pistols, enveloping them in a handkerchief, and then presenting them to one of the combatants, he took his weapon, and the other was delivered to the antagonist. The ends of the handkerchief were respectively placed in their hands; they raised their pistols; the word was given; they fired and the slanderer fell back, shot through the breast, a torrent of blood gushing at the instant from his mouth and nostrils.' One British army officer, a Captain Stewart, took this format to its logical conclusion and insisted that he and his opponent should duel in a grave which had been dug for the purpose. As it was, his opponent's nerve failed as he climbed down into the pit and picked up his end of the handkerchief, so the captain thrashed him for his cowardice. In another, perhaps more horrible version of the duel *au mouchoir*, both the pistols were loaded, which the historian Victor Kiernan said was 'equivalent to a suicide pact' and 'can never have been popular'. An even more bizarre version was the so-called 'American duel', something that was briefly popular on the continent and appeared to have absolutely nothing to do with America. While being witnessed by their seconds, the duellists would choose lots. Whoever chose the short straw was obliged to die by his own hand, normally in private. Amazingly some young men who lost these duels did indeed retire to their rooms and put a bullet in their heads. In 1905, the *New York Times* was most put out that these encounters were still described as somehow American. 'If it must receive a racial or national designation, [it was] thoroughly German, but if it had not been described as "American" we would have been content to apply to it some such adjective as "silly" or "stupid".'

Some pistol duels took place on horseback, the challenge being to hold the weapon steady while galloping at full pace. Sometimes the pistols were loaded with small shot as well as a ball to make it easier to score a hit. The combatants would keep their distance by charging down two parallel lines, like two knights in a tournament, armed, though, with pistols and not lances. Other duellists simply chose to ignore the rules and do things their way. On January 6 1882, Messrs Benjamin Constant and Forbin des Issarts duelled from chairs at ten paces 'on account of the rheumatism of the former'. In May 1812, just outside Reading, two French officers on parole fought with just one weapon, a single fowling piece, at fifty paces, the idea being to swap the gun round until one man was hit. As it happened, the first to fire shot his opponent dead.

Perhaps the most bizarre ballistic duel took place in 1808 when two Frenchmen fired at each other with crude blunderbusses 'as pistols could not be expected to be efficient in their probable situations'. For Monsieur de Grandpré and Monsieur de Pique had chosen to duel from the baskets of two balloons floating over Paris. The men had quarrelled over a famous opera dancer called Mademoiselle Tirevit who was mistress of one and lover of the other. They chose this form of combat, they said, because they had 'elevated minds'. So, at 9 a.m. on May 3, watched by a huge crowd, these two eccentric Parisians climbed into their aircraft near the Tuileries and rose gently up into the morning air. At about 2000 feet, when the balloons were about 80 yards apart, de Pique fired his blunderbuss and missed. 'Almost immediately after, the fire was returned by M. de Grandpré, and the ball penetrated his adversary's balloon, the consequence of which was its rapid descent, and M. le Pique and his second were both dashed to pieces on a house-top, upon which the balloon fell.' De Grandpré and his second, however, drifted happily away in the light north-westerly breeze before landing safely twenty miles away.

For David Landale and George Morgan, standing opposite one another in a Fifeshire field that dank morning in August 1826, there would be no such exotica. The duel they were about to take part in would follow tradition to the letter, a straightforward combat but no less lethal. Both men would stand facing each other, and at a signal, they would fire simultaneously. But before this could happen, their seconds, William Millie and William Milne, had work to do.

Their first task was to agree the distance both men should stand apart. Although the duelling codes offered some guidelines, few were specific or dogmatic about this most important of decisions. Some duellists, particularly the better shots, liked to put a little distance between them and their opponents. Not only did it make it slightly safer for them, it also allowed them to demonstrate their ballistic skills. The most successful pistol shot on record was made by the American duellist, Alexander McClung, who in October 1833 shot dead his opponent from a distance of 100 feet. He told his antagonist, a General Allen, that he would shoot him in the teeth and 'casually raised his pistol and fired. The ball hit Allen in the mouth, knocked out a couple of teeth, took out a section of his tongue and imbedded itself in the spine. [He] slumped to the ground and died on the spot.' Other duellists preferred closer encounters, often just a few feet apart. This not only allowed them to demonstrate greater courage, it also gave them a better chance of hitting their opponent. There were, however, risks: in March 1796, a Captain Sweetman demanded a distance of just four paces because he was short-sighted. Unfortunately, this just made it easier for his opponent to shoot him through the heart. (Not that myopia was always a problem. One purblind duellist shot dead an opponent simply by using his voice to locate him – the unlucky antagonist had fired first and exclaimed: 'By God, I have missed him!') So it was largely up to the participants to decide the distance. Too far apart and the lack of danger would render the duel a mockery. Too close and the encounter would be little short of murder. Lieutenant Milne suggested that David Landale and George Morgan should stand fifteen paces apart. This was reasonable and perfectly within the rules, but for some a touch on the long side, a distance that would favour the experienced and accurate shot over the greener gunman who might prefer his chances over a shorter ground. 'If a man has a good shot for his opponent, and is but an indifferent shot himself, it is decidedly to his advantage to fight at the shortest distance,' Andrew Steinmetz concluded. 'If a good shot and opposed to an inferior, he should then choose the longest distance.' So Millie, all too aware of David's unfamiliarity with a pistol, said he would prefer twelve paces, and Lieutenant Milne did not demur. Millie was extremely lucky to find his counterpart so accommodating. Many seconds fell out over how far apart their principals might stand. And even once that was decided, they still had to agree what constituted a pace. Some seconds argued that a pace was the thirty inches of a single step, others that it was the sixty inches of two steps. The latter distance rendered twelve paces almost the length of a cricket pitch, much reducing the chance of a hit. That morning, the seconds agreed a pace was the more conventional single step.

David and George stood by, waiting patiently, as the two seconds continued their work. Lieutenant Milne tossed a sixpence to decide who would measure out the ground and give the signal to fire, a toss that he won. But should there be a signal or an oral command to fire? Some seconds preferred a visual signal, such as the dropping of a handkerchief, because it forced both combatants to look away from each other until the last moment and thus limited their aim. But William Millie thought a command would be 'more decided' and Milne said he had no objection to that. The word of command agreed upon was: 'Gentlemen, are you ready? – Fire!' with the strict stipulation that neither man should raise his pistol until the word 'Fire'.

They then had to agree exactly where their principals would

stand. The canny second would do everything he could to ensure that the position was to his man's advantage. He would choose a spot where the adversary was silhouetted by a hedge or a wall or some other background. This would help his principal's aim. At the same time, he would try to ensure that his principal blurred into his background as much as possible. And obviously, he would try to ensure that the sun was not shining into his face, 'a caution,' Traveller observed, 'almost unnecessary to persons in this country, as we are so seldom favoured with its appearance in the morning'. On that rainy morning, in August 1826, Milne had no such concerns as he marked out twelve paces in a line running broadly east–west. William Millie 'paced them after him and found them correct'.

The seconds then 'proceeded to load the pistols in the usual manner in presence of each other and to mutual satisfaction'. This was right and proper. The Irish code established that: 'The seconds load in presence of each other, unless they give their mutual honours they have charged smooth and single, which should be held sufficient.' This was a crucial job for a second and his principal's life would depend on it. Pistols at the time were prone to misfire – damp powder, a broken flint, a faulty percussion cap, a loose ball that falls out of the muzzle – and the rules were quite specific: a misfire of any kind was counted as a shot. Even worse, a badly loaded pistol could be lethal to the duellist: too much powder or a blocked barrel could result in the weapon exploding in his hands. Abraham Bosquett witnessed one duel where 'the Principal [was] killed by his own pistol bursting, a part of the barrel having entered the temple'. On another occasion, 'the Principal shot his own Second through the cheek, knocking in one of his double teeth, not by the ball, but a part of the pistol barrel.'

William Millie observed to Lieutenant Milne that his principal, David Landale, was using detonating [percussion] pistols while George Morgan had brought his flintlocks. Did Milne mind? Would he like one of David's pistols? Milne replied: 'No, let each have their own.' Milne later recalled: 'It is usual when both gentlemen have pistols on the ground, that each takes his own, and from Mr Morgan telling me before this period that he knew his own pistols well, I thought it best that he should use them himself.' The experienced naval lieutenant also had his own views about these newfangled detonating pistols: 'I do not conceive that in a matter of this sort, detonating locks are superior to flints, having myself experienced that detonating locks are liable to miss fire.' And the supposed ability of the new pistols to fire more quickly would have no impact over such a short distance: 'I [do not] consider that detonating locks would give any advantage to a person firing with them in a duel, the word being given so as that no advantage can be taken by either party.' William Millie said nothing but privately disagreed. In such circumstances, he said later, '[he] would prefer percussion locks himself'.

Everything was now ready; it was time for David Landale and George Morgan to take up their positions. Once again, Traveller knew exactly how this should be done. 'When called upon to leech [take up his mark], he should step up boldly and firmly, as though he was going to shake hands with an old friend, instead of shoot one,' he wrote. 'Having taken his station, he should cast his eyes closely upon his adversary, and mark if there is any nervous tremulation in his movement: as to observe it is encouraging; because when a man trembles his fire is seldom effectual. He should also be very careful to remain himself as firm and stiff as a statue. Not a muscle in his face or movement of his body should portray any extraordinary degree of feeling or excitement.' Such advice was probably easier to read than to follow but both David Landale and George Morgan appeared calm. George took off his coat, laid it carefully on the ground and took up the position closest to the track, facing east where the dawn was slowly breaking. David walked to the other mark and turned to face his opponent. The two seconds handed their principals the cocked, loaded pistols and backed away ten yards to a position of relative safety away from the line of fire. The moment of truth had come.

The codes of duelling were nothing if not specific and detailed about how a man should behave on the field. They covered every aspect of his behaviour: what he should wear, when he should speak, how he should fire, how he should die. Such is the detail that many golf club secretaries today would not be unfamiliar with their precision or their phraseology. But like all rules, they were many and varied and often inconsistent. Some claimed that the man who had been challenged had the right to choose the weapons and the ground. Others said precisely the opposite. Some, like the Irish code, established that 'any wound sufficient to agitate the nerves and necessarily make the hand shake must end the business for that day'. But others said it was perfectly acceptable for a wounded duellist, if capable, to continue, either firing off his first shot, or even taking part in a second or third exchange. Often it was simply up to the seconds and the surgeons to decide on the day, at the moment. The wisdom of firing again while wounded was uncertain. In October 1783, a Mr Green met a Captain Munro in Battersea Park, south London and was severely injured in the first exchange. Green insisted on continuing unless Munro apologised. The captain would not do so, so Green declared: 'Then one of us must die', which was quite right, for he perished in the next exchange of fire, shot through the heart. By contrast, General Andrew Jackson, many years before he became the seventh president of the United States, was more fortunate. In a duel with another crack shot, Charles Dickinson, in May 1806, Jackson appeared to allow his opponent to fire first and was struck in the chest. There is a suggestion that this was his deliberate tactic – to risk being injured so that when his turn came, he had enough time to make sure that his shot was lethal. Apart from clasping his left hand to his chest, 'the General stood firm, while Dickinson recoiled, crying out: 'Great God! Have I missed him?' A moment after, Jackson took deliberate aim and pulled the trigger . . . Dickinson reeled and his face turned white, and as his friends hurried toward him, he sunk to the ground.' Only then did anyone realise that Jackson had been injured too, albeit not fatally, even though the bullet would remain lodged in his flesh until the day he died almost forty years later. After the duel, he boasted to his second, saying that 'he would have lived long enough to have killed his antagonist even if he had been shot through the heart'. Jackson lives on today on the back of the twenty dollar note.

One of the most disputed issues was whether or not a duellist should be able to fire harmlessly in the air. This was known in duelling parlance as deloping. The Irish code was categoric: 'No dumb shooting or firing in the air is admissible in any case. The challenger ought not have challenged without receiving offence; and the challenged ought, if he gave offence, to have made an apology before he came to the ground; therefore children's play must be dishonourable on one side or other, and is accordingly prohibited.' The Irish framers were clearly determined to protect the integrity of their traditions. The historian Victor Kiernan said the Irishmen had a point: '"Deloping" or firing in the air, might be generous, but might be taken as an admission of being in the wrong; if both men deliberately fired wide, things became farcical.' It could also be interpreted as a craven hope that the gesture might be reciprocated. For honour to be established and courage displayed, there had to be an element of danger. But by the 1820s, *The British Code of Duel* declared deloping acceptable behaviour, within reason. Andrew Steinmetz certainly saw nothing wrong in a duellist firing wide. 'This is quite proper in every way,' he wrote. 'But if such be his intention, he should be cautioned to keep it carefully concealed until his antagonist has discharged, and to raise his pistol with the same nerve and accuracy as if he intended to fire. Because when a principal is aware that the opposite party does not intend to fire at him, his aim is likely to be much more accurate.' Steinmetz also considered that a delope ended the duel. 'The seconds should never permit another discharge,' he wrote. 'When a man fires in the air, it is considered an acknowledgement that he has been at fault.' There were, however, exceptions. A man who received a shot and then fired wide showed both courage and mercy. The most famous example of this, albeit in fiction, involved the heroic cad, Harry Flashman. In his first outing under the pen of George MacDonald Fraser, the cowardly imposter takes part in a duel with another officer. Flashman ensures that his opponent's pistols are loaded with nothing but powder. After he has 'survived' his opponent's fire, Flashman fires deliberately wide. By a lucky fluke, the shot takes off the top of a bottle thirty yards away. His reputation for mercy is thus enhanced by his supposed marksmanship and he is the envy of the regiment. Flashman's only critic is his father who tells him: 'Don't be such an infernal fool another time. You don't fight duels in order to delope, but to kill your adversary.'

Some rules said men should fight bare-chested to show they were not cheating by wearing protective undergarments – it did happen, men sometimes binding their torsos in silk in the belief that bullets would more easily slide off their person. Other rules said this was absurd because no man prepared to establish his honour in a duel could act so dishonourably. Some codes went the other way and said duellists should wear formal dress. One Italian code insisted that it was 'de rigueur that he shall wear an English frock coat and a high hat. As for the trousers, it shall have been determined by previous agreement whether they shall be supported by a belt or suspenders.' Experienced duellists would wear black coats with buttoned up collars with no buttons or white collars to offer as a target. Yet more rules said that duellists should be searched to make sure that they carried no books, coins, watches, wallets or cigar cases that could impede a bullet. Some rules even banned eye glasses. This was not taken lightly because there were many occasions when even something as little as a button saved the life of a duellist. In 1704, the world of music escaped a great loss when a duelling sword broke against a button on the coat of one George Frederick Handel. In one duel in Ireland in 1823, a duellist was saved by a lucky horseshoe. He had found the shoe on the ground while on the way to the duel and was encouraged to pick it up as a good omen. 'He put it in his pocket and his adversary's ball actually struck it over the region of the heart, and glanced off at an angle.' In another duel, a man survived when a bullet lodged in some gingerbread nuts that he had in his pocket. One French nobleman hoped for similar luck by lining his chest with thick slabs of paper. It worked and stopped the bullet. However, 'notwithstanding this device, the blow from the bullet created a sore on the left side, which was never effectually cured. The Marquis died shortly afterwards.' When, in a duel between two Frenchmen, one survived when his opponent's ball struck a five franc piece in his breast pocket, his second is supposed to have remarked: 'That's what I call money well invested.'

There were sundry other rules: no duelling on a Sunday or a saint's day; no duelling near churches; no duelling between fathers and sons. And as the rules of judicial combat had declared half a millennium earlier, there was to be no duelling involving men over sixty. Perhaps the most depressing thought is that there were even rules for how a duellist should behave as he died. This was because most duellists died slowly. A few were spared this torture, expiring instantaneously from a fatal wound to a life-giving organ, or, in the case of one French duellist in January 1812, a heart attack at the moment of truth. Most duellists, however, would die lingering, excruciating deaths from blood loss, botched operations or infection, hours, days and even weeks after the encounter. One nineteenth-century American writer, only slightly tongue in cheek, described the possibilities thus: 'If a man could be sure of a ball in the right quarter – say the fleshy part of the arm, or of the thigh, or a grazing shot upon one of the ribs . . . or not hit at all, it would be well enough. But it is not pleasant to anticipate . . . a bullet in the shoulder-joint, occasioning infinite pain and a crippled limb for life: or a ball in the hip, badly scratching the femoral artery and bloating up into aneurisms; or in the articulation of the lower jaw, splintering bones of importance; or one in the lungs, producing great wheezing and weak wind for the residue of life; or in the stomach, allowing much gastric juice to escape and spoiling the thought of dinner forever.' The most gruesome death was that of a wounded duellist for whom there was no thought of dinner at all. The unfortunate Lieutenant Newman 'was shot through the nose, lived a considerable time in the greatest agony, and after literally starving to death in consequence of the obstruction to his swallowing nourishment, he left a wife and four unprovided children to lament his loss'.

So with all this time on their hands, dying duellists needed some rules of behaviour and Traveller, as ever, was ready to provide them. 'If upon the discharge, his adversary's ball has taken effect, he must not be alarmed or confused, but quietly submit the part to the examination of his surgeon, who should close round him, with his Second, the moment the discharge has taken place,' he wrote. 'I cannot impress upon an individual too strongly, the propriety of remaining perfectly calm and collected when hit: he must not allow himself to be alarmed or confused, but summoning up all his resolution, treat the matter coolly, and if he dies, go off with as good a grace as possible.' This rule showed duelling at its most absurd. Perhaps the best example of these deathly good manners came from Lord Camelford after he had been mortally wounded by his friend Captain Best. 'You have killed me, Best, but the fault is wholly mine, and I relieve you of all blame,' the peer said. 'Shake hands with me and forgive me, and then fly and save yourself from arrest.' Such sentiments, to some, could appear noble and courageous. Yet from the mouth of a cruel, murderous and eccentric seeker of duels such as Lord Camelford, the words sound distinctly phoney.

Away from the field, two hundred yards down the track into the wood, the two chaise drivers were minding their horses and gossiping. There were 'some conjectures' as to what was going on. Gilbert Garner, George's driver, knew what was up. He told John Mason that after what he had seen, 'he would wager a thousand pounds that some of these gentlemen were going to fight a duel.' But before Mason had time to reply, Dr James Johnston came hurtling up the road on an exhausted pony. Panting for breath, he asked the drivers which way the gentlemen had gone and they pointed him on his way. He rode on without a word. He reached the gate, tethered his horse, jumped the wall and burst through the bushes onto the field where David Landale and George Morgan stood, twelve paces apart, pistols in their hands. He could not believe what he was seeing. For although Johnston knew he was attending a duel, 'he had all along supposed Mr Morgan a second from calling on him for his professional assistance'. He had never expected that it was Morgan himself who was one of the principals.

He did not know Lieutenant Milne but was acquainted with William Millie and immediately ran up to him. 'Millie, Millie, for God's sake, stop!' he cried. 'What the devil is the meaning of this?' He 'begged an explanation and declared that he was totally ignorant of the circumstances and said can no arrangement be effected?'

David, seeing Johnston talking with Millie, said loudly: 'Doctor, you have no right to interfere.' He was quite right: doctors were not supposed to get involved.

Johnston replied curtly: 'You have no right to speak.' He was equally right: on the duelling ground, both principals were expected to remain silent and let their seconds do their talking for them. But David was determined that everything should be done fairly and that regardless of what happened, no one could say later that the duel had not been conducted properly. He insisted: 'Let there be no conversation with one second while the other is not present.'

So Lieutenant Milne came up and joined Millie and the doctor. 'Milne said to Dr Johnston that he had made every effort the evening before to reconcile the parties but without effect.' He tried to show Johnston the piece of paper outlining his plan for a mutual apology from both parties. But the doctor, belatedly remembering his duty, said 'he could not listen to what Milne had to read from the paper, and that this was not the proper place for it'. But at the very least, he had to know the cause of the dispute.

William Millie said: 'Doctor, Mr Landale was struck yesterday on the open street in Kirkcaldy and can do nothing.'

Shaking his head, Johnston said: 'God, that's certainly very bad.'

By now, the two principals, unable to listen to this conversation, were growing frustrated. 'Depend upon it, doctor, you are only wasting time,' David Landale cried out. 'No apology,' shouted George Morgan again.

Realising there was nothing he could do, 'Dr Johnston considered it better to be out of the way as fast as possible.' So he told the seconds: 'It is time I was off' and walked quickly back towards his horse. But on his way, he spotted Dr Smith lurking among the trees and headed in his direction instead.

★

David Landale and George Morgan readied themselves again, both seeking Conrad's focused, homicidal mood. Throughout the doctor's interruption, quite properly, neither had moved from their marks. David took out his watch and handed it to his second. 'Millie, if I fall, keep that for my sake,' he said. Morgan did likewise. The two seconds withdrew. Milne looked at both principals to make sure they were ready and began the words of command: 'Gentlemen, are you ready?' But before he could say: 'Fire', William Millie cried out and brought the duel to yet another unexpected halt. For he had spotted that George Morgan was literally trying to jump the gun. On the word 'ready', the banker had raised and presented his pistol, earlier than he was supposed to.

'Morgan, that is not fair,' Millie exclaimed. 'Drop your weapon until the word fire is given.'

'Oh, very well,' said Morgan and let his pistol drop to his side.

Another, agonising pause, as again Milne looked at both principals to make sure they were ready. Then, the command: 'Gentlemen, are you ready? – Fire!'

This time both men fired. A single report echoed off the trees. Millie 'distinctly saw both pistols go off' but 'both pistols went off so instantaneously that [he] could not distinguish them from one shot'. He, naturally, was looking in David Landale's direction 'and conceived that Morgan's ball passed close by Landale's back'. But as the smoke cleared and he looked at George Morgan, he knew the banker had been less fortunate.

The ball from David Landale's pistol had penetrated George Morgan's ribcage, just below the fifth rib on the right; it had then passed through his lungs and possibly his heart, and exited under his left armpit. The former soldier gave what Milne described as 'a sort of groan' in disbelief and stood there for a moment as if his mind and his body refused to accept what had happened. Millie thought Morgan stood for about ten seconds: 'He did not fall down instantaneously but dropped his pistol and gently fell on his right side.' The doctors came running, Dr Smith reaching Morgan first. 'I got up to him just as he was falling and observed him struggling hard for breath and bleeding profusely from the mouth. When he fell, I endeavoured to untie his neck cloth and called for Dr Johnston's assistance.' Dr Johnston, who was by then at his side, exclaimed: 'The man is dead, as dead as John Brown, by God.' Dr Smith continued his examination: 'On turning the body on its back, I discovered a wound about the middle of the right side of the chest and another immediately below the left arm pit, of such an appearance as to leave no doubt of their fatal nature as blood and air were escaping from both.' The air was clear proof that the lungs had been penetrated. Dr Johnston said there was 'bleeding much at the entering wound and at the exit'.

The men standing in that Fifeshire field suddenly became aware of what had happened, the bloody reality of the duel sinking in, overpowering all high minded conceptions of honour. This was what duelling meant – death. Alexander Pushkin caught the mood exactly when he described the moment when Onegin shot Lensky:

> He lay quite still and past all feeling;
> His languid brow looked strange at rest.
> The steaming blood poured forth, revealing
> The gaping wound beneath his breast.

One moment back – a breath's duration –
This heart still throbbed with inspiration;
Its hatreds, hopes and loves still beat,
Its blood ran hot with life's own heat.
But now as in a house deserted,
Inside it – all is hushed and stark,
Gone silent and forever dark.
The window boards have been inserted,
The panes chalked white. The owner's fled;
But where, God knows. All trace is dead.

David Landale remained at his position, watching the doctors tending to his fallen adversary. Unabashed, he told his second: 'Millie, I consider that a just retribution of providence.' But he added: 'We had better be off.' As they began to leave, according to Millie, Lieutenant Milne cried out: 'Mr Millie, you had better not go away. This is all your fault. Had it not been for you, this might have been prevented.' Milne later denied saying this, insisting he had told Millie and Landale 'there was no use in them remaining'. Either way, Millie said nothing but walked away with David, carrying both his pistols. He fired off the second pistol for safety 'to prevent accidents on going into the chaise'. According to Gilbert Garner, both men 'came running towards the chaises'. David 'desired him to drive up to Mr Morgan as he wanted the chaise'. Gilbert thought David looked extraordinarily calm. 'From Mr Landale's appearance, I would not have known that he had been engaged in anything,' the driver later recalled. 'He appeared quite composed.' John Mason agreed. He said that Mr Landale 'did not appear agitated but rather paler in the face than usual, and his eyes thrilled a little and on the whole looked rather steely-like'. In fact, it was William Millie who appeared most shaken. 'I thought Mr Millie had been one of the persons engaged in the duel and paid most attention to his appearance,' Gilbert Garner recalled. 'He was very white in the face and appeared confused and agitated.'

As David and Millie got into their chaise, Dr Smith came up to them and 'told them that George's wound was mortal and that they had better be gone'. He took out his instrument and dressing case 'in case anything could still be done' and returned to the field. David and Millie looked at each other but said nothing, save to order the coach away. Honour had been satisfied but now they were outlaws and needed to flee.

Gilbert Garner drove in the opposite direction, up the track to the gate. Dr Johnston came running up to him and said: 'Gilbert, Mr Morgan is shot.' He cut the rope tying the gate and opened it up to allow the chaise into the field. There the doctors began the grisly task of dealing with the body. Dr Smith 'assisted Dr Johnston to tie [Morgan's] arms down by his side' and then used one of the dead man's handkerchiefs – and one of his own – 'to wash the blood from his face'. Then Dr Johnston ordered the body to be put into the chaise and taken home. But Dr Smith disagreed: 'I objected to this being done so immediately in case life might be extant, or any blame attached for rashness, and proposed that a cart or litter should be procured from the neighbouring farm.' So Dr Johnston took his pony and headed up towards the Cardenbarns farmstead.

While the rest of them waited, according to Dr Smith, Lieutenant Milne 'expressed his regret at what had taken place but that he had done everything to prevent it, but without success. He remarked however that Morgan had got fair play.'

Gilbert said Milne appeared 'much vexed and agitated on the ground'. The driver, meanwhile, came up for a closer look at the body. He dismounted the chaise and although himself 'much agitated' at the gruesome sight 'he . . . went and put a hand on the body to satisfy himself whether Mr Morgan was dead. He was quite dead, bleeding much from the right side and a little from the mouth.' A short while later, Dr Johnston returned empty handed. 'The Devil, a horse cart or man could be found about the whole town,' he exclaimed irritably. Both doctors examined Morgan's body a second time and again confirmed to Milne that the banker was quite dead. 'The body had lain by this time about 30 or 40 minutes.' Milne, still dazed by what had happened, gathered up Morgan's coat and hat and pistols. He asked Dr Johnston and Gilbert Garner to fire off the spare pistol that remained primed and loaded. Both refused so he 'drew the shot' so that the pistol was now harmless.

The body was then put into the chaise. 'Mr Milne seemed most concerned and sorry for Mr Morgan's death,' Dr Johnston later recalled. He suggested that Milne should sit in the chaise alongside the body. But Milne 'declined and said he would not do so'. It was clearly going to be too much for Milne to sit inside with the body of his late acquaintance so instead he jumped up onto the dicky – the driver's seat – next to Gilbert Garner. Dr Smith, who was now without a ride, also hitched a lift on the dicky next to Milne. The lieutenant tried to show Smith the plan he had proposed for a mutual apology but, like Dr Johnston before him, Smith 'positively refused' to hear any word of it. The doctor then came across one of his colleagues riding by and got down from the carriage to join him. Milne now had no one but Gilbert Garner to hear his protestations of innocence. 'Milne said to me that he had done everything in his power on the preceding evening to get the affair sorted without effect,' Gilbert recalled. 'He was extremely sorry for what had happened but always thought up to the moment of the duel that the quarrel would be made up.'

Dr Johnston rode off on his pony and headed back into town, his heart heavy with the task before him. For it was he who would have to tell David Morgan that his brother was dead.

6
On the run

It is astonishing that the murderous practice of duelling should continue so long. A man says something which another man tells him is a lie. They fight – but whichever is killed, the point remains unsettled.

Benjamin Franklin, cited in *The Art of Duelling*, 1836

Between Torbain and Cardenden,
A bloody duel was fought:
Morgan fell and Landale fled
From off the bloody spot.

Fifeshire rhyme, anon., cited in *Kirkcaldy 1838–1938*, 1939

The paradox of duelling was that, in Britain and across the continent, it was almost universally illegal and yet almost universally tolerated. The monarchs of sixteenth-, seventeenth- and eighteenth-century Europe ostensibly opposed duelling and established laws against it. They had enough trouble already keeping the peace among their feuding barons and few wanted that conflict legitimised by the rituals of duelling. Europe's rulers were also loath to see so many noblemen die in duels when they could be much better deployed fighting the many wars that ravaged the continent. So most monarchs made clear their opposition to duelling both by legislation and by condemnation. In Britain, Elizabeth I formally decried the practice. James I 'could not abide fighting' and worried about the number of Scots who followed him down to London and died in duels with Englishmen. In 1612 James asked an eminent lawyer, Sir Edward Coke, to spell out exactly what the common law said about duelling and he concluded that 'to kill a man in a duel was murder, but there was no bar to sending a challenge or acting as a second'. This prompted James, the following year, to write – insufficiently anonymously – a tract entitled *Proclamation against Private Challenges and Combats*. His attorney general, Francis Bacon, boasted that he would 'prosecute if any man appoint the field, though no fight takes place; if any man accept a challenge, or consent to be a second; if any man depart the realm in order to fight; if any man revive a quarrel after the late proclamation.' A few years later the court of the Star Chamber unanimously condemned the idea 'that the private duel in any person whatsoever had any ground of honour'. After the Civil War, the Puritans came down hard on what they considered a Cavalier practice. In 1651, a committee of MPs proposed that duelling should be punished by property confiscation, banishment and the loss of the right hand. Oliver Cromwell was not quite as anti-dextrous as that but in 1654 he did pass an ordinance formally banning duelling. This made the sending or accepting of a challenge punishable with six months' imprisonment; anyone who failed to report a challenge within twenty-four hours was considered to have accepted it; and death by duelling was murder. When duelling experienced a bloody renaissance after the Restoration, Charles II threatened his duelling nobles with 'the utmost rigours of the law' and, perhaps more importantly, banishment from court.

Queen Anne said duelling was an 'impious practice'. Similar laws sprang up on the continent. The Spanish formally prohibited duelling as early as 1480. One Italian ruler, the Prince of Melfe Caraccioli, was so frustrated at his inability to stop the practice that he ordered all duellists to fight on the parapet of a Turin bridge, something that virtually condemned both combatants to falling into the river. In France, the duel was made a capital offence in 1609. Cardinals Richelieu and Mazarin both issued edicts and laws against duelling throughout the seventeenth century. Richelieu in particular was obsessed with banning the practice; his elder brother had died in a duel and, in 1627, he personally ordered the beheading of two nobles who had called each other out. He told Louis XIII: 'We must cut off the heads of some of these distinguished duellists or the time will soon arrive when they will pay no attention whatever to the edicts of your Majesty.' Louis XIV, the Sun King, clamped down hard on duelling and was more successful than his predecessor. Frederick the Great of Prussia told his officers that they could duel only with his permission. But on the first occasion that that permission was granted, the two combatants were dismayed to find the king waiting for them next to a gibbet. The challenger asked what this meant and Frederick replied: 'It means, Sir, that I intend to witness your battle until one of you has killed the other, and then I will hang the survivor!' Not surprisingly, duelling was for a time rare in the Prussian armies.

He and other European monarchs were aided by the Catholic Church which, after a slow start, was equally condemnatory. The Church believed that duelling was a sin because only God had the right to take life. And not only was the successful duellist threatened with hell and damnation, the dead duellist was equally sinful, being guilty, in the Church's eyes, of the crime of self-murder. The Council of Trent in 1563 thus threatened excommunication not only for duellists but also for those rulers who neglected to suppress them. It declared that 'the detestable custom of duelling which the Devil had originated, in order to bring about at the same time the ruin of the soul and the violent death of the body, shall be entirely uprooted from Christian soil'.

But despite this wave of legislation, prohibition and proclamation, duelling continued. In part, this was because the concept of law in those days was much laxer than it is today. Legislation was considered more instructional than literal, such were the practical difficulties in enforcing laws except at the point of a sword. Laws could simply be ignored. Yet duelling survived in the main because Europe's secular and spiritual leaders did not practise what they preached. For all their condemnatory rhetoric, monarchs were often privately supportive of duels. In fact, it was the apparent willingness of one king to duel that legitimised the combat for many of Europe's nobility. In 1527, Francis I of France challenged Charles V of the Holy Roman Empire to a duel. Charles accepted, Francis had second thoughts, they fought a war, Charles won and kept Francis in prison until he apologised and paid a ransom. The impact was widespread, as the American historian Major Ben Truman wrote: 'From that moment, upon every affront or injury which seemed to touch his honour, a gentleman considered himself entitled to draw his sword and demand reparation from his adversary.' Some monarchs, such as Charles II, granted hundreds of pardons to feuding courtiers. One king, George III, actually wrote out *pro forma* standing pardons so his favourites could duel without fear of retribution.

Some monarchs were just very human and enjoyed the sport, the gossip and the intrigue of duelling; a good combat brightened up a dull court. Other kings, as many historians have pointed out, were from aristocratic stock themselves and shared the same belligerent tendencies as their fellow noblemen. But as well as class sympathy and morbid fascination, Europe's kings and queens also tolerated duelling because they recognised they lacked the authority to stop it. For all the talk of absolute monarchy, their power was in practice circumscribed. Few monarchs could afford to crack down too hard on a nobility without whose support they could not rule.

As the years passed, duelling came to be seen as less of a threat to the state and the rule of law. Not only were rulers and governments more sturdily established, but the duel itself became more manageable, ritualised and self-regulating. Where once the murderous affrays and pitched battles of knights and their retainers had challenged the rule of law under a weak monarch, the private, controlled duel between two individuals on a cold dawn was now all but an irrelevance to the order of a modern, European state. But while many European monarchs subsequently appeared to tolerate duelling, few ever got round to repealing those laws which declared it to be a capital crime.

With the fatal shot still ringing in their ears, David Landale and William Millie sat back in the chaise and ordered John Mason to drive them as fast as possible from the sodden field in Fife where George Morgan's body was slowly growing as cold and damp as the earth beneath him. The two men were now on the run. Honour was satisfied, courage proved, yet both had broken the law. David had killed a man, and Millie was an accomplice. So they had to flee, they had to leave Fife, Scotland even, to evade the authorities. But if one of the first rules of crime is to ensure an adequate getaway vehicle, then David failed utterly. For when he ordered John Mason to drive to Stirling, about fifty miles to the west, he cannot have expected the coachman's response. He refused. He said it was too far, his team were too tired. 'I said my horses were not able to,' Mason later recalled. 'Mr Landale then said, "Drive to Queensferry" [a coastal village ten miles to the south west]. I again said my horses were not able to go that length. Mr Landale then ordered me to drive to Burntisland [four miles away]. Same answer.' At this point, David lost his patience and angrily ordered Mason 'to drive to the nearest place where fresh horses could be got'. You can only imagine the turmoil in David's mind. He had just killed a man in a duel and yet here he was, unable to flee, because some disobliging driver was refusing to push his horses. If it had been absurd for George Morgan to get lost on his way to the duel, it was equally undignified for David Landale to get stuck on his way from it.

John Mason scratched his nineteen-year-old chin and said he could probably take David as far as Kinghorn, a village just a couple of miles south of Kirkcaldy, no distance at all. David had no choice but to nod his agreement. To some extent, it was William Millie's fault. He had assumed that Mason would understand their urgency but the driver was clearly a little slow on the uptake. He claimed afterwards that he 'knew nothing about Morgan being shot until he came back to Kirkcaldy'. Millie could also have done more to ensure that fresh horses were used. But how could he have planned for the aftermath of a duel? He might just as easily have needed the coach to make a short, mournful return to St Mary's. Presently they arrived at Kinghorn and David and Millie stepped out of the chaise 'without saying anything to Mason'. David told him to have the bill for the ride sent to St Mary's but, despite the short distance travelled, still 'paid the driver for his own trouble'.

David now had to think on his feet. His planned escape route, as he had described in the letter to his land agent John Anderson, was in ruins. He had hoped to drive to Stirling, from where he could slip secretly into southern Scotland without having to catch a very public ferry across the Firth of Forth. From there he intended to go straight to Glasgow where he was not well known. Yet here he was, just a few miles south of Kirkcaldy in the opposite direction of where he wanted to be in an area where everyone knew his name. There was no alternative. With fresh horses and a new chaise, the two fugitives drove on a few miles down the coast to Burntisland, the little town where Lieutenant Milne lived, and from there they caught the 9 o'clock morning ferry across the water to Edinburgh's docks at Newhaven. There they employed the first coach they could find and headed west to Glasgow where they arrived later that afternoon, hoping for the best that they had not been spotted.

All that driving left David a lot of time to think and he spent that first day coming to terms with what he had done. He knew he had acted properly and honourably but that still did not get away from the fact that he had killed a man. It would be too much, at this stage, to say that his conscience was troubled but it was at the least uneasy. As he turned the affair over and over in his mind and began to rationalise what had happened, he decided who should shoulder the greater responsibility: George Morgan and God. Throughout the journey, according to William Millie, 'Landale never expressed any regret for having killed Morgan. His regret seemed to be, and he expressed it, that he had been forced into such an affair by Morgan, and repeatedly mentioned that Morgan's death was an intercession of the Almighty, and that the Almighty had stirred up Morgan to be instrumental in his own death.'

David took this view not only because he had strong religious convictions but also because he had not expected to escape unscathed in a duel with a former solider. Many, too, in Kirkcaldy would wonder how the inexperienced gunman had aimed true while the experienced shot had fired wide. In practice, there is little evidence to suggest that soldiers were better marksmen than civilians. A study of many duels involving officers leads one to conclude that soldiers were undoubtedly more familiar with firearms but no more likely to point them in the right direction than the next man. David, however, did not know this; he believed that God had played his part, a belief that many found easier in a pistol duel than a sword fight. The historian Victor Kiernan wrote that 'a bullet's direction being less predictable than that of a sword-thrust, possibly some of the more religiously minded, or fatalistic, found it easier to see the hand of Providence, or fate, on the trigger than on a sword-hilt.'

That night, from his hotel room in Glasgow, David wrote to his agent John Anderson, and again excused his actions with self-righteous confidence. 'My dear John,' he wrote. 'You will long ere now have heard of the fatal result of Morgan's insult to me. Providence decreed it. I always felt it would be so, and the consciousness of the rectitude of my conduct both in the sight of God and man enabled me to go through it with manly firmness and bear up now against the least compunction for the act, as I feel I have done my duty.' In this one, brief paragraph David revealed much. The words were an echo from the past, beliefs that could just as easily have been spoken 500 years earlier by a knight who had survived trial by combat. God, it was believed, did indeed determine the outcome of such encounters. Yet the significance is not that David felt the need to reach back down the centuries to justify his killing of George Morgan. It was the fact that he felt the need to justify it at all.

The glory days of the duel were glorious indeed. Encounters were celebrated, revelled in, endlessly retold, just as ancient minstrels and bards had gloried and exaggerated the tales of knights errant saving maidens in distress or ridding the world of dragons. Duellists were fêted as heroes, brave warriors who placed honour above life. Few felt the need to flee, let alone justify their actions. Duelling was a craze, a fashion both for those who indulged in it and those who followed it. In some social circles, two questions would be asked of a man: 'Who was his family? Has he ever blazed?' A young gentleman would not be considered fully educated until he had 'smelt powder'. From the royal court to the lowly inn, duelling was hot gossip, a source of excitement for many who lived essentially dull lives. 'Who fought today?' they would ask one another, desperate for the smallest detail. Many would disapprove but all were fascinated. They wanted a full account of the dispute that caused the duel, the names of all concerned, and of course, a blow by blow, shot by shot description of the combat. Sometimes this would come by word of mouth. But many seconds considered it their duty to give a brief account to the evening newspapers so that their side of the story would be heard. *The British Code of Duel* even had some guidance for how these reports should be compiled: 'This should be a simple and unornamented narrative of the facts in few words. No expiation on the conduct of either party is admissible.' If the papers had nothing fresh, there were always the memoirs of famous duellists to fall back on. There was rarely much sense of shame from the participants, or disapproval from the public.

Duelling was not just something that was followed from afar, a private event to resolve a private dispute. On occasion duelling was witnessed by thousands. The duel's forebear, the tournament, had of course been a public spectacle, a deliberate display of military prowess, personal honour, and superior breeding designed to impress and subdue the local peasantry. Trial by combat was equally open, a demonstration of public justice. In 1571 more than 4,000 spectators turned up at Tothill Fields in London, drawn by the prospect of a rare trial by combat. Sadly for them, even in those days, Elizabeth I thought that trial by combat was a bit much and, at the last moment, banned the encounter, much to the disgruntlement of the assembled masses.

But the public loved a good duel and if they knew one was to take place, they would be up early with their picnics to secure a good spot from which to view the encounter. In the late eighteenth and early nineteenth centuries, many Londoners would gather at dawn at Covent Garden, Chalk Farm, or Lincoln's Inn Fields just to watch the duels. In one Irish horseback duel in 1759, between Colonel Jonah Barrington and a Mr Gilbert, 'the entire country for miles around attended to see the combat which had been six months settled and publicly announced'. The crowds were seated 'as at a horse race and the ground kept free by the gamekeepers and huntsmen mounted'. In 1808 two Irishmen standing for election quarrelled over some votes in their rotten borough. John Colclough and William Alcock duelled the next morning and 'many hundred people assembled to witness the affair, among whom were several magistrates'. The two short-sighted men were placed eight paces apart, they fired and Colclough was shot through the heart. 'The bystanders were almost petrified with horror, when on a sudden, a loud and horrible yell burst simultaneously from every quarter of the field.' In 1833, almost 2,000 people witnessed a duel near Paris between a nobleman and an officer who had courted but refused to marry his sister. They too were not disappointed by the spectacle: in the first fire, the aggrieved nobleman was grazed by his adversary's ball; in the second, he shot his dishonourable opponent dead through the head.

Duelling was celebrated in the arts. Plays were full of them; the theatre could rarely resist the tragedy and melodrama of an honourable death. Duelling, in fact, fulfilled many of the requirements of tragedy – you knew the outcome was likely to be fatal, the interest derived from how and why it happened. While the middle classes supposedly disapproved of duelling, they were also titillated by the tales of aristocratic passion and honour. According to Victor Kiernan: 'A good many novels after 1815, when so many British families had members who had served on the Peninsula, were written by military men, who could be relied upon not to neglect the story-telling value of the duel.' Even those authors who aspired beyond the horizons of the hack novelist were obsessed with duelling, in particular the Russians. Like Pushkin, Chekhov,

Dostoevsky and Tolstoy all understood the dramatic usefulness of a duel and frequently included them in their work. Chekhov even wrote a novella called *The Duel*. Sir Walter Scott wrote obsessively about duelling, and based the encounter in *St Ronan's Well* on the duel between Sir Alexander Boswell and James Stuart of Duncarn. Charles Dickens used duels in his novels to mock the aspirational middle classes. Even Charlotte Brontë has Mr Rochester boast to Jane Eyre about his duelling past that left a French *vicomte* with a crippled arm. It all added to the glamour of the duel.

Doctor James Johnston wiped George Morgan's blood from his hands and coat, mounted his horse and plodded slowly back to Kirkcaldy with his dreadful news. 'I proceeded directly to the house of David Morgan and found him standing at his gateway,' the doctor later recalled. He did not hesitate. 'I addressed him and told him I had unfortunate intelligence to communicate to him and immediately said his brother had been shot dead.' To be told of a brother's death is, under any circumstances, an awful thing that would explain any amount of shock and grief. To be told it was murder would excuse all expressions of anger and thoughts of revenge. Yet David Morgan, so far as we know, felt little of these emotions. According to Doctor Johnston, he asked simply: 'Was everything fair?' His thoughts were not ones of sadness, regret or despair; they were about the propriety of what had taken place. David Morgan had accepted in his own mind that his brother had tried to resolve his dispute 'as a military man' and if that meant he had died in the process, so be it. As long as the duel had been proper and 'fair', then sadly, there was nothing he could object to. Public attitudes to duelling might have been changing but David Morgan was of the old school who still believed it was a legitimate and acceptable practice so long as it was properly carried out. The only sign of grief on David Morgan's part would come a few days later when he was interviewed by the authorities about the duel. The clerk to Kirkcaldy's justices of the peace, Will Douglas, wrote that the interview was a 'painful duty and severe upon him as his brother was witnessed only two hours before it'. But on that day of the duel he kept his emotions in check and asked simply about the justice of the encounter. In answer to David's question, Dr Johnston said 'he had no reason to doubt' that everything was fair. David nodded but said nothing. Dr Johnston urged him to go down to his brother's house 'and arrange for receiving his body'. This he did, before going out to see a man called John Leslie who lived down the road. Leslie was a wright by trade. But in Kirkcaldy, he was also the man who made the town's coffins.

By the time David Morgan returned, Lieutenant Milne had delivered George's body to his former home in Kirk Wynd. Milne did not linger at the house and left soon after, but he did not exactly rush: he took the same ferry to Edinburgh as David Landale and William Millie but not until half past two that afternoon. We do not know if he dared protest his innocence to the brother of the man he was supposed to protect.

If David Morgan's response to his brother's death was cool, then he cannot have been surprised by the rather unfeeling reaction from the Bank of Scotland's head office. Once he had sorted out the arrangements for dealing with George's body, David dutifully sent word to his superiors in Edinburgh about the unhappy outcome of the duel. George Sandy, one of the bank's secretaries wrote back by return: 'Sir, the death of Mr George Morgan Junior, your brother and colleague, is communicated to the Bank by Mr Richard Tosh, sent by you to make that melancholy communication and the Directors heard it with the deepest sympathy.' But after this less than effusive note of grief, the banker did what bankers do and moved swiftly to secure the bank's business. 'Official system requires the Bank immediately to represent to you, and you to remember, that the charge and trust – to which the Bond 21st and 23rd February 1818 is relative – continues with you as the survivor, and through this Bond, continues in full force and effect of security to the Bank for you as the survivor in official capacity, charge and trust of agent or cashier of the Governor and Company of the Bank of Scotland in and for the District of Kirkcaldy.' In other words, the bank wanted David Morgan to stay on. Despite the lack of sympathy, David would have been content with this. For the bank could always have concluded that these Morgans were no longer worth the trouble and shopped around for new agents. Yet they continued their trust in David.

Word of the duel spread round Kirkcaldy fast. In such a small, gossip-ridden community, such a secret would not last long. In fact, it was already being talked of around Kirkcaldy's breakfast tables before George Morgan was even cold. James Aytoun, heard about it at 'nine o'clock . . . when one of my servants acquainted me that Mr Morgan had been that same morning shot in a duel with Mr Landale'. At that same moment, David was still waiting to catch the ferry at Burntisland.

The duel 'caused a great sensation' in Kirkcaldy, not least because it had happened so soon after the Boswell–Stuart encounter just down the road. The general response from

Kirkcaldy society, such as it was, appeared to be this: that George Morgan was an impudent, ungentlemanly fellow who few would miss, but that David Landale should have tried harder to avoid a duel. It was a view expressed by George Mitchell, one of David's friends and colleagues in the linen trade. That Wednesday morning, just a few hours after the duel, Mitchell happened to be in Edinburgh and bumped into William Moneypenny, Kirkcaldy's collector of customs, and Richard Tosh who was on his way to inform the Bank of Scotland of George Morgan's demise. As they chatted, Mitchell talked in a 'contemptuous manner from his opinion of George Morgan's general character'. In particular, he said that 'had Mr Morgan died a natural death, he did not believe there were many men in Kirkcaldy who would have said they were sorry for him'. Yet Mitchell also expressed his surprise at the duel 'and observed that all he regretted was that Mr Landale should have allowed himself to be hurried away so far as to fight such a fellow as George Morgan.'

This note of regret was reflected in the newspapers. For duelling was by now rare enough always to warrant at least a few paragraphs. And when the duel was as interesting as this one, those paragraphs became columns. On Thursday August 24, the day after the duel, the *Edinburgh Evening Courant* reported briefly: 'We are sorry to learn that a meeting took place yesterday morning to the north of Kirkcaldy, between George Morgan, junior, Esq., and David Landale, Esq., both of Kirkcaldy, when at the first exchange of shots, Mr M received his adversary's ball in the chest, and unfortunately died on the spot. As the cause of this meeting must undergo judicial investigation, we refrain from giving particulars connected therewith.' A day later the *Scotsman* added a few more details, such as the names of the seconds, and spoke of the 'unfortunate difference' between Landale and Morgan, and its 'regret' at the banker's death. By the time the weekly papers came out, the reporters were almost lyrical in their sorrow. The correspondent for the *Edinburgh Weekly Journal* began his report thus: 'It is with no ordinary feelings of regret that we have this day to record the fatal issue of one of those unfortunate rencounters [*sic*] which the world calls an *affair of honour.*' The sarcasm almost drips off the page. By the following week, news of the duel had even reached London where *The Times* picked up the story. Even in those days page three of *The Times* was the depository of salacious crime stories. On August 28, the Monday after the duel, the paper printed the brief outlines of the story. The following day, it reprinted a version of events first published in the *Caledonian Mercury*, it too describing the duel as a 'melancholy rencontre'. It was clear that public attitudes to duelling were no longer quite as celebratory as they had once been.

Aaron Burr was the Al Gore of his day. In 1800, he missed out becoming president of the United States by a handful of votes. His victorious opponent, Thomas Jefferson, was obliged by the rules at the time to make Burr vice-president in an attempt to heal wounds and unite the nation. Yet Burr remained bitter and always blamed his defeat on Alexander Hamilton, one of the great figures of the American Revolution. Hamilton – a close friend of George Washington, a co-framer of the constitution, a leading Federalist, and a former head of the army – had successfully persuaded a tied electoral college to swing behind Jefferson. So when Vice-President Burr discovered a few years later that Hamilton had bad-mouthed him in a letter, he issued an instant challenge. Hamilton – by then retired from politics – was opposed to duelling on moral and religious grounds. But his duty of honour was greater than his ethical beliefs and so on July 11 1804, both men crossed the River Hudson with their seconds to what is now New Jersey. Burr was determined to shoot his rival dead, which he did. Hamilton, as he was hit, discharged his own pistol harmlessly. There was huge public revulsion, not just at the death of such a popular figure but at the practice of duelling as well. 'The affair had the effect of arousing the public mind of the people in the Northern States to a positive horror of duelling,' the American duelling expert, Major Ben Truman wrote. 'With the exception of the assassination of Lincoln and the deaths of Washington and Garfield, no public or private event has ever created the deep and general sorrow which was manifested over the melancholy termination of this most unfortunate affair.' Burr was castigated by the press, deprived of his New York citizenship, indicted for murder and forced into hiding. He was shunned by society. One of his biographers recalled: 'The city was not a safe place for Burr. He fled for his life and his terrified Myrmidons hastened to avail themselves of the protection of obscurity. Never again could that blood-stained man redeem his reputation before mankind, so infinitely more fatal was that duel to the survivor than the victim.' Burr tried to restore his law practice but died destitute on Staten Island in 1836. In contrast, Hamilton is a revered founding father and his face still adorns the modern ten dollar note.

Duelling has no better morality tale, at least not from the United States. But such public disapproval was beginning to find expression in Britain too. In September 1809, at the height of the war against France, the Tory defence secretary, Lord Castlereagh, challenged his colleague George Canning, the foreign secretary, to a duel. Castlereagh, with some justification, believed Canning had been plotting against him. Both men, who resigned their posts amid a political crisis a few days before the duel, met at dawn on Putney Heath. Canning, who had never fired a pistol in his life, missed twice but Castlereagh, with his second shot, lightly wounded his opponent in the leg. The public were outraged that two supposedly distinguished statesmen could act like this. 'To suppose it possible, after the disgusting exhibition they have made, to form out of their dispersed and disordered ranks a government that could stand, is the height of absurdity,' wrote the *Morning Chronicle*. Both men came in for a lot of criticism and although their careers survived in the short term, the duel was frequently held against them. Shortly after the encounter, Canning hoped to become prime minister when the ailing Duke of Portland resigned. But he hoped in vain. George III chose instead a man called Spencer Perceval who three years later secured the dubious honour of becoming the first and only British prime minister to be assassinated, shot dead in the House of Commons by a disgruntled merchant. Instead, Canning had to wait another eighteen years before he became prime minister. It was a long wait for a brief premiership; after just four months in the post, he fell ill and died. Castlereagh's career fared better; he went on to become one of the architects of post-Napoleonic Europe at the Congress of Vienna. But he never achieved popularity. The great Tory aristocrat and statesman committed suicide in 1822 amid allegations of homosexuality. His funeral procession was booed as it entered Westminster Abbey.

But this was as nothing compared to the public outcry caused by a duel in 1829 which involved no less a man than the then prime minister, the Duke of Wellington. More than a decade after Waterloo, following several years of political uncertainty, George IV had turned to the aging war hero to re-establish a little order in the Tory party and the country. One of Wellington's first acts was to give Britain's Catholics a greater role in public life in an attempt to avoid unrest in Ireland. The policy divided the Tory party and one peer, the Earl of Winchilsea, a hardline Protestant, questioned Wellington's motives. Many letters were exchanged and eventually the duke demanded satisfaction in the field. Wellington was supposed to be opposed to duelling; he had spoken out against it, arguing that it fostered indiscipline and wasted good officers. Yet he was so upset at Winchilsea's claims that he felt he had to challenge the earl to a duel. The fact that he was sixty-one years old and prime minister did not appear to worry him in the slightest. So, at dawn on March 21 1829, the conqueror of Napoleon and an unimportant peer met on Battersea Fields with a view to killing each other. In the end, Winchilsea realised that he was on a hiding to nothing – however right his cause, he did not want to be known as the man who killed Wellington – and he refused to point his pistol, firing instead in the air. Wellington fired deliberately wide as well and accepted a written apology. Courageous and honourable, said some. But the public were not impressed. They could not understand their prime minister's willingness to risk life and limb for such a trivial matter and Wellington found himself openly mocked in the press. The *Morning Herald*, among others, was utterly contemptuous. The paper said London had been 'thrown into great ferment' by tales of a duel which seemed 'utterly improbable', a fiction 'only fit to amuse male and female old ladies' and 'gossipers in and out of petticoats'. A full account of this gossip was then given, the improbable tale of how the two peers had met 'in Battersea Fields, among the cabbages'. Strange, declared the paper, but true: 'Yes, reader, the Duke of Wellington, the conqueror of a greater conqueror than either Alexander or Caesar, the first warrior of his day, the victor of a hundred battles, the Prime Minister of Great Britain . . . setting all these things at nought, placed himself in a situation where it was probable that he might have become a murderer; might have committed a deadly crime, which would have brought him to the bar of his country to plead for his life as a felon of the blackest dye. And all this risk was run, forsooth – all this wickedness was to be perpetrated – merely because a noble lord, in a fit of anger, wrote a pettish letter, which even his best friends and warmest admirers laughed at. Truly it is no wonder that the multitude should break the laws when we thus see the law-makers themselves, the great, the powerful and the renowned, setting them at open defiance.' Thus where once duels had been celebrated, now they were condemned. Fascination had become open disapproval.

If such were the public attitudes to duelling, it is no surprise that David Landale knew he would have to work hard to clear his name and protect his honour. The man he chose for this task was his yarn agent, John Anderson. His job was to act as David's spokesman while he was on the run, to put his side of the story and keep David up to date with how the duel was being seen. In his letter to Anderson from Glasgow on the evening after the duel, David gave the agent his commission and urged him to ensure that 'my fellow citizens will protect my honour during my absence'. And he entrusted Anderson with his first task – the world must know that David was prepared to hand himself in to stand trial. He wrote: 'In a few days, when I see the affair in public papers, I shall write to the Lord Advocate stating my readiness to meet the charge.' Anderson did well. Within a few days, the papers reflected David's views. The *Fife Herald*, the *Scotsman* and *The Times* all reported: 'We have authority from the friends of the survivor of the late duel at Kirkcaldy to state that measures are taking place to bring forward his trial as early as the forms of court will admit to. Mr Landale will most readily present himself before a jury of his country so soon as a day shall be appointed, temporary absence being only intended to avoid unnecessary confinement.'

For that was David's more pressing concern. Public opinion was one thing, but avoiding the strictures of the law was another. There might not have been any regular standing police force in Britain at the time but the authorities had more than enough constables on stand-by. With surprising swiftness, the law ground into action. Within hours of the duel, Andrew Galloway, the local public prosecutor, formally asked Kirkcaldy's magistrates to issue arrest warrants. In his petition, he wrote:

> May it please your Honours to grant warrants to Constable and assistants to search for and apprehend the persons of the said David Landale, Lieutenant William Milne and William Millie and bring them before your Honours for Examination . . . and thereafter to commit the said David Landale, Lieutenant William Milne and William Millie to the Tolbooth at Cupar or other sure Jail, there to remain for the crimes charged against them until liberated in due course of law.

As it happened, the duty justice of the peace was George Millar, Kirkcaldy's tax collector, and the town's mayor. He also happened to be a friend of David Landale and a colleague in the chamber of commerce. But in his official role that day, he had no choice. He replied to Galloway immediately:

> 'Having considered the foregoing petition, grant warrant to Walter Grant, Constable, and assistants to search for and apprehend the persons of the said David Landale, Lieutenant William Milne and William Millie wherever they may be found within the county of Fife and to bring them before any one or more of the Justices of the Peace of the said County for Examination.'

As Walter Grant and his constables fanned out across the county, George Millar JP ordered all potential witnesses to be subpoenaed so they could describe what had happened. In Scotland, this was known as precognition, a legal fact-finding process that established whether or not there was a prima facie case for a trial to take place. This was a task that fell to Andrew Oliphant, a member of one of Kirkcaldy's big shipowning families who was sheriff depute for the county of Fife. He and a handful of clerks spent the whole of Wednesday taking witness statements from twenty-nine people, some of whom had been directly involved with the duel and others who knew David and George well. The following day, Thursday August 24, Oliphant wrote to Adam Rolland, the crown agent in Edinburgh, giving him all the details of the duel. He concluded, wrongly as it turned out, that David Landale and William Millie were probably in Edinburgh and Lieutenant Milne was hiding out in Burntisland.

But Oliphant's letter was crucial because of the tone it set for the investigating authorities. First he pleaded the case for Millie and Milne. 'The seconds, more especially Mr Milne, seem to have done all in their power to accommodate matters but without effect,' he wrote. And if they were to hand themselves in, would they be allowed bail, he asked? 'In the last unfortunate business in Fife, I believe both seconds were allowed this privilege.' But second, and most importantly, Oliphant told the story from David Landale's point of view. He wrote that the quarrel had originated in some banking transactions 'and Mr Morgan seems to have been the aggressor as he laid his umbrella over the shoulders of Mr Landale in the public street.' He insinuated that David Morgan had not done enough to stop the duel: 'It appears that the whole arrangement was known to Mr David Morgan, brother of the deceased, who did not choose to give any information on the subject.' And then, crucially, this, the last sentence of the letter, next to which Oliphant wrote the word 'Private', which he then under and overlined: 'I may state that Landale is a man much respected here. The other by no means so.' It was a damning letter. David Landale's friends were protecting him well in his absence.

But as the wheels of justice began to turn, and the constables hunted their man throughout Fife and Edinburgh, David Landale fled further afield. On Thursday August 24, the day after the duel, he wrote again to his agent, John Anderson. He was still in Glasgow, but not for long. 'I am just setting off for Carlisle,' he wrote, 'where you will address me in the name of D.L. Lindsay, Post Office.' Not only was David Landale having to flee, but he was also having to live under an assumed name. He asked Anderson to send him a parcel of clothes and other necessaries: 'blue camblet cloak, cap and brown grey coat, common breeches, long gaiters to match, white cordovan do [a soft leather garment], two pairs of shoes, writing desk and dressing box.' Thus encumbered, David Landale was ready to run for England. His destination – the wilds of Cumbria.

A man who survives a duel should, in theory, celebrate. He has demonstrated his courage and defended his honour. He has risked his life and still his heart beats. He can hold his head up high in society, where his name will be revered as a man of valour and honour. An account of his actions will be published in the newspaper. His friends will look up to him, and, perhaps, even fear him a little. Women will flock to his door. Duelling, so it was said, required coffee for two and champagne for one. Yet more often than not, the corks remained firmly in the bottles. For although society accepted duelling, the law did not and many duellists were obliged to play the criminal. They indulged their lethal habits in private and, having taken their opponent's life, they had to flee like common felons to avoid the reach of the law.

Some duellists would do their fleeing before the duel and journey abroad to conduct their combat. For many years, British duellists would cross the Channel to places like Calais or Boulogne where they could fight beyond the reach of the Crown. At least they did until 1829 when the law was changed so that British coroners' juries were empowered to investigate murders by British nationals overseas. Other duellists would not flee at all, trusting that the lack of testimony from the seconds would protect them from prosecution. More unscrupulous duellists went further and deliberately removed all identifying marks from their dead opponent. Andrew Steinmetz described one such occasion: 'The seconds proceeded to examine the pockets of the dying man, whilst the echoes of the forest repeated the frightful death-rattle of his agony, amid fitful convulsions. They removed his watch, his papers, everything that might give any clue to the actors in the hideous tragedy, and then all disappeared, like assassins after a murder, already pursued by the pangs of remorse.'

But most duellists would flee to avoid capture, in the hope that they could return later once the scandal had died down. For some, that took a long time. One evening in May 1790, Captain James Macrae was escorting a lady home from the theatre in Edinburgh when he quarrelled with a drunken servant of Sir George Ramsay over who had prior claim to a sedan chair. Correspondence and a duel ensued. Ramsay was shot dead, and Macrae fled to France where he was forced to remain for twenty-six years to escape conviction and prison. In August 1807, a young officer called Lieutenant John Sargeaunt served as a second in a duel between two fellow servicemen, one of whom died. Such was the outcry that he fled to America where he spent the rest of his life in self-imposed exile, returning home just once to visit an aging father.

Yet David Landale fled for different reasons. Rather than wanting to begin a new life in another country, he simply wanted to avoid temporary imprisonment while he waited for his trial. This cannot have come easy to a man like David. Here was a proper, devout, mostly law-abiding member of society having to hide like an outlaw, skulking in discreet hotels, using an absurdly unconvincing alias. Yet not only had he planned to do this, he had also considered it a price worth paying. The paradox is that it was not considered dishonourable to flee the scene of a duel. An affair of honour allowed a duellist to flee to escape the strictures of the law, which is why David Landale found himself in a bumpy coach heading south across the border into England.

As George Morgan's body was lowered into the family grave in Kirkcaldy, an interment left unrecorded on the headstone and noted discreetly only in the sexton's book, David Landale headed for Carlisle, in the north of the Lake District, where he spent the first weekend after the duel. From there he wrote again to John Anderson to sort out his finances. Fugitives need money and he had to send a 'procuratory letter' to his bankers which would allow Anderson to draw money on his account. David was still accompanied by William Millie, who had loyally stayed at his principal's side. On Monday, they headed further south, to Keswick, in the very heart of the mountains. The following day, Tuesday August 29, almost a week after the duel, David wrote again to Anderson who had apparently become quite disturbed by Morgan's death.

> My dear John,
>
> I have received your letter of the 25th inst. Your feelings about the late affair appear to have agitated you by far too much and caused you to be alarmed at your shadow. I beg that you throw the late event entirely out of your mind, as I have already done from mine, and go on in the management of my business in the usual way, for I see nothing whatever to annoy you, more especially as you have always me to advise within a few days, as I have now fixed upon remaining in Britain, and will very likely pay you a visit in a week or two of an evening privately. Mr Millie has just arrived from a tour among the mountains,

lakes etc. and making the most of our time and keeping
ourselves fully employed.

Regardless of what he felt inside, David was showing some
considerable sang froid.

Not all duellists were so phlegmatic – some were racked
with guilt for their actions. Many steeled themselves adequately
for being shot but rarely prepared for the psychological impact
of being responsible for the death of another human being.
In 1815, the celebrated Irish politician Daniel O'Connell shot
dead a Dublin councillor called John D'Esterre in one of
Ireland's most notorious duels. 'O'Connell, together with his
second, repaired to a church, and took a solemn oath, or made
a vow to heaven, that he would never fight another duel. He
also offered a pension to the widow of his unfortunate adversary, equal in amount to what her husband had been earning.'
He never again attended church without first wrapping up
'the guilty hand' in a handkerchief 'declaring that he could
not approach his Redeemer with the hand exposed which had
taken the life of a fellow man'. Captain Best, the man who shot
dead Lord Camelford in 1804, claimed he was subsequently
visited by his opponent's ghost. 'No moment of my life has
been an entirely happy one since I killed that man,' he once
said. 'I often see poor Camelford standing up before me.' Others
were even more distressed. The inveterate American duellist,
Alexander McClung, was said to be so haunted by his many
victims that he eventually shot himself in the head. A French
diplomat known only as Monsieur S once shot dead a fellow
consul in Valparaiso on the Chilean coast. 'He ran off like a
madman, with haggard eye, and tearing his hair,' Andrew
Steinmetz recalled. 'The man who had hankered after revenge

for a twelvemonth, now that he had got it to his heart's content, cursed the skill which had served him so well. He died of remorse a few years after. Before breathing his last, he called his son to his bedside, and pointing to the fatal pistol, hanging on the wall and covered with crepe, he said: "Keep that weapon as the best part of your inheritance. The remembrance which it will ever call to your mind will, perhaps, render you less a slave than I have myself been to the cruel laws of the point of honour. At any rate, it will teach you what it costs to kill a man."' Around 1850, a Kansas politician called Franklin Elliott was so upset by his role in a duel that he lived as a hermit for the rest of his life. His girlfriend, Olive, had fallen in love with another man, whom he had felt obliged to challenge. At twenty paces, Elliott had shot his opponent dead but was so distraught that he withdrew from public life. He lived in a small and isolated cave up in the hills miles from town which he visited once a year for powder, shot and salt. More than twenty years later, in November 1871, hunters seeking shelter from a storm entered the hermit's cave and found him dead, wrapped up in an animal pelt, with a copy of Shakespeare and a likeness of his love by his side.

One Kirkcaldy writer believed that David Landale felt similar pangs of remorse. Jessie Patrick Findlay claimed: 'To his dying day . . . he was subject to attacks of profound melancholy, to fits of morose silence, haunted with visions of the tragic field of Cardenbarns.' And yet there is no evidence for this melodrama. All the accounts instead suggest that while David was undoubtedly upset by the duel and would have preferred not to have killed Morgan, his conscience, at its core, was untroubled by the banker's death. He told John Anderson he had thrown the event 'out of his mind'. And while he fled from justice in the Lake District, he was calm and self-possessed, and not without cause. For he was busy doing everything he could to prepare for the coming trial, communicating, albeit indirectly, with the authorities in Edinburgh. There was a plan and after David had been on the run for a week and a half, on Saturday September 2, events began to move fast. That afternoon William Millie and Lieutenant William Milne handed themselves in to the constables in Fife. Both, like David Landale, had written to the authorities to say they would surrender at the appropriate time. Once it had been agreed that the seconds would not be indicted, there was no need for them to remain in hiding so, according to the local justice of the peace at Cupar, they came that day 'from different places at a very considerable distance – one hundred miles upwards – to surrender themselves'. The acting sheriff depute, Andrew Jameson, granted warrants for both men to be imprisoned within the Tolbooth at Cupar, a town north of Kirkcaldy, for the crimes charged against them, 'therein to be detained until liberated in due course of law'. The due course of law ran quickly and both men were freed on bail, for Millie at a cost of £100, for Milne just £60.

On the same day, the state, in the form of George IV and his representatives, formally charged David Landale – in his absence – for the murder of George Morgan. The charge stated that 'murder is a crime of an heinous nature and severely punishable'. It claimed that David Landale, 'having conceived malice and ill will against the late George Morgan', did 'wickedly and maliciously challenge the said George Morgan to fight a duel' during which he 'wickedly and maliciously discharged at the said George Morgan' who died 'almost instantly and was thus murdered by the said David Landale'. It added that 'the said David Landale, being conscious of his guilt . . . did abscond and flee from justice'. David was ordered to turn up at the 'Criminal Court House' in Perth on September 21 at 10 o'clock in the morning. If he failed to do so, and did not hand himself in within fifteen days, the consequences were grave: 'If he fail, the said fifteen days being bygone . . . thereafter ye denounce him our rebel, put him to our horn and escheat and inbring all his moveable goods and gear to our use for his contempt and disobedience.' In other words, his entire property would become forfeit to the state.

David, meanwhile, left Cumbria and headed secretly back to Edinburgh. On Tuesday September 5, he wrote again to John Anderson, expressing his confidence about the trial. 'I have no fear,' he wrote, 'as I am convinced the Crown lawyers will submit such a respectable jury as will at once clear me of all crime.' And, enigmatically, he added: 'But I approve highly of the active measures of my truly active friends, as it is our duty to be guided in such matters by the advice of counsel.' It is not clear what he meant by this, what these 'active measures' were. But while it might be going too far to suggest that David was trying to rig the jury or fix the court, one can suppose that he was doing everything he possibly could to swing the balance in his favour. Such was his attention to detail that he even chased up various witnesses to ensure they had recalled events as he had. In a letter to Anderson the following week, on Monday September 11, he said he wanted to discuss with Mr Cumming, the bookseller, 'the threat which G Morgan gave me one day in passing him on the street the week before I received the first letter from him. As it took place a few yards to the eastwards of Mr Cumming's door, I mentioned the circumstances to him, which he must recollect perfectly. I think the expression [Morgan] made when passing him was: "I'll be damned if I don't make you pay for what you have done" at the same time as clenching and shaking his cane as if in the attitude of striking me. All this I told Mr C, the moment it occurred.'

For this last week or so before the trial, which had been postponed by a day to September 22, David was hiding out in Edinburgh in what the newspapers would call an undisclosed location. His friends knew where he was because he was in contact with them by letter. But David was obviously unable to go out, just in case he was spotted and recognised in the street. He was trapped indoors and it was clearly unsettling for him. Two days before the trial in Perth, he wrote to John Anderson from his Edinburgh safe house. He thanked his yarn agent for getting more money: 'I won't require so much but there is no saying what will be required at Perth and it is proper to be prepared.' And, collected as ever, he even sorted out a little business: 'The yarn purchases had better stand over till my return. We had better purchase from Craig at two shillings, two and a half pence and two shillings three pence than at Dundee just now.'

David urged Anderson to talk his way into court so he could give his friend moral support at his side: 'I shall wish to have you beside me on Thursday evening or Friday morning before I go to court. By acting as a clerk and carrying a few papers for Mr [George] Dalziel [one of David's lawyers] will get you admitted.'

David insisted he was not nervous. He wrote: 'My mind maintains its usual calmness. I only feel a little enervated by keeping within doors so much.' But some nerves were beginning to show: 'If Dr Smith has not for certain sent me the stomach powders by this day's coach at eleven o'clock, be there to bring one or two with you, or by himself, as the confinement here has put me out of sorts, and as I am afraid of cold feet in court, which would unhinge me completely, I beg you will send in Dr Smith's carriage the large pair of shoes in my bedroom.' Thus, despite all his preparations, the accused man was anxious. And he was right to be. For in the eyes of the law, the killing of a man in a duel was no different from wilful murder, and of this David Landale was undoubtedly guilty.

7

The trial

Express malice . . . takes in the case of deliberate duelling, where both parties meet avowedly with an intent to murder: thinking it their duty as gentlemen, and claiming it as their right . . . and therefore the law has justly fixed the crime and punishment of murder on them and their seconds also.

William Blackstone, *Commentaries on the Laws of England*, 1765–9

Everyone of them makes himself judge in his own cause, condemns the offender without a jury, and undertakes himself to be the executioner.

Benjamin Franklin, cited in *The Art of Duelling*, 1836

Deep within the vaults of the National Library of Scotland in Edinburgh lies a manuscript, a bound volume containing thousands of words of closely written copperplate. It is entitled simply, '*The Case of David Landale*'. It comprises a collection of witness statements, court records and personal recollections that were laboriously copied out by the clerk of a celebrated nineteenth-century Scots lawyer called Henry Cockburn, who wished to keep a record of the trial for his files. When he died, his trustees handed the manuscript and many other papers to the library for safekeeping and there it has lain, unnoticed and unread. Yet, dusted off and painstakingly transcribed, these papers make it possible to re-create in vibrant detail the events in a Scottish courtroom on a warm day in September almost 180 years ago.

In the 1820s, justice in Perth was dispensed from the county courthouse, a large, two-storey structure on the banks of the River Tay. The building dominated the eastern skyline, telling the world that while the river protected the town, it would defend the law. This was a modern seat of justice: brash, new, built in the flamboyant neo-classical fashion of the era. The Greek revival was in full, nostalgic swing: a colonnade of twelve Doric pillars held up a solid, sandstone pediment, presenting a façade described as 'one of the handsomest fronts in Scotland'. So handsome, in fact, that it was for a time a tourist attraction, a site marred only by complaints from visitors who said the river was so wide that it stopped them getting a good view. They were told to wait for low tide 'when the quay in front partly supplies a pediment that [it] can be seen to advantage'. As with any new building, not everyone was happy. A contemporary guidebook complained that the portico was 'much hurt by the introduction of iron railings between the columns. It is expected that the good taste of the County Gentlemen will order their removal.' But most Perth citizens considered their new court house 'a model of good taste – correct, simple and dignified, yet not deficient in ornament'. The aesthetics, however, could not disguise the underlying purpose: felons arriving here in 1826 were supposed to look up at the imposing frontispiece and feel the full weight of the law upon them before they even stepped foot in court.

On the morning of Friday September 22 1826, the court

was packed, filled with people eager to witness a celebrated trial. 'The court . . . was crowded in every part, soon after the doors were open, it being known that the case of Mr David Landale was to come on early in the day,' the *Perthshire Courier* reported. Such was the press of people that 'they considered themselves fortunate who could gain an admission upon any terms'. And it was not just ordinary folk who queued patiently outside; the local aristocracy was also in attendance. 'Many of the neighbouring nobility and ladies of distinction were present', including Lady Gray, the three Ladies Murray, the Earl of Mansfield and General Stewart of Garth. They too had to queue but, once inside, avoided the indignity of the public galleries by finding seats in the relative calm of the magistrates' bench to the judge's left. To the judge's right, supporting him on the bench, sat Lord Ruthven and Viscount Stormont.

The court was noisy, boisterous and silenced only when the judge in question, the Honourable Lord Gillies, swept in and began dispensing justice. Lord Gillies knew the Landale trial would take most of the day, so he dispatched his first cases with all due haste. George Nicol confessed to housebreaking, Andrew Hind admitted theft; both were sentenced to transportation for fourteen years. A weeping, well-dressed twelve-year-old called Elizabeth Miller was charged with stealing eight shillings of silver at Dundee vegetable market. After a diatribe against 'youthful depravity', Lord Gillies sentenced the girl to seven years' transportation. William Davidson, who robbed a man of some bread, books, and a towel, was transported for life. Robert Leckey, who pleaded guilty to stealing a watch, a pair of stockings, a vest and some silver spoons from two houses in Fife, was sentenced to death. Another man, after being sentenced to fourteen years' transportation for stealing, was heard muttering as he left the dock that at this court 'there was plenty of law but damned little justice'. A sense of foreboding swept through the public galleries; it was clear to every onlooker that Lord Gillies was not slow to pass sentence in the harshest of terms.

Being a modern building, Perth courthouse had all the latest refinements of Georgian law enforcement, and, in the 1820s, this meant a secret tunnel. On the other side of the road from the courthouse were two new prisons, one for felons, the other for debtors, and 'from the Jailor's House, which fronts the gate, there is a private passage under-ground leading to the Prisoners' Box in the Justiciary Hall.' No longer were prisoners frogmarched into court through the public halls. Now they emerged without fanfare from a hole in the ground straight into the prisoner's box, a journey that modern defendants still take today. David Landale, however, having not actually surrendered to the authorities, was spared this indignity. Instead, at 11 a.m. sharp, he was allowed to walk into the court with honour, escorted not by jailors but by friends and relatives. John Anderson, his agent, was there, holding legal papers so he could sit at the counsels' bench; Provost Gavin Haddon had come all the way from Aberdeen; William Moneypenny, the customs collector, and James Peters, had come from Kirkcaldy, as had the brother of David's late wife, Thomas Spears, and his son, Thomas Jnr.

The court fell silent as David took in the view from the bar. To his right sat the lawyers, to his left the jury. Over his right shoulder were the public galleries, each man and woman following his every glance, desperate to know his mood. And before him, above him, sat Lord Gillies, the man who would determine his fate. The clerk rose and read out the charge, rolling the lurid details around his tongue.

'Murder,' he said, 'is a crime of an heinous nature and severely punishable. Yet true it is and of verity that the said David Landale is guilty of the said crime.' For David Landale, 'having conceived malice and ill-will against the late George Morgan . . . did, upon the 22nd day of August 1826, wickedly and maliciously challenge the said George Morgan to fight a duel with him'. The following day, at Cardenbarns Farm, Mr Landale did 'wickedly and maliciously discharge at the said George Morgan a pistol loaded with ball, whereby the said George Morgan was mortally wounded, the ball having entered on the right side, penetrated through the chest, and escaped at the left arm-pit, of which mortal wound the said George Morgan died almost instantly, and was thus murdered by the said David Landale.' He added: 'The said David Landale, being conscious of his guilt in the premises, did abscond and flee from justice.' The clerk laid down the charge sheet, and the court held its breath. Lord Gillies looked up at David and asked if he was guilty of these charges. In what was described as 'a firm tone', David answered: 'Not guilty, my Lord.'

On June 23 1808, on a parade ground in Armagh in northern Ireland, Major Alexander Campbell and Captain Alexander Boyd had a quarrel over the correct way of giving a command. They subsequently fought a duel against many of the rules of honour – at night, in a room, at less than seven paces, without seconds, only twenty minutes after their quarrel – and Boyd was shot and mortally wounded. As Boyd lay dying, Campbell urged him several times to assure the fellow officers who had entered the room that everything had been fair. But Boyd refused and accused Campbell of being a 'bad man' who had rushed him into the duel without seconds. 'You know I wanted you to wait and have friends,' he said. Nevertheless, as he died, Boyd did forgive his adversary. Campbell fled to England and lived in London under a fictitious name for many months before handing himself in. The following year he was tried. Despite many officers testifying as to his good character, Campbell did himself no favours by publicly predicting that he would be acquitted. The jury, not wishing to be taken for granted and concluding there had been breaches of the *code duello*, found him guilty of murder and he was sentenced to be hanged. Then began a desperate campaign by his wife for clemency. She decided to appeal directly to the king for a royal pardon. But such was the weather that she had trouble crossing the Irish Sea. 'It blew a perfect hurricane and no reward could tempt the captain of any vessel to venture to sea,' wrote Andrew Steinmetz. 'While she was running up and down the shore in a distracted state, she met a few humble fishermen, and these poor fellows no sooner heard the cause of her agony than they offered her their services and their boat, in which she actually crossed the channel.' She arrived at Windsor late, after George III had retired for the evening, but the queen took pity on Mrs Campbell and presented her written plea to the king that night. He and his council, however, decided the law should take its course.

Although Campbell had a temper that had on this occasion got the better of him, he was much liked and his conviction was hugely unpopular. The night before his execution, he acknowledged the errors of his ways: 'I suffer a violent and ignominious death for the benefit of my countrymen, who, by my unhappy exit, shall learn to abhor the too prevalent and too fashionable crime of duelling.' He also turned down the chance of escape. 'The night before the execution, Mrs Campbell had managed to perfect methods of escape, as it was pretty generally understood that, although no royal mercy could be extended, no particular means of vigilance had been adopted,' wrote Ben Truman. But Campbell told his wife: 'The greatest struggle of all is to leave you, my darling, but I am still a soldier and shall meet my fate like a man.' And so he refused to dishonour himself further, although the guard was asleep, the doors of the jail unlocked, and horses and confederates were close at hand.'

Campbell had begged to be shot but this request was refused, so the following morning, October 2, after several hours of prayer, he climbed up a scaffold in the centre of Newry. The place was packed with soldiery and public alike, as Ben Truman described with all due drama: 'There stood before him nineteen thousand sympathizing men with heads uncovered; and among them Fusiliers, with whom he had intrepidly charged the enemy upon the burning sands of Egypt. The hum of a single bee might have been heard in that respectful crowd, as Campbell addressed it. "Pray for me" was all the poor soldier said, and while the diapason of an impressive "Amen" went up unbroken by a single other utterance, or even whisper, the unfortunate man let fall his own cambric handkerchief as a signal that he was ready, and simultaneously he dropped through the dreadful trap and went off on that uncertain pilgrimage to the unknown beyond.' The melodrama of the historian, the sympathy of the fishermen, the blind eye of the jailors, and, above all, the unprecedented turnout at the execution, all pointed to one thing. The law might disapprove of duelling, but the public disapproved of the law.

Henry Cockburn rose to his feet and surveyed the court. He loved a full house and he loved a challenge and with this case, he had both. At the age of forty-six, he was one of the finest lawyers of his generation; David Landale had not skimped in his choice of brief. Alongside Cockburn sat his close friend and fellow counsel, Francis Jeffrey. In future years, they would both become peers and be appointed respectively Scotland's solicitor-general and lord advocate. Cockburn did not concentrate on the questioning of witnesses; his speciality, rather, was making opening and closing speeches. 'He was thought to be a great pleader,' wrote his biographer, Karl Miller. 'He and Jeffrey excelled with juries, and he many a time melted the heart of Midlothian.' To the people of Perthshire and Fife, he and Jeffrey were well known, not least for their celebrated performances during the trial of James Stuart of Duncarn for the killing of Sir Alexander Boswell in the duel outside Kirkcaldy in 1822. Cockburn was a Whig; in other words, a social reformer who had swapped his Tory past for a radical present in an Edinburgh that was enjoying the fruits of the Enlightenment. He was, according to Miller, 'a small, wiry man, a talker, walker, swimmer, skater, bowls-player, and devotee of the open air . . . a great light in Edinburgh, very popular, an esteemed eccentric and sage'. He was 'no dandy': his hat was 'the worst in Edinburgh' and 'he designed his own very clumsy shoes.' Nonetheless, he was exactly the man to choose to defend life and limb in a court of law.

The jury before Cockburn was one that would have been familiar to him: fifteen local men picked from the heart of Scotland's mercantile and agricultural classes. There was a corn merchant, a wood merchant, a forester, a founder, a weaver, an inn keeper, a handful of farmers and just four gentlemen who bore the title esquire after their names. Cockburn knew very clearly what he wanted to do, how he would appeal to this jury, how he would play the trial. Yet he was not short of advice. For David Landale was a particularly diligent client. Hidden within the surviving court papers lies a detailed memorandum that David wrote for Cockburn, setting out precisely how he wanted his case put.

What is clear is that David was concerned that his business might be hurt by revelations about his working practices that would come out in the trial. Referring to himself typically in the third person, he wrote: 'As the credit or stability of a commercial man is of the greatest consequence to him, and as any case like the present when money transactions are brought to public view, must tend to affect the stability of the parties, Mr Landale is particularly desirous that his counsel should take every fair opportunity to give a favourable tone to those transactions, which, if unexplained, might lead to very hurtful impressions going abroad respecting him, particularly when connected with a dispute with his Banker.' His concerns might indeed have been justified. But it is hugely significant that David expressed them. For he was acknowledging that victory in a duel was no longer enough to restore reputation. His personal honour might be satisfied but he still felt the need to ensure that his reputation as a businessman was protected. Twenty years earlier, the duel would have been enough. Not any more.

To that end, David Landale wanted David Morgan hauled into the witness box and cross-examined under oath. The banker could be asked about his letter praising Landale's surety, his decision to invite the merchant to dinner with Mr Campbell, why none of his customers had become insolvent. This, David suggested, would do much to prove his respectability and 'would shew that [the Morgans] had no foundation for their conduct by an unaccountable alarm, and in so far calm the minds of the public in my favour'. David also wanted Cockburn to emphasise that the £5,000 cash credit or overdraft that he got from the bank was to 'enable me to meet any disasters rather than any own wants'. The proof, he said, was that the money was used to help some of his customers who had run into difficulties. 'Not one of the manufacturers in our own District has become insolvent, while in other districts where the linen manufacture is carried on, whole towns have become bank-rupt, such was the unprecedented convulsion that then existed in the commerical world.' David also wanted it pointed out that it was more honest for him to have gone directly to his bankers rather than privately mortgaging his whole property.

He took Cockburn through the allegations he made in his letter of complaint to the Bank of Scotland head office, specif-ically providing evidence of the Morgans' 'silly ignorance' and 'base and ungenerous spirit'. David wrote that he 'particularly requests his counsel to impress upon the jury that that letter was not so much a letter of complaint as one of vindication for his removing his business from the Bank of Scotland'. David was still upset at the Morgans' refusal to pay his bill for £1,000 at Coutts Bank in London 'thereby putting to hazard my credit'. David said he 'should like much that my counsel question Mr David Morgan, as by his letters to the Bank on that subject, he appears to have written evasively and the refusal to fulfil that promise was the ultimate cause of the separation'.

But above all, by reading these papers, it becomes clear that David Landale wanted Cockburn to go for George Morgan's jugular. He said his lawyers should emphasise that 'the confi-dence of the public [was] completely shaken in them, by the numerous quarrels of one of the Agents with his townsmen at large, and the notoriety of his imprudent remarks respecting the Banking transactions at their office'. He said he wanted the court to know that the Morgans' 'refusal to do any banking business was to say the least of it ill-judged and imprudent, but that the conduct of the deceased was base and malicious, and not proceeding from any discernment or caution which ought to regulate the conduct of a banker.' David now was in full, self-righteous flow:

That the consequences of a very humble member of society declaring doubts, hazarding surmises and quoting the private transactions of some of his more respectable neighbours is sufficient at any time to do injury to his credit and respectability in society, which it is at all times difficult to restore. But what calculation can be made of the injury that might be done to such a person as Mr Landale, who besides his general business as a merchant and manufacturer, has, as a Commission Merchant, been entrusted for nearly 20 years by some of the first Mercantile Houses in Britain with their property to a very large extent. The period at which the slanders of the deceased were propagated and confidential transactions divulged, was an era in the commercial world that few of us will ever forget; and in place of Morgan supporting the credit of Mr Landale as he ought to have done, the whole of whose banking transactions had passed under his eye for almost 10 years, it is evident that he conceived the malicious design to ruin him as a commercial man, for what reason, God only knows. For Mr Landale is not conscious of ever having given him any offence up to the commencement of the transactions alluded to, and had not Mr Landale been a person possessed of considerable property, there is no doubt he must have sunk under such reports propagated from such a quarter.

Under these circumstances, no language was too strong for Mr Landale to make use of in his letter to the Directors. It is only astonishing that so respectable a Bank should have retained such an Agent a single day after such a representation was made from so respectable a quarter. The exculpatory evidence is so complete, both as respects the character of Mr Morgan and Mr Landale; the assault made, the previous notoriety of Morgan's character, that it would have been impossible for Mr Landale to have existed one day comfortably if within his reach, if he had not challenged him, and the fairness with which everything was gone about on the field, must with the powerful eloquence of his counsel induce the jury to pronounce a unanimous acquittal.

Henry Cockburn needed no further encouragement. He stood up and read out the formal argument of the defence. David Landale, he said, admitted that he had a quarrel with George Morgan 'the result of which he sincerely laments'. But it was Morgan who 'brought that quarrel and all its consequences upon himself'. The banker, Cockburn said, 'being of rash and quarrelsome habit . . . not only spoke of the Defender's affairs to strangers, but attempted to ruin his credit'. David's letter of complaint to the Bank of Scotland was 'fully warranted by the facts'. Morgan's assault 'left the Defender no course but one to follow; but to the very last, he was always willing to accept of an apology – which was going farther towards a reconciliation than most men in the Defender's situation would have thought proper or safe'. The banker refused to apologise so 'if Mr Morgan fell by the hands of the Defender, this was a catastrophe for which he had himself alone to blame'.

Cockburn laid down the piece of paper, gathered his thoughts and looked up at the jury. His strategy was clear. He would admit that David had broken the law, he would blame Morgan for having given him no choice but to do so, and he would emphasise David's willingness to accept an apology. But first, he told the jury, they should know something of David Landale's character. 'His reputation, as well as that of his father to whom he succeeded, stood as high as that of any mercantile gentleman in this country.' If proof were needed, then it could come from no less a man than George Morgan himself. Cockburn pulled out of his file the letter that George and his brother had written about David Landale's creditworthiness in January of that year and read it out in full. His security was 'quite good', he gave 'active and great circulation' to the bank's notes, his business was all 'fair value accommodation' and he kept 'steadily by the bank'. But what then of George Morgan's character? Cockburn declared: 'It is my wish, Gentlemen, to tread as lightly on the ashes of the deceased as his best friend could wish and is consistent with the justice due to the living.' Such was Cockburn's wish, but accounts of the trial show that he proceeded to stamp over Morgan's reputation without restraint. A banker, he said, as a 'depositary of many important transactions', should run an office which 'demands the strictest secrecy'. Everyday gossip did not matter. But none could come from the bank. 'Now, mark the conduct of the deceased. During a time of great commercial distress – a distress considerably augmented by panic – when a word, a whisper, were able to overturn the highest characters and the firmest credits – the deceased not only made the most highly improper disclosures in matters connected with Mr Landale's business, but had indulged in insinuations deeply injurious to his credit.' Such behaviour left David no choice but to leave the bank. His letter of explanation to head office, 'although no doubt calculated to irritate Mr Morgan, was yet justified by the facts'. But when Edinburgh 'rashly and inconsiderately' sent a copy of David's letter to the Morgans, George's response was extraordinary. He sent a letter 'containing no expressions of regret for what he had done, no apology for his false insinuations, no explanation for his unaccountable conduct' and subscribed himself as 'George Morgan, Lieutenant, Half-pay 77th Regt of Foot!' Cockburn was incredulous: 'Here, a man known only as the Agent of a Bank, and charged with having betrayed the trust committed to him as such – throwing off the only character in which he was recognised, and adopting one which he had laid aside for years – defends his injurious insinuations, refuses all explanations and declines all apology.' What kind of reply, Cockburn asked the court, was this? It was nothing less than an attempt by Morgan to persuade David Landale to challenge him to a duel. His use of his military rank made it 'plain that the deceased intended to provoke the gentleman to whom he wrote to challenge him'. Cockburn told the jury how Morgan had incorrectly believed that only the challenger was liable to transportation, how he had told people he would horsewhip David, how he had ordered dozens of bullets to be prepared for his pistols.

Having trodden on Morgan's reputation with clod-hopping abandon, Cockburn now showed the court he could tiptoe as well. David Landale's response to all this, he declared, was blameless. 'My client, Mr Landale, although warned of Mr Morgan's proceedings, would not give credit to them, nor would he go armed, although advised by his friends to do so. The gentleman at the bar never courted any reencounter [*sic*], he never meditated malice, nor thought of personal conflict, unless absolutely forced upon him. And even after being grievously injured, he was still disposed to accept of apology.' Few men, Cockburn said, would have had the courage to accept an apology after such an assault. But Morgan refused all apology so David had no alternative. 'Shut out from society, marked and dishonoured – how few are there who have the courage to think that their disgrace can be expiated but by arms? The challenge was thus forced upon him. But even at the last stage of the proceedings, when on the ground, and an opening being made by their mutual friends for an understanding and reconciliation, the gentleman at the bar expressed his willingness to accept of apology. Again this was peremptorily refused; and I now ask if any one can conclude in the terms of the indictment that my client was actuated by preconceived malice? Or whether it did not lie on the other side?' Cockburn wound up his peroration: 'Well, the melancholy catastrophe took place, and the unfortunate survivor is here this day to abide its consequences. I call him unfortunate, for however strong the provocation, however imperious the necessity, and irreproachable his conduct, from first to last, in this affair, still, as often as that day recurs, on which a fellow-creature was by his hand deprived of life, it must, to the latest year of his existence, be accompanied with feelings of humiliation and pain. The consciousness of having been left no alternative – of having been compelled to the course that he had followed – dictated the line of conduct he had pursued since that lamented event. He did not abscond from justice, he merely wished to avoid unnecessarily the disgrace of confinement, and at once intimated his readiness to attend at that tribunal. I again put it to the Jury whether Mr Landale had any alternative. Excepting females, children, judges and clergymen – and those whose situation or feebleness prevented and excused it – no honourable mind could follow any other course than that my client has done.' With that, Cockburn sat down, his work done. Lord Gillies told Cockburn that 'the Court and the Jury were under an obligation to the learned counsel for the eloquent and perspicacious statement that he had given'.

One of duelling's many roots was, of course, the law itself. The judicial duel sanctioned combat as a way of resolving a dispute between two men. But by the sixteenth century, judicial duels were extremely rare 'and men were turning away . . . from public vindication to the private satisfaction of the duel'. And that private satisfaction was obtained entirely outside the law. James VI of Scotland – before he headed south and became James I of England – had in 1600 made duelling without royal sanction a capital crime. Almost 100 years later, the law was tightened further, making the giving or accepting of a challenge punishable with banishment and the confiscation of property – regardless of whether or not the duel took place. In practice, both laws were rarely enforced and subsequently repealed. But in their place came new laws which were unequivocal. For most of the eighteenth century, the sending of a challenge or any other incitement to duel was a summary offence in common law. From 1803, after the passage of what became known as Lord Ellenborough's Act, the fighting of a duel was, regardless of outcome, a statutory,

capital offence. If the outcome was the death of one participant, the survivor and the seconds were guilty of murder.

The law was so unambiguous on this because duelling, by
definition, could not be manslaughter, or in Scotland, culpable
homicide. While manslaughter is an act of the moment, murder
is a deliberate, premeditated act, carried out with malice afore-
thought. 'Because of this, no duelling death could logically be
interpreted as manslaughter,' wrote the historian Anthony
Simpson. 'Duellists could never attempt to plead passion in an
effort to mitigate their crime, as this would have laid them
open to public accusations of inappropriate behaviour in the
field.' Thus David Landale could never claim that he had killed
George Morgan in a fit of anger in the face of extreme provocation. The irony was that the more the duellist stuck to the
code of honour in ensuring there was a period of reflection,
normally overnight, between challenge and duel, the more he
was ensuring he would be charged with murder.

The distinction between duel-murder and manslaughter
might have been clear in British law but it was not so on the
continent. However illogically, the laws of France, Italy and
Austria continued to treat a duel killing as manslaughter. And
in Britain, many judges muddied the water. In an attempt to
prevent their fellow noblemen being convicted of murder, they
frequently allowed juries to convict duellists of manslaughter
which was subject to ridiculously light punishment. 'The
maximum punishment was a token fine, branding in the hand,
and one year's imprisonment,' wrote Antony Simpson. 'From
the late eighteenth century, duellists so convicted were rarely
imprisoned, and the corporal part of the punishment was miti-
gated to the literal slap on the wrist – mock branding with a
cold iron.' In 1712, Lieutenant-General Maccartney, second to

the Duke of Hamilton in his notorious and lethal duel with Lord Mohun, was 'tried for murder and acquitted and was discharged of the manslaughter by burning with a cold iron to prevent an appeal of murder'. But in 1822, four years before David Landale's duel, the laws were tightened up. Manslaughter became a more serious offence in law, the punishment for it increased to involve automatic imprisonment or transportation, and it became less easily applicable in duelling cases. 'The options of the jury were accordingly limited and a full acquittal became the only alternative to a capital conviction.' Thus one possible escape route for David Landale was closed off.

In practice, the law was rarely taken to its fullest conclusion. But on those few occasions when it was, the result was uncompromising. In 1786, an Irishman called George Reynolds advised his mother to sack her attorney, one Robert Keon. The lawyer was so furious that he horsewhipped Reynolds at the County Leitrim assizes. Reynolds, a reluctant duellist, knew he had no choice but to issue a challenge. On the morning of the duel, Reynolds arrived on the field, walked over to Keon and attempted to engage him in conversation. Yet before the seconds had even measured the ground or loaded the pistols, Keon exclaimed: 'Damn you, you scoundrel, why did you bring me here?' and shot Reynolds through the head. Such was the extreme breach of the laws of honour that Keon suffered the extreme penalty of the laws of the land. In early 1788 he was convicted of murder and sentenced to a traitor's death, namely to be hanged and then, while still alive, disembowelled, decapitated and quartered.

Outside the court the witnesses sat in silence waiting their turn. First to be summoned by the prosecution was William

Millie, David's second. He gave his account of the duel calmly and with detail, emphasising above all how both he and Lieutenant Milne, Morgan's second, had been 'anxious to bring about an amicable settlement but feared it was impossible'. He described how Morgan had cried out 'No apology' on the field, how he had raised his pistol too early, how he had died instantly. It is clear from the transcripts that David's lawyers clearly felt this was not quite enough so Francis Jeffrey rose to his feet to cross-examine. He teased out of Millie the fact that David Landale had 'expressed no intention to challenge' unless he was struck, and that David had been willing to accept in principle a written apology. Perhaps most importantly, he got Millie to tell the court how, in the carriage on the way to the duel, David had said again that he would accept an apology on the field, that he did not wish for Morgan's life, 'I merely wish reparation for the injuries done me.' Millie declared that he 'never heard Mr Landale at any time express anything, in the course of all their correspondence, inconsistent with this resolution to accept an apology'. Jeffrey was clearly happy with that and put no further questions.

William Milne was called. He was less comfortable. He was at pains to emphasise how he had agreed to be George Morgan's second before he knew the nature of the quarrel with David Landale, and how, when he found out in the carriage on the way to Kirkcaldy, he 'objected strongly to be his second for this as it was the last thing one gentleman should do to another, that of horsewhipping'. Milne said he only consented to be Morgan's second 'principally that he might effect an amicable arrangement'. He urged Morgan repeatedly to make an apology, but in vain. Like Millie, the naval lieutenant emphasised how he had tried to resolve the quarrel by getting both sides to meet halfway. Francis Jeffrey was quite happy with this – the second was defensive and making his own excuses rather than protecting his principal. But he still got Milne to tell the court how David Landale had taken 'no aim' and that 'everything was quite fair and honourable'.

Then came the doctors. Dr Johnston described how he had tried but failed to halt the duel, how he had heard one report, how he had been summoned, and how he had found George Morgan bleeding to death. Dr Smith confirmed the sequence of events. Francis Jeffrey again rose to his feet, just to re-emphasise the argument that ran throughout the defence of David Landale. Dr Smith, as someone who had accompanied Landale and Millie on the way to the duel, would be in a position to confirm David's willingness to accept an apology. Smith confirmed this was true: he heard Mr Landale say that 'if Mr Morgan would make an apology, he would accept of it on the ground before them . . . He had no object whatever but to repair the injury his character had sustained.'

The defence witnesses were then called. Intriguingly, David Morgan was never called to the stand. The prosecuting authorities certainly wanted him there, not least because they believed he had not done enough to prevent his brother's death. On August 26, just a few days after the duel, one of the Crown lawyers had written to a colleague: 'It appears to me that he is partly to blame and that he is truly chargeable with his brother's death. For he had an opportunity afforded him by Mr Cumming's information which he did not use to prevent mischief. He must be examined and must be made a witness . . . at the trial both to make apparent and comment on his conduct.' David Landale too was keen to get David Morgan in the stand, not least so he could testify as to his credit and financial responsibility. But such was the determination of Henry Cockburn and Francis Jeffrey to hammer home David's lack of malice, they took a firm decision – against their client's wishes – not to call David Morgan as a witness. They did not want to get into the murky complications of who said what to whom in the original quarrel over David's finances. Instead, they wanted the court to hear evidence about how David Landale was an honourable man and how he had repeatedly offered to accept an apology from George Morgan. The defence witnesses did not disappoint them.

The accountant James Fleming testified that his friend, George Morgan, had told him he wanted to 'put his cane across Mr Landale's shoulders first time they met'. He confirmed, too, Morgan's reluctance to call David out. '[He] was afraid to give the challenge as he understood that by law a challenger was liable to transportation – he would therefore take the other recourse, assaulting him.' Robert Stocks, the linen merchant to whom Morgan had first expressed doubts about David's creditworthiness, confirmed the banker's loose-tongued allegation. He praised David, a friend of more than twenty-five years, as 'one of the most orderly and correct gentlemen among his acquaintance, and never found him disposed to quarrel'. But he admitted rather shamefacedly that he had indeed asked David to pay back a £1,000 loan the moment Morgan raised doubts about his solvency. The bookseller, James Cumming, made the most of his time in the witness box, proudly taking the court through the events that had taken place in or outside his shop, culminating with Morgan's assault on David Landale. William Todd, the blacksmith, confirmed that Morgan had asked him to make thirty-three bullets for his pistols. Provost Haddon hailed David as 'a

man of the greatest probity and honour, of mild and gentle
manners, and most unlikely to provoke quarrels'. Walter Fergus,
former provost of Kirkcaldy and an old family friend, said he
had known David since he was a child and 'esteemed him as
a man of strict honour and every way a gentleman'. He had
'scarcely ever seen his temper ruffled'. The customs collector,
William Moneypenny, praised David as a man of 'much mild-
ness and honourable feeling'.

Yet murder was murder and such high praise from a few
friends was not, in the eyes of the law, enough to excuse a
duel to the death. Alexander Wood, the advocate depute, rose
to his feet and addressed the jury. He comes across clearly as
a man who was uncomfortable in his role. He agreed with all
the witnesses that the man standing before them now was
indeed 'of the highest character and respectability'. He accepted
that, whatever the verdict of the jury, 'the unfortunate
gentleman must ever bear the fatal day on which he deprived
Mr Morgan of life in painful remembrance'. But David Landale
'had the misfortune to deprive a fellow creature of life and
was consequently at their bar to answer a charge for the crime
of murder'. Wood admitted he had a 'difficult and unpleasant'
task in prosecuting David but he had no choice. He said he
'could not disguise from himself, nor from the Jury, that the
law of the land was at variance with the practice and feelings
of society on a subject of this nature. But it was incumbent on
him, at the same time, to say that the act of killing in a duel
constituted, in the eye of the law, the crime of murder.' There
was no need to go into the evidence, he said. 'It was clearly
demonstrated, and not attempted to be denied that Mr Morgan
had met his death at the hands of the unfortunate gentleman
at the bar.' But how should the jury respond? 'Whether they

might find such alleviating circumstances in the case as might dispose themselves to give a verdict which would avert the necessary consequences inferred by law, was for them to judge,' Wood said. 'But as the law stood, he was justified in craving a verdict of guilty.' He sat down to a silent court.

The truth is that the law against duelling was widely ignored, sidestepped, and deliberately misinterpreted. Few prosecutions took place. There was a wealth of legislation that could have been used against non-fatal duels. The candidly named Stabbing Act of 1604, the Coventry Act of 1682 and the Black Act of 1723 were all on the statute books and could have been deployed. But few of these acts ever seem to have been applied against duellists. There were common laws, too, that could be used against duelling, crimes of assault and affray that were punishable by fines and prison. When these laws were enforced, they were effective; the threat of a substantial but realistic fine was always much more of a deterrent than the prospect of a rarely enforced capital prosecution. But these laws were enforced all too rarely.

As for fatal duels, there were just as few prosecutions. Statistics about duelling are notoriously inaccurate; records about private events being, by definition, private. But it is possible to draw some conclusion from analysing records of those duels which reached the public eye. And though the precise figures may change, the broad thrust is identifiable. Andrew Steinmetz claimed that there were 172 duels during George III's sixty-year reign, of which 91 had fatal results. Of these only 18 came to trial, from which just 2 men were executed. Between 1803 and 1832, according to one nineteenth century historian, Humphrey Woolich, the Old Bailey convicted only 11 people under the anti-duelling laws, of whom just 6 were executed. None of them was considered a genuine duellist. Regardless of the inconsistencies, Victor Kiernan said the trend was clear: 'Duellists . . . could kill each other and go scot free, when a poor man could be hanged for stealing a few shillings.'

Duellists escaped punishment because the courts tolerated their behaviour. Most juries in those days were deeply middle-class: tradesmen, shopkeepers, farmers and the like. By and large, they refused to convict their aristocratic betters. 'Those few duellists who were tried went largely unpunished because men of lowly social position acquitted them, and in so doing demonstrated considerable tolerance for the duel as an institution,' wrote Antony Simpson. Juries reflected the popular view of the time that duelling was a consensual act between adults and thus no business of the state, as long as fair play had been ensured by the seconds. They also considered execution for duelling a draconian and disproportionate punishment for the crime. A law which failed to distinguish between wilful murder and ritualised single combat between two consenting adults was viewed as an ass. At the same time, juries often lacked enough evidence to convict because seconds, doctors and other witnesses were allowed to escape taking the stand. They could do this because they themselves faced possible charges as accessories and might reveal evidence which would harm their defence. Juries therefore tended to accept the old common law principle that a witness could not be forced to incriminate himself. As such, they frequently had insufficient evidence to convict – how could a man be guilty of duelling if no one would testify that he was even on the field at the time? One mid-nineteenth-century court in India found a way around this. Once the duellist had been cleared through lack of evidence, the two seconds were charged as accessories. The duellist was summoned back as a witness. There was now, however, no risk that *he* might incriminate himself because, under the law, he could not be charged with the same offence twice. Thus he was no longer able to keep his silence. He was forced to confess to the seconds' roles and both were convicted of manslaughter. Such neat legal footwork, however, was the exception rather than the rule.

If the juries were reluctant to convict, so were the judges. Many of them were of the same aristocratic background as the duellists. Some had themselves duelled in their long-lost youth. Few were enthusiastic to enforce a law their class considered illegitimate. So they bent the law. Many advised their juries of the correct legal position but did so in such a manner as to encourage them to reject it. Others were more open and simply acknowledged the truth, namely that the law on duelling was at odds with popular sentiment. One judge told his jury: 'Gentlemen, it is my business to lay down the law to you and I shall do so: where two persons go out to fight a duel, and one of them falls, the law says it is murder, and I tell you by law it is murder, but at the same time, a fairer duel I have never heard in the whole course of my life.' One Italian judge went further and simply ignored the law. Up before him was an actor called Signor Rossi who had duelled and injured a man who had rudely interrupted his performance of Hamlet. The next day Rossi was desperate to get to Milan for another performance but was forced to court. 'You deserve five years' imprisonment,' the judge began ominously. 'But now that the man of law has spoken, the playgoer must add the last word. I was at the theatre last night. You acted like a god and you did very well to chastise this good for nothing. I know that you are expected in Milan, and take this ring as a remembrance of how I look upon your conduct.' The bottom line, wrote Antony Simpson, was that 'the criminal justice system was completely ineffective in curbing the duel . . . This was not so much due to deficiencies in the law as to the unwillingness of all social classes to cooperate in its application.'

From time to time, the judges and juries would convict. Not on the basis of law however, but on the basis of the code of honour and the notorious *code duello*. 'The fairness of the bout became the concern of the court, and not the legal questions at issue,' wrote Simpson. This was undoubtedly the basis on which Major Campbell was judged, who, having broken the rules by rushing his opponent into a duel without seconds, was convicted and executed. Such a breach of the codes almost did for another soldier, albeit of rather more senior rank. In September 1840, in the dying, dogdays of the British duel, the 7th Earl of Cardigan became embroiled in a quarrel with a fellow army officer, a Captain Reynolds. The earl, an arrogant man who had spent many thousands of pounds buying his way up to his current rank of lieutenant-colonel in the 10th Dragoons, had insulted Reynolds who had responded with a challenge. Cardigan correctly refused the challenge because it was strictly against army regulations for officers of different rank to fight. So one of Reynold's friends, a Captain Harvey Tuckett, took up the case and wrote an insulting article about Cardigan in the *Morning Chronicle*. One of the many accusations was that Cardigan was obsessed with ensuring that wine was always served from decanters. The peer had apparently reprimanded Reynolds for allowing Moselle to be served in the officers' mess from the bottle. This time Cardigan ignored the rule book and sent Tuckett a challenge. They fought on Wimbledon Common and Tuckett was wounded. The local constabulary arrested them all and the magistrates dispatched Cardigan to be tried by his peers in the House of Lords. Few expected Cardigan to be convicted, but the peer did himself no favours, for it emerged during the trial that he had broken the *code duello*. 'The most serious piece of evidence against him turned out to be the fact that he had, against accepted practice of the day, used rifled pistols,' wrote Antony Simpson. Rifled pistols were more powerful and more accurate than the smooth-bored weapons required by the rules, and thus not considered an appropriate weapon for a gentleman. In the end, however, the trial was a farce. The attorney general, no less, Sir John Campbell, advised the witnesses to refuse to answer any questions for fear of incriminating themselves. Campbell also insisted that the peer had broken no rule by using rifled pistols because he had been apparently willing, in theory at least, to allow Tuckett the use of them. Cardigan was acquitted and fifteen years later led the ill-fated Charge of the Light Brigade at the Russian guns in the Crimea. He survived with only a small wound and retired to his home in Northamptonshire where many years later, at the age of seventy-one, he died after falling from his horse.

Francis Jeffrey rose to his feet. Henry Cockburn had begun the day with his opening statement, now he, Jeffrey, must finish the job with his closing. Jeffrey was in many ways the right man for the task. For not only did he bring his undoubted powers of advocacy to the court, he also brought his experience as a near duellist. Twenty years before, Jeffrey had been challenged to a duel by an angry poet called Thomas Moore, whose work the lawyer had mocked in the *Edinburgh Review*. As it was, the duel was interrupted by some constables and both men were bound over. There were, however, subsequent rumours that both men had realised the idiocy of duelling and had secretly tipped off the constables and loaded their pistols with paper pellets. Jeffrey's oratory that September afternoon was long, his phrases melodramatic, and his repetitions frequent. But from reading the transcripts, it is obvious that he had a clear, razor sharp strategy. He had to establish beyond doubt that David Landale had not acted out of malice, he had to emphasise that few duellists were ever convicted, and he had to flatter the jury without shame or restraint. Almost two centuries on, it is possible to say he achieved his aims without exception. He said David Landale was to be congratulated 'that the honour and purity of his motives had so soon been laid before the world'. He told the jury to consider 'the unsullied purity of [David Landale's] general character, the original and grievous wrongs he had sustained, the meek, temperate, and even business-like manner in which he at first and for some time endeavoured to obtain redress, the most intemperate and unreasonable manner in which it was withheld, the reluctance with which he adopted the last extremity and painful alternative, or the calm and generous manner in which he had consented to adopt even of a verbal apology on the fatal scene of the catastrophe: each and all gave him strong claims to their commiseration and acquittal.' Jeffrey may appear now to be laying it on thick but on that day it had the desired effect. 'Every part of [David's] conduct in the final affair itself was allowed on all hands to have been cool, fair and honourable, everything proved his motive to be only the redress of injured feelings, the restoration of that honour of which he had been unjustly deprived.'

Thus, Jeffrey came to his first point. 'No mode of killing could constitute murder, unless malice could be proved,' he said. 'That the bare fact of taking away life in a duel constituted murder he would deny. He denied that it could be law . . . On the contrary, [duelling] was a remedy for injuries for which law tribunals could afford no redress.' The argument was simple: David had not acted maliciously and therefore could not be guilty of murder. 'Unless the facts could convince the jury that the deed was maliciously committed, it was of no consequence what his learned friend opposite might denominate law,' Jeffrey said. 'It was evidence of malice only that could confirm the fact and render [the duel] criminal.'

It was this, Jeffrey argued, that had led to so few convictions for duelling in the past. He claimed that duelling had been 'frequent and common' during the fourteenth and fifteenth centuries because of the 'romantic spirit of chivalry which prevailed'. But now he pointed out that duels actually were remarkably rare. 'During the reign of his late Majesty [George III], not more than two hundred authenticated duels had taken place in England, Scotland and Ireland. For these, only from twenty to twenty-three trials had been instituted, and not one conviction ensued, except in a very few instances in which it evidently appeared that the practice was abused by making a challenge a pretext for accomplishing murderous purposes.' Jeffrey's figures differ slightly from Steinmetz's but they both make the same point, and, in the court on that day in September, it was a point well made. 'During the last 150 years, not one conviction has taken place in Scotland. Now our blood was not colder, nor our sense of honour more obtuse than that of our neighbours. But the reason was, that the investigations uniformly terminated in the development of circumstances rather honourable than otherwise to the survivors. They were therefore acquitted.'

So who had made these judgements? Jeffrey came to his third point. It was, he said, the juries who had shown such good sense. He told his own jurymen that when he had spoken of the paucity of convictions, 'he could assure them that it was not on account of the ignorance of the juries, or their disqualification to discriminate, that this had arisen.' Nothing could be further from the truth, he said. 'Juries, on cases of duelling in this country, had been composed of men rather of superior intellect. The practice of law therefore, notwith-standing the doctrines of judges or men of law, had been uniformly established by intelligent, discriminating and consci-entious men in opposition to the principle laid down that killing in a duel inferred murder, unless accompanied by circumstances proving deadly malice.'

Jeffrey summed up his argument. It was proper that David should answer for his actions. He maintained, however, 'that his client had not committed a crime but had rather sustained a grievous misfortune. He was unfortunate in having been injured, he was unfortunate in having been the instrument of depriving his neighbour of life.' But, he concluded, 'under the circumstances, there was no rule, no practice, no prin-ciple upon which they could find guilt in this case, when it was proved no malice had existed.' Jeffrey lingered, staring at the jury, daring them to disagree before resuming his seat.

If such grandiloquence had not swayed the jury, it certainly won over the judge. Lord Gillies began his summing up thus: 'Nothing I mean at present to address to you is intended to weaken the effect of what you have just heard from the Counsel for the panel.' The judge was right: he did nothing to dilute Jeffrey's oratory and instead merely continued in a similar vein, all but directing the jury to acquit. Yes, he admitted, 'the general rule of law is that killing in a duel is murder'. But that law accepted qualifications and 'I consider that the panel at the bar is within the qualified rule of law.' He said that in none of the cases 'which ever came under my observation could less blame be attached to the survivor in a duel'. The testimony to David Landale's character was 'as high as is possible for man to receive'. Throughout this affair, the Kirkcaldy merchant had lived up to that reputation: 'His whole demeanour has been manly, temperate and fair. Mr Landale did not challenge on receiving the first insulting letter, not thinking the laws of honour applicable in such a case, but his antagonist thought differently and evidently forced on the duel.' He continued: 'You have clear and undeniable evidence of the reluctance of the panel to fight, and that his great and sole object was the reparation of his honour and character. It has been said, indeed, that from the fact of killing, the law presumes malice. But this is a presumption which may be rebutted by evidence, and of the sufficiency of that evidence, in this case, you, Gentlemen, must be the judges. The great provocation endured was another alleviating point. The insult sustained led to the contempt and scorn of the world, the provocation was permanent and continuous, and the wound thereby caused, the lapse of time would only augment and render more intolerable. I will not trouble you farther than to say that in all the cases quoted, if the juries were just and reasonable in acquitting the prisoners, I do not see how the panel at this bar can justly and reasonably be condemned. Gentlemen, this is all I have to say. If you think this case falls under the general rule, you may convict. If you think it falls under the milder construction adopted by former juries, you will return a verdict of not guilty.'

The court fell silent as all eyes turned to the jury. The fifteen men consulted quietly among themselves. It was now four in the afternoon and the trial had lasted a full five hours. But the jury took just a couple of minutes to reach a decision. The foreman – or chancellor – George Campbell Esq. of Edenwood announced that they would not need to retire. The jury, he said, had found unanimously that David Landale was not guilty of the charge laid before them. Lord Gillies replied: 'Gentlemen, this is just such a verdict as I expected from you.' He turned and faced David: 'Mr Landale, you must be aware that the only duty I have now to perform is to dismiss you from this bar, with a character unsullied. I assure you I feel the greatest pleasure in performing this duty, and in congratulating you on the result of this day's proceedings. I am confident all who now hear me participate in these sentiments.'

The judge was not wrong. The crowd erupted and cheering broke out in the galleries. The court reporter noted dryly: 'The decision seemed to give high satisfaction to an extremely crowded court.' David's friends shook his hands as he stepped down from the box. At last, his ordeal was over.

8

Epilogue

*The duel is one of those provisional arrangements which, like canni-
balism, slavery, polygamy and many others, belong to certain stages of
society, and which drop off as decayed and dead matter when, no
longer necessary, they become injurious excrescences upon the body
social.*

Richard Burton, *The Sentiment of the Sword*, 1911

*Squeezed from below by the hostility of the middle classes, from above
by the mounting apathy of the aristocracy, and from without by the
opposition of law and religion, the practice of duelling attenuated and
withered until it was finally abandoned in the mid-nineteenth century.'*

James Kelly, *That Damn'd Thing Called Honour*, 1995

At dusk on May 20 1845, four men gathered on a scrap of
coastal wasteland six miles west of Portsmouth. A chill sea
breeze was blowing in off the Solent sending sprigs of furze
rolling across the isolated shingle dunes. Out in the Channel
stood several yachts at anchor riding the evening chop and
tide. Two of the group on the beach busied themselves loading
pistols. Their partners stood silently, fifteen paces apart, both
looking out to sea. One was Henry Hawkey, a young lieu-

tenant in the Royal Marines, the other James Seton, a former captain in the 11th Hussars. Once they had been friends, but that evening, there on that cold, lonely strand, they were enemies, divided by the love that Mr Seton felt for Lieutenant Hawkey's wife. Isabella Hawkey was twenty-four years old, 'eager, vivacious and gay . . . a good dancer, fond of boating and riding to hounds. It was only natural that she should attract the admiration of her husband's friends'. Yet James Seton's admiration had turned to love, and in time, to obsession. Despite being married himself, he had pursued Isabella through the salons and tea rooms of Southsea. She led him on but never quite succumbed to his wolfish charms. But at a party the night before they had gone too far. In the full gaze of the husband they were cuckolding, Seton had given Isabella flowers and she had danced with him all night. Hawkey, realising suddenly what most of Portsmouth already knew, quietly challenged his wife's suitor to a duel. Seton declined and defiantly shared the last dance with Isabella. For Hawkey, this was too much. As the final chords of the quadrille sounded, he walked over to Seton, kicked him in the shin, and declared loudly: 'You are a blackguard and a villain, Seton. You can either fight me or be horsewhipped down the Portsmouth High Street.' Seton was trapped. He could not escape such a public challenge and thus, twenty-four hours later, found himself standing on a breezy beach facing the consequences of his passion.

'Fire!' cried one of the seconds. A single report echoed across the flats as Seton discharged his weapon, the ball whizzing past his opponent's head. Hawkey's pistol, mistakenly kept half-cocked for safety, did not go off. The pistols were reloaded and correctly cocked. Again the seconds stepped back. This time, at the command, the duellists fired together and Seton slumped to the ground clutching his stomach. Hawkey moved as if to approach his wounded opponent but, thinking better of it, checked himself and fled, crying 'I'm off to France.' A local coastguard, alerted by the shots, helped Seton's second row the bleeding duellist to one of the yachts so they could get him to medical help in Portsmouth. Seton lingered for ten long and painful days until he died from his wounds and a botched operation. Thus, in the sordid, bloody sheets of a dingy Portsmouth hotel, ended the last recorded duel between two Englishmen on English soil.

The encounter was almost a cliché, an event that included everything that was hackneyed about the modern European duel: two military men crossed in love, a crude insult, a reluctant participant, a misfiring pistol, a wasted life. It was almost as if the duel as an institution was saying that this was as good as it got. But in 1845, the message from the British people was that this was no longer good enough. There were one or two other duels on British soil but they were paltry encounters between foreigners. British men did, of course, still duel overseas, in far-flung colonies where boredom, dipsomania and claustrophobia provoked lethal encounters between expatriate merchants, soldiers and administrators. But at home, the duel had had its day. Andrew Steinmetz, that great chronicler of duelling, concluded that the Seton-Hawkey encounter was 'the last duel of Englishmen in England; at any rate I have been unable to find the record of any other.'

This curious phenomenon that had laid a scar across Europe's nobility for several centuries had been ailing for some time but now, in Britain at least, it was no more. It did not disappear overnight but the seeds of its passing were sown over many years. Historians still argue over why duelling declined.

There are those, inevitably, who favour a Marxist analysis, believing that duelling was a bastion of feudal aristocracy that withered at the hands of a growing industrialised middle class that sought to impose its own social priorities and ideological concerns. There are others who argue instead that those middle classes actually embraced duelling in a fit of aspirational social climbing and thus the practice died out only when those middle classes found something else to do. There is some truth in both suggestions but neither tells the whole story. In fact, duelling declined because of a complex set of social and historical events and trends that robbed it of its cultural legitimacy. It simply became absurd to duel.

Like many minority activities, duelling suffered the moment it became popular. The last decades of the eighteenth century and the first of the nineteenth saw duelling flourish, particularly as a result of the Napoleonic wars. As Andrew Steinmetz wrote: 'The perpetual excitement of the long war had utterly unsettled the morals of the nation – warlike sentiments and martial aspirations imbibed with mother's milk . . . how could it be otherwise than that duelling should be popular, being only a war between individuals?' What was once a privilege for a narrow class of aristocrats and gentlemen became common practice among lower orders. The duel, wrote one historian, had become 'vulgarly popular'. The first blow was struck by technology. The newfangled pistol replaced the sword and instantly allowed anyone to be a duellist. In the past, a man would have required the years of training in swordplay. Now anyone, of any class, could stroll into a gun shop, buy a pair of percussion pistols, and shoot his opponent dead in the morning. Editors fought to defend their columns, doctors to defend their procedures, judges to defend their decisions. Another assault on duelling's elitism came from the youthful middle classes themselves. They loved to duel, not least because they thought it made them posh. Duelling was seen as a vehicle for social aspiration and its greatest drivers were snobbish soldiers. Thousands of middle-class officers, who had spent the years fighting Napoleon aping their aristocratic betters, returned after the peace in 1815 and duelled like men possessed. At the same time the professional middle classes – the lawyers, the vicars, the journalists, the civil servants – had a constant injection of new duelling blood from the second and third sons of aristocrats who were forced to earn a crust by the unrelenting laws of primogeniture. In 1817, Abraham Bosquett wrote that 'no country is at present more addicted to duelling.'

This apparent democratisation of duelling had the curious effect of preparing the way for its decline. The upper classes were horrified to see what had once been their privilege become common practice. As a result, one of the strongest codes of duelling, namely that a gentleman could not refuse a challenge without risk of ostracism, began to weaken. Men no longer considered themselves automatically obliged to accept a challenge if so many of their potential opponents were not of the same class. The duel was no longer in itself a definition of gentle rank and thus the upper classes duelled less.

The older, established members of the industrialised middle classes were as horrified as their aristocratic counterparts. They had been quite content for the landed classes to shoot each other occasionally. But the prospect of young middle-class men getting involved was much more serious. Duelling suddenly became a threat to everything their class represented. The middle classes saw duelling as a dangerous and destabilising antithesis of their bourgeois values of restraint, reliability, and rule of law. Duelling was a threat to profit, prosperity and the public peace. 'There was a world of difference between throwing away your life and saving for a rainy day,' wrote the historian Kevin McAleer. A dedicated capitalist could not afford to risk a duel every time he was involved in a business dispute. Such disorderly public behaviour was an anathema to him, a symbol of the excesses of the last century. More than that, a genuine bourgeois would naturally put his business and family before some spurious and anachronistic concept of personal honour. According to Antony Simpson, the middle classes believed that 'as duelling became more pervasive, it became less manageable and therefore more of a social threat'. As a consequence it was vital for the state to take responsibility for arbitrating between individuals in dispute.

The concern felt among the industrial middle classes spread. Where once the press had gloried in the notoriety and excitement of duelling, the public prints now began to mock. In the wake of the ridiculous duel in 1840 between the Earl of Cardigan and Captain Tuckett, *The Times* was unstinting in its condemnation: 'What the effect upon society in general must be of letting it be understood that there is a crime which must not, or cannot, be restrained or punished because peers and "gentlemen" think proper to commit it while the law declares it to be a felony, we leave those to judge who know the power of example and the aptness of the lower orders to learn evil from their betters. We are firmly convinced that no more pernicious or anarchical principle than that of the defenders of duelling was ever broached by Chartism or even Socialism itself.' Strong stuff and note the inverted commas. In the cheekier popular press, duelling was lampooned in cartoons, a once solemn act rendered ridiculous by scrutiny.

Fake duellists were exposed and mocked for fighting with pistols charged only with powder or bogus bullets made out of paper or mercury. Notorious duellists were ragged in the street. On the day Lord Cardigan was acquitted by the House of Lords, he attempted to attend a play in Drury Lane but a riot broke out: 'Yells, hisses, shrieks, groans made it impossible for the performance to begin; it being feared that the Earl would be attacked, he was taken out of the theatre by a side door.' Groups and societies were set up to oppose duelling. The most influential, the Anti-Duelling Association, was set up in 1843 'consisting of 326 members, so many of whom were of the two services, or noblemen, baronets and members of parliament'. They denounced duelling 'as contrary to the laws of God and man and eminently irrational as well as sinful'. One of the outspoken anti-duelling activists was an Irishman called Joseph Hamilton who called for stringent new laws. All seconds, he declared, should be fined £1,000 and forced to surrender half their property to the poor. And as for the duellists: 'Let the body of the deceased be soldered up in a leaden coffin to prevent an offensive smell; let it be drawn on every anniversary of the death for one hour upon a sledge through the most public parts of the town or city next to the scene of action, accompanied by the survivor.' Not surprisingly, Hamilton's ideas did not trouble the parliamentary draftsmen.

Some of these changing views began to filter further down the social chain and opposition grew among ordinary, labouring folk. Above all they resented what they saw as a privilege of aristocracy. Why, they asked, should a gentleman killer escape the law when a thieving peasant could be strung up at the gallows without a moment's thought? Why should there be one law for the rich and one for the poor? The 1820s and 1830s were already a time of huge social and industrial unrest in Britain and the agricultural and emerging working classes welcomed yet another reason to hate the toffs. The landed classes were not immune to this sentiment. They had not forgotten the fate meted out to their fellow gentry on the other side of the English Channel during the French Revolution of 1789. So, many aristocrats simply decided to give up duelling, considering the practice no longer a bastion in defence of their class but a potential weakness that should be removed. The nineteenth century has been seen by many historians as a progression of tactical concessions by the old power, the landed classes, to the new, the growing industrialised middle classes – Catholic emancipation, the abandonment of the Corn Laws, the enfranchising Reform Acts. Many gentlemen simply added duelling to this list of sacrifices that they believed were necessary to ensure the survival of their class.

This view was not shared across the water. Europe's nobilities were horrified at what their British cousins were doing. They held on ever more firmly to their right to shoot each other, seeing it as a badge of their class against the onslaught of the growing, wealthy middle classes. And they mocked the British nobility. 'The old sense of honour and prejudices of the [English] upper classes were scattering before the superior strength of money, whilst the German nobility remained poor but chivalrous,' wrote the German – and noble – historian Heinrich von Treitschke in the 1890s. 'The duel fell into disuse and disappeared completely; the riding whip ousted sword and pistol and this victory of brutality was celebrated as a triumph of the Enlightenment.' This desire to protect their class privilege and identity betrayed a greater nervousness and sense of vulnerability among continental nobilities than among their

British counterparts, who had a longer heritage and larger accumulation of aristocratic institutions and symbols. While the British nobility were strong enough to give up duelling, the European aristocracies felt less secure in their newer and less stable nation states and the popular uprisings which swept across Europe in 1848 appeared to prove them right.

If duelling suffered from its class origins, it also came under pressure from changing social and cultural attitudes. A duel was at its heart an act of extreme individualism. Both participants had to believe that their sense of personal honour, their reputation among their peers, were more important than anything else in their lives. Their families, friends, dependents, profession, they all came second to honour. Perhaps the duellist who most exemplified this was the British prime minister, William Pitt the Younger, who chose to put his honour before even his country. In 1798, in the dark, uncertain days during Europe's struggle against Napoleonic France, an Irish MP called George Tierney criticised Pitt's plans to beef up the navy to counter the threat of invasion. In his typically florid style, Pitt – now thirty-nine and not so young – questioned Tierney's motives on the floor of the House of Commons, refused to retract them and found himself challenged to a duel the next day. Amazingly, he accepted. So at 3 o'clock on Sunday May 27, Pitt found himself standing on Putney Heath in south-west London, facing an armed adversary twelve paces away. They exchanged two shots and thankfully missed both times. Thus a highly effective war leader, at a crucial stage in Britain's conflict with France when the threat of invasion and rebellion was real, chose to risk his life in a trivial dispute with an insignificant MP. Even at the time this was considered absurd, at least by some. George III was furious with his prime minister. 'I trust what has happened will never be repeated,' he wrote. 'Public characters have no right to weigh alone what they owe to themselves; they must consider also what is due to their country.'

So duelling was among the most selfish things a man could do, and over time, many came to realise this. And naturally it was the families that fought back first, for the prospects for a widow and children, shorn of their breadwinner, were not good. In Jane Austen's *Pride and Prejudice*, Mrs Bennet has a genuine fear that her husband will impoverish the whole family by dying in a duel while seeking their errant, eloping daughter, Lydia. Gradually families impressed upon their foolish menfolk that duelling was a risky business. John Wise, a US congressman, expressed this change in attitudes when in 1884 he turned down a challenge from a man called Page McCarty. 'With a sweet home, filled with merry children, with enough to live comfortably, with a paying profession, I am happy and want to live,' he wrote. 'In God's name, what would a man like Page McCarty put in stake against this when we stood at ten paces with pistols? His abuse of me has no more effect than a dog barking at the moon. His invitation comes too late. Time has been when I might have been fool enough to indulge in such folly, but with age, and a broader view of life and its responsibilities and duties, I have bidden farewell forever to the McCarty type of manhood.' The Irish writer, who hid behind the pseudonym of 'A Christian Patriot', described one man who deliberately invited his opponent to breakfast so he could avoid a duel: 'After breakfast, the challenger reminded his host of the engagement. [The host] replied: "That amiable woman, and the six little innocents who you saw at breakfast, depend upon my energies for their support, and until you can stake something of equal value, I think we shall be badly matched in mortal combat."' The challenger accepted the argument and both men shook hands as friends. Another family man, an unnamed bureaucrat from Rosenberg in West Prussia, avoided a duel by making a specific demand of his challenger. 'I have, as you well know, a wife and five children, for whom I am bound to care in the event of my death at your hands,' he wrote. 'My present yearly income is forty-five hundred marks. I require you to pay over to a bank a capital sum the interest of which will correspond to my present income, so that it may yield a livelihood to my widow and fatherless children.' Not surprisingly, the challenger declined. The official replied: 'In that case, I fear that our duel can never take place. A man who has nothing to lose except his own life will scarcely expect me to allow him to shoot me and to beggar my widow and children without any sort of equivalent.'

The duellist's individualism was challenged equally by new social trends that emphasised the group rather than the individual. On one level this saw a gentleman's sense of personal honour begin to be replaced by a sense of collective duty. A man had a duty not to himself, but to his family, his society, his nation, his monarch. This was the self-sacrificing duty that forged an empire, that encouraged young men to ride into the valley of death without reasoning why, that a century later would urge them to climb over the top of a muddy trench *pro patria mori*. In some countries, it would later lead to the extremes of nationalism and communism where the individual was subordinate to the state. On another more simplistic level, the same trends led to the growth of team games where the self had to be subsumed in pursuit of the common goal. '[Duelling] . . . lost cultural legitimacy,' wrote the historian, Richard Cohen. 'New pastimes had emerged: organised football, cycling, competitive yachting for the well-off, and the pleasurable risks of mountaineering, barely known in 1800, yet by 1900 it was one of the glamorous new outdoor activities. Increasingly popular team games such as cricket and football promoted the tendency to regard the individual as primarily part of a larger group, and individual interests and needs were subordinated to those of the collective.' The growing interest in sport saw duelling replaced in particular by boxing as an obsession of the upper classes. Some historians point as well to the changing attitudes towards alcohol. Hundreds of duels in the hard-drinking eighteenth century were provoked by bar-room quarrels at a time when inebriation was for many a permanent state. A century on the early Victorians disapproved of such intemperance and thus drank and argued less.

Intelligent people began to question the rationale of duelling. In the past, many had defended the practice as a civilising force for the nation. 'It is strange,' wrote the eighteenth-century pamphleteer, Bernard Mandeville, 'that a Nation should grudge to see half a dozen Men sacrific'd in a Twelvemonth to obtain so valuable a blessing as the Politeness of Manners, the Pleasures of Conversation and the happiness of Company in general.' Defenders of duelling believed it checked incivility by making men think twice before being rude; it held men accountable for their actions and their words; it prevented greater violence by providing a controlled outlet for conflict resolution; it provided an opportunity for a swift end to disputes rather than the lasting vengeance of the vendetta; it perpetuated a concept of manly honour that could be only of benefit to society; and it was a demonstration of individual freedom against the overpowering might of the state. 'The duel makes each of us a strong and independent power,' wrote the nineteenth-century French writer, Jules Janin. 'It takes up the cause of justice the moment the law abandons it; alone it punishes what the laws are unable to punish, scorn and insult . . . We are a civilised people today because we have conserved the duel.'

But now more questions began to be asked. Some men began to wonder if this thing called honour that all the duel-lists went on about should be based more on a love of glory than a fear of shame, as it had been in ancient Greece and Rome. Others wondered if honour was actually more akin to virtue, something that could be demonstrated by a pattern of behaviour rather than a single act of violence. Some men thought simply that the codes of honour and duelling, far from being civilising forces, were in fact 'mouldering remnants of bygone barbarism' that challenged the rule of law by promoting and not preventing violence. Some were just pragmatic. The moralist William Paley doubted duelling's efficacy as a means of justice: 'Duelling, as a punishment, is absurd, because it is an equal chance whether the punishment falls on the offender or the person offended.' One mathematics don at Cambridge prevented a duel between two pupils with a similar display of logic. 'What is all this about, why do you fight?' he asked one of the would-be duellists. 'Because he gave me the lie,' replied the student. The don thought a minute and then said: 'He said you lied, eh? Well, let him prove it. If he proves it, then you did lie, of course. But if he does not prove it, why, then it is he who has lied. Why should you shoot one another?'

One of the more effective assaults on duelling came from the simple onset of modernity. Duelling was simply seen as an old-fashioned, eighteenth-century way of doing things. Contemporary advances in industry and science combined to make duelling look just silly in an era that would produce the Great Exhibition of 1851. 'To the age of railways, steamers and gaslight, of popular education and popular science, duelling appeared criminal and absurd,' wrote the biographer, Cecil Woodham-Smith. Like slavery and witch hunts, the duel was no longer acceptable in a civilised society. Perhaps the least effective curb on duelling was the law itself. Legislation down the ages repeatedly failed to stop men wilfully stepping outside the law to shoot one another. Yet two legal changes did have some impact. First, the growth of the civil courts began to persuade some men that they could look for redress there rather than on the duelling field. The prospect of financial damages appeared more attractive than the risk of physical injury. The Libel Act 1843 in particular rebalanced the law in favour of plaintiffs by stopping defendants pleading truth as a defence in a criminal libel suit. But more importantly, one particular law introduced in 1844 changed the whole way the army looked on duelling.

Queen Victoria never really liked duelling. But she did nothing to stop it until one duel finally spurred her into action. On July 1 1843, Lieutenant Alexander Munro of the Royal Horse Guards shot and wounded his brother-in-law in a duel in Camden Town, north London. Lieutenant-Colonel David Fawcett of the 55th Regiment lingered for a couple of days before he died in his wife's arms. The duel provoked outrage not only among ordinary Londoners but also among those who resided at Buckingham Palace. Victoria made her feelings known and the next year they were acted upon. On March 15 1844, Sir Henry Hardinge, the secretary for war, told the House of Commons that the Queen was desirous of 'devising some expedient by which the barbarous practice of duelling should be as much as possible discouraged'. Few noticed the irony: Hardinge had been Wellington's second fifteen years earlier in the duel against Lord Winchilsea. The following month, the Articles of War were changed so that 'every officer who shall send a challenge, or who shall accept a challenge to fight a duel with another officer, or who, being privy to an intention to fight a duel, shall not take active measures to prevent such duel, or who shall upbraid another for refusing or not giving a challenge, or who shall reject or advise the rejection of a reasonable proposition made for the honourable adjustment of a difference, shall be liable if convicted before a general court martial to be cashiered or suffer such other punishment as the court may award.' Where once the army rules had encouraged duelling by implicitly making it a court martial offence to refuse a challenge, they now declared that duelling *itself* was an offence. The change could not have been more stark. And as if to ram the point home, Sir Robert Peel, the prime minister, changed the law further so that the widow of a duelling officer would be denied an army pension. His argument was that 'an institution predicated on the affirmation of courage and the demonstration of manliness could . . . be subverted if it brought destitution to the dependent and the weak'. He was right. Duty to family now overrode duty to the self and, almost overnight, the duel lost its greatest disciples, the military. Thus, by the end of the 1840s, duelling, in Britain at least, was no more.

It was a tired but relieved David Landale who travelled slowly back to Kirkcaldy after his acquittal in Perth. He knew he had behaved with honour but it was not an experience he wished to repeat. Not only had it placed great strain on him and his family, but it had also disrupted his business. John Anderson could not be expected to run Landale & Co. by himself. It was time to pick up the pieces.

Some in Kirkcaldy had disapproved of the duel. Further afield there were one or two pamphlets written by those who opposed duelling. One such scribe was George Buchan Esq. of Kelloe who wrote a masterly tract about David's trial, summoning every legal and spiritual argument he could master against the outcome. But even he made clear that he had nothing against David personally. 'Not an unkindly thought is entertained,' he wrote, 'with regard to the character of an individual, as to whom the chief feeling ought to be that of deep concern for the painful circumstances in which he has been placed, in having unhappily shed the blood of a fellow creature.' If there was any disapproval in Kirkcaldy, it was short lived. Unlike some duellists who found themselves shunned by society as the nineteenth century drew on, David was welcomed back into the fold. 'For many years after, he continued to do a large business, and to be held in honourable respect by all who had commercial transactions with him,' his obituary would later record. David was soon back in the saddle as chairman of Kirkcaldy's chamber of commerce. The minutes of the first meeting after the duel, on November 14 1826, show that David 'begged the indulgence of the committee' for forgetting to set a date for their annual general meeting. With typical understatement, he blamed his absentmindedness on what he called the 'peculiar circumstances under which he had been individually placed of late'. He would remain their chairman for another four years.

David even tested his post-duel reputation in the ballot box. He was successful and entered local government, campaigning hard in favour of what would become the 1832 Reform Act that swept away the rotten burghs and extended the popular franchise to the middle classes. 'Burgh politics had . . . due attention from Mr Landale,' his obituarist recorded, 'and during the struggle that preceded the passing of the Reform Bill, he took warm interest in the fortunes of that measure, and several times addressed public meetings in support of it.' In 1835, nine years after the duel, the people of Kirkcaldy expressed their ultimate confidence in David and elected him their provost.

David's personal life flourished as much as the political. After eight years alone since the death of his first wife, the widower found love again. He had known Mary Russell since she was a child. She was the daughter of one of his closest family friends, a fellow linen merchant called William Russell. The two families had been close for years and were already bound by marriage. In 1814 David's elder brother, James, had married another of William's daughters, Helen. Now, many years later, their two younger siblings fell in love and on March 19 1828, almost two years after the duel, David Landale and Mary Russell were married. He was forty-two, she was twenty-three. It was clearly a loving relationship: over the next two decades, they had no fewer than eleven children – four sons and seven daughters.

Meanwhile, his company recovered. Things went well enough for David to branch out into new trades: he picked up a little dry salting business and became part owner of a couple of ships. According to the census records, in 1851 Landale & Co. employed fifty women and sixteen men, both in its portside warehouses and bleachfield just up the road at Lochty. David's two eldest sons, James, then aged twenty-one, and Robert Russell, seventeen, were both learning the trade, working as clerks for their father. And at home, Mary had help bringing up the growing family from a nursemaid, a housemaid and a cook.

Life for David Morgan was less sweet. Apart from the birth of his seventh child in November 1826, there was little in the aftermath of the duel to cheer him up. For a time, he struggled to run the bank by himself. The people of Kirkcaldy did not forget George Morgan's behaviour towards them and they took their revenge on his brother. 'It is easy to overlook the fact that the Bank's business in any town depended crucially upon the character and abilities of the agent,' records the Bank of Scotland's official history. 'One outcome of the duel in Kirkcaldy was that the Bank's business among the town's linen manufacturers faded away.' When, a few years later, David Landale's old friend and fellow linen merchant, Walter Fergus, decided to get into banking himself and set up the Union Bank, he stole most of the Bank of Scotland's business. 'Even Head Office acknowledged that little could be done until the agent, David Morgan, was gone and that new accounts would depend on new industries. It was the growth of the jute trade, the harbour development and the invention of the linoleum manufacturing process in the 1840s and '50s that gave the Kirkcaldy branch a second lease of life.' The Bank of Scotland also learned its lesson, banning any of its Kirkcaldy apprentices from serving in the local branch, a rule it only repealed in 1940.

For a time, money was clearly tight. In July 1830, David was forced to sell the family pew in the local church. There is a suggestion that the Morgans might have bent the rules to keep claiming George's army pay for several years after his death. Although George was shot dead in 1826, he is named in the Army Lists as a registered half-pay lieutenant in the 77th Regiment of Foot until 1831. This could, of course, have been nothing more than an understandable inaccuracy at a time of poor communications and record keeping. But George

Morgan's death had made headlines in *The Times*. Someone in the regiment would have heard about it and amended the records. For some reason, however, this did not happen. And that reason could have been that someone was continuing to claim the half-pay for as long as they thought they could get away with it.

Relief came in the shape of David's son, Alexander Gibson Morgan, who joined his father at the bank in 1839. Alexander was born on May 2 1817, the fifth of David and Margaret Morgan's seven children. He was clearly capable. He actually started working for his father at the bank when he was fourteen – unpaid according the records. But he later became one of the first of the family to go to university, reading chemistry at St Andrews in 1835. A year later, however, at the age of nineteen, he chose to rejoin the family business, going to work as a teller for the Bank of Scotland in Perth, earning £50 a year. Within three years, he had done well enough to come back to Kirkcaldy to work as a clerk for his father. By all accounts, Alexander, who had been nine years old at the time of the duel, was the opposite to his late uncle George: he was steady, dour, and respectable. He was of 'a quiet, rather retiring disposition and most gentlemanly bearing,' his obituary would later recall, a man who had been 'an esteemed townsman' and 'most respected in our midst'. He was also a devout Christian, and after the schism in the Scottish church, joined the breakaway Free Presbyterian 'Wee Frees' Church. In 1841, as his aging father continued to buckle under the strain of running the bank, the twenty-four-year-old Alexander became joint agent, earning £300 a year, and slowly began to take over the ropes from his father. Such was the continuing bad feeling among the linen merchants that Alexander concen-

trated on building new business among the growing industries. And in Fife, that meant the new linoleum trade for which
Kirkcaldy would later become famous. Alexander was a particularly close friend of Sir Michael Nairn, the great Kirkcaldy
linoleum baron. Gently, the bank directors in Edinburgh
encouraged David to retire, which, in August 1849, he did,
leaving the whole agency to Alexander.

Duelling might have died out in Britain by the 1850s, but
elsewhere it died hard. In the United States, it continued to
prosper for several more decades. Like so much else, duelling
had been exported to the colonies with the early immigrants
and the first recorded encounter on American soil took place
in June 1621, albeit between two servants. Such was the disapproval of Edward Doty and Edward Lester's masters that they
punished the men severely, binding them together by hand
and foot for twenty-four hours, regardless of their wounds.
The early Americans – the Puritans, the Quakers, the Dutch
– were not keen duellists. But by the time of the War of
Independence against Britain, duelling was hugely popular,
particularly in the South. The presence of such large British
and French armies did much to spread the duelling habit.
American combatants followed the European duelling codes
but both more laxly and more imaginatively. They did not
have to be gentlemen – the duel was open to all comers. They
used more weapons, preferring frequently rifles at sixty paces,
shotguns at forty and bowie knives at close quarters. On occasion, they even used revolving pistols as the technology developed and became more reliable. This, however, stretched the
definition between the ritualised duel and the uncontrolled
gunfight, something that was exaggerated further on the big

screen. The free-for-all firefight so beloved of the Western film genre had little to do with the heritage of the European duel. And the man-to-man, quick-draw combat between two cowboys pacing down a dusty street was the pure invention of Hollywood, with a little help from the back writers of late nineteenth-century Western novels. The reality of the Western gunfight was more mundane: a man would send word to his opponent that he would shoot him next time they met. Both would go around armed until this time, when a gunfight would ensue and one would survive. Andrew Steinmetz, writing in 1868, captured the real mood: 'In the States, men fight in earnest. Revolvers are ever revolving. No objection to fowling pieces, to rifles, to bowie knives. Put up your hand to scratch the back of your neck and the man nearest you will whip out a bowie knife. The walls of the hotel bedrooms, even in Washington, the capital, are riddled with bullet holes . . . the bartender always has a revolver on the shelf behind him.'

American duels were often about securing revenge rather than that rather Old World concept of satisfaction. Alexis de Tocqueville wrote in 1831 that 'the duel based on extreme susceptibility to points of honour . . . is almost unknown in America'. The duels there, he claimed, were simply a way of killing one's enemy outside the law: 'In Europe, one hardly ever fights a duel except in order to be able to say that one has done so; the offence is generally a sort of moral stain which one wants to wash away . . . In America one only fights to kill. One fights because one sees no hope of getting one's adversary condemned to death.' Many Americans mocked the European duel as a farce. If you were prepared to go as far as killing a man to resolve a dispute, you did so. You didn't appoint a second to prevent the combat, you didn't give your opponent the choice of weapons, you didn't risk your own life any more than you had to. 'I thoroughly disapprove of duels,' said Mark Twain with only half a tongue in his cheek. 'If a man should challenge me, I would take him kindly and forgivingly by the hand and lead him to a quiet place and kill him.' Thus the American combat was less about establishing honour and more about resolving a dispute through violence. This is illustrated above all by the large number of American duels caused by political disputes rather than issues of honour. The history books list numerous senators, congressmen, state governors who duelled, and even a president or two, such as Andrew Jackson. The politicians fought over election campaigns, property rights and, above all, slavery. And in the body politic, opinion had to be defended with a pistol just as much as policy. Campaigning newspapermen were frequently forced to fight the readers they libelled. Many press rooms had firearms ready just in case an angry victim stormed through the door. One nineteenth-century San Francisco editor even had a note pinned to his door: 'Subscriptions received from 9 to 4, challenges from 11 to 12 only.' The states' legislators naturally made laws against duelling – Massachusetts declared that duellists would be executed, have a stake driven through their bodies, and be buried without a coffin – but as in Europe, the laws were mostly ignored or unenforceable. Duelling declined first in the North, particularly after the Civil War, but it lingered longer in the South where the landed, slave-owning classes held on more firmly to what they saw as their badge of social distinction. But by the late nineteenth century, duelling had all but died out in the United States.

Yet on the European continent, duelling was experiencing a renaissance. In Italy, in the ten years between 1879 and 1889,

some 2,759 duels were recorded, most of them still fought
with swords. In Germany and the Austro-Hungarian empire,
duelling was rife, driven on by ideals of imperial militarism.
As well as the traditional pistol duel, there also flourished,
particularly in the German universities, special sword fights
known as *Mensuren*. These very German combats were not
strictly duels as such. Instead, they were more like gruesome
sporting encounters between representatives of competing
student fraternities or corps. Rarely had the combatants any
meaningful dispute between them. Nor were they expected
to put their lives at risk. But they were driven by extreme
concepts of honour and courage, they adopted many of the
codes of duelling, and they spilt a lot of each others' blood.
The two students would fight at arm's length with sharp edged
but non-piercing swords, standing relatively still while they
hacked at their opponent's head with whip-like wrist move-
ments. They wore leather gauntlets on their hands and thick
lederhosen from chest to knee, they bound their arms with tight
silk bandages and special protective pads, they wrapped their
throats with thick stocks and they strapped on thick glassless
goggles to protect their eyes. And there, in a crowded inn,
standing in a 12-foot-square, chalked-out ring from which
they could not withdraw, surrounded by hoards of drunken
students, their aim was quite simple: to gash or slash their
opponent in the head, preferably in the cheek or the top of
the forehead. These were not duels, one historian concluded,
but instead 'more elaborate ritualistic facial operations'. Scars
on the cheek were seen as a badge of courage and honour by
men, and, the loss of ear, nose and scalp notwithstanding, as
sexually attractive by women. Often the duellists would rub
in specially prepared salt mixtures or even horse hair to preserve

the scar. Some early plastic surgeons were known to provide a discreet scar cutting service for those students lacking the courage to fight. The duellists were also expected to endure being stitched up by drunk medical students with the same stoic bravery as they received their wounds in the first place. Any display of weakness or pain could result in ostracism from the student corps. These *Mensuren* were naturally illegal but actively encouraged by German elites as a suitable vehicle for both fostering and proving character in a young man's education. As a student in the 1830s, Otto von Bismarck reputedly fought seventy-eight such combats. The future kaiser, Wilhelm II, was born with a withered left arm and practised fencing for many years to beef up his right arm. He believed unashamedly in the benefits of *Mensuren*: 'As in the Middle Ages, manly strength and courage were steeled by the practice of jousting or tournaments, so the spirit and habits which are acquired from membership of a corps furnish us with that degree of fortitude which is necessary to us when we go out into the world.' *Mensuren* are still illegal, still lunatic and yet still practised in some German universities today.

In France, duelling survived the revolution – the newly empowered bourgeoisie picked up the blades the guillotined aristocracy left behind – and flourished. The French upper classes, military and fourth estate fought with bloody abandon. As Marilyn Monroe sang: 'The French were bred to die for love, they delight in fighting duels.' Yet towards the end of the nineteenth century, the duel – still overwhelmingly sword based – became more ritualistic and less lethal, often halting at first blood. Among some, this provoked mockery. The American satirist, Ambrose Bierce, defined the French duel as 'a formal ceremony preliminary to the reconciliation of two enemies'. But to the French, the practice remained popular as a demonstration of the classic individualism of their nation. French philosophers defended duelling as an act of patriotism, a tool of civilisation, a vehicle of justice – anything in fact that could restore national morale and identity in the wake of the country's devastating defeat by Germany in 1870. At the turn of the century, France found an ardent advocate of duelling in Georges Clemenceau, its prime minister. Clemenceau, who led France between 1906 and 1909, and 1917 and 1920, fought twelve duels: seven with pistols, five with swords. 'He preferred the sword but in most of his encounters he was the challenger and rarely had choice of weapons,' wrote Richard Cohen. 'His rivals generally chose pistols, possibly because they believed he would never aim to kill and might opt to miss altogether; whereas with an épée he might satisfy himself only with a significant bloodletting.'

After a slow start, duelling also spread through Russia's elites. Initially they were distrustful of what was considered a deeply foreign practice. But as Russia fell in love with France, and as its armies fought wars deeper and deeper into the western European continent, the duel ended up in Moscow along with so many other cultural icons. The tsars, like most monarchs, were divided. Catherine the Great's son, Paul I, believed Europe's monarchs should fight duels – with prime ministers as their seconds – to avoid the mass bloodshed of war. Accordingly, he challenged Napoleon Bonaparte to a duel in Hamburg, a challenge that not surprisingly never received a reply. But earlier tsars like Peter I disliked the practice and ordered men hanged just for contemplating a duel. In later times, Nicholas I banned even the mention of duelling in the press: Pushkin's fatal duel was not reported until six weeks after his death. However, 'by the end of the nineteenth century, with Moscow and Saint Petersburg in love with all things French, no self-respecting officer or gentleman could ignore the new sensation.' Many young men, in particular those in literary sets, duelled in particular to demonstrate their independence from the tsar. But in the end, like so much else, the revolution ended all thoughts of duelling in Russia.

Eventually, it was a war, World War One, which killed off the pistol duel. On one level, the sheer scale of the slaughter rendered it pointless and absurd to risk more death over a trivial slight or a misguided sense of personal honour. There was also a generation of would-be young duellists whose bodies instead now lay rotting in Flanders' fields. On another level, duelling was discredited by its very similarity to the nature of the war itself. Many historians have claimed comparisons between war and duelling − Carl von Clausewitz, the classic Germany military theorist, claimed that 'war is nothing but a duel on an extensive scale'. But World War One has always drawn most comparisons, historians arguing that the nature of trench warfare − the trading of fatal blows, the stubborn refusal to seek reconciliation − meant the war was itself a form of duelling between nations. The war was, of course, fought by many military officers and commanders − particularly on the German and French sides − who had wide experience of duelling. 'The Great War may not have been a war to end war,' wrote Victor Kiernan, 'but it might be called a duel that virtually ended duelling.'

After 1918, lethal duels were rare and in many cases publicity stunts rather than serious combat. In a reaction against all things Prussian, duelling was banned in the Weimar Republic. Yet duelling with swords did experience a brief Indian summer among the fascist societies of Germany and Italy in the 1930s which adopted anachronistic dreams of knightly chivalry to give spurious historical legitimacy to their regimes. Benito Mussolini loved to duel, and did all he could to encourage fencing among his *fascisti*. In Germany, the Nazis were initially cautious of the university duelling fraternities, considering them a possible threat. But the students refused to abide by a ban on *Mensuren* and after several years of confusion, the Nazis switched tack. Suddenly the codes of honour became codes of national socialism and national pride. Leading Nazis, such as Heinrich Himmler and Reinhard Heydrich, who also happened to be obsessive fencers and duellers, did all they could to encourage swordplay. But World War Two put an end to all that and in modern European society, the duel had finally reached its end.

The story of David Landale does not end happily. For, many years after the duel, on a hot summer's day, the linen merchant suffered a massive seizure and was paralysed. He was sixty years old. According to the correspondent known only as 'C' in the *Kirkcaldy Advertiser*. 'In his declining years, Mr Landale became paralysed on one side and latterly had to be moved about in an invalid's chair as he became quite unable to walk.' A daguer-rotype photograph taken at the time shows David sitting stiffly upright in a chair, wearing a smartly buttoned coat, his face set in grim concentration. His right hand holds the top of a cane for balance while his left hand lies limply on his thigh, hooked round into a claw that bears every hallmark of a severe stroke. Such was David's disability that the family could not cope on their own. A male 'sick nurse' called Archibald Sinclair from Inverkeithing was employed; he would stay at St Mary's and look after David until the day of his death. Other things, however, could not be solved with medical help. David's paralysis had a huge impact on his business. He was no longer able to keep an eye on things and gradually Landale & Co. declined. His obituary recorded that after his 'attack of paralysis', David had further 'repeated shocks, at intervals, of that disease' which 'gradually unfitted him for attending to business, and his extensive commercial concerns lost his personal oversight and superintendence'. In 1853, he was forced to bring in his two eldest sons, James and Robert Russell Landale, as co-partners to help run the firm. Clearly business did not get better. A correspondent known as 'F' told the *Fifeshire Advertiser* in 1907 that he could still remember 'the high principles of [David's] large family in the days of their adversity, after they had great financial losses'. Such was the severity of the paralysis that David appears even to have lost the ability to speak; he was, according to one legal document, 'incapacitated by illness from making any alteration' to his Will during his last years.

Yet David lingered on and survived many uncomfortable years until he died shortly after 5 o'clock in the morning of October 4 1861 in his bed at St Mary's. His death certificate declares his cause of death to be 'paralysis' and, horrifyingly, it states that the duration of the disease was fifteen years. In its long and affectionate obituary, the *Fifeshire Advertiser* noted David's death as melancholy but not altogether unexpected. 'For the whole course of a long lifetime, Mr Landale's name has been intimately connected with the trade of the town, and notwithstanding that difficulties, unfortunately, overtook him towards the close, we believe all acquainted with the deceased will bear us out in saying that, before bodily affliction and commercial misfortune united to bear him down, he uniformly showed the spirit of a gentleman, and the uprightness and integrity of a British merchant.'

Naturally, the obituary could not avoid mentioning the duel, but even after all those years, there was a delicacy to be observed. 'At this period in Mr Landale's life, there occurred a tragic incident which it is impossible to pass over without mention, although we certainly have no desire unnecessarily to stir up painful reminiscences – we need not say that we allude to the duel between Mr Landale and Mr Morgan, in which the latter had the ill fortune to fall mortally wounded. It would be unjust to the memory of Mr Landale not to state that he has always been acquitted for his part in this most unfortunate affair by his fellow townsmen, as having been forced into it by great provocation.' Yet even then, by the early 1860s, duelling was seen as a rather unfortunate anachronism. The obituary explains away George Morgan's behaviour by stating that he, 'being in the army, would have the high notions of honour then prevalent among gentlemen of the military profession'. And as for David Landale's reaction to being assaulted with an umbrella, the obituarist feels he has to explain that the merchant 'felt that he could not stand a blow as he stood angry and insulting words, and he took the course to resent it then common among gentlemen'.

By the time of David's death on October 4 1861, Landale and Co. was insolvent. His sons, James and Robert, clearly did not have their father's aptitude for business. James had slunk off to Mauritius some years before and so it fell to Robert to sort out the estate. 'His object in so doing,' declared one legal document, 'is to make up a title to said personal estate for the purpose of realising the same and dividing the proceeds amongst the creditors of the said David Landale who, as partner of the firm of D Landale and Company, merchants, was insolvent at the time of his death, and his estate is now insolvent.' Robert had wanted to wait until James, his fellow executor, returned home to Scotland. He was believed to be on his way home from Mauritius but no one knew when he might arrive. But such was the burden of debt that Robert simply could not wait. In a deposition to the lawyers, he wrote: 'There is an absolute necessity for the immediate realisation and division of said personal estate, the creditors being urgent in their demands for the same, and that further delay in doing so will be attended with considerable expense and loss to all concerned.'

David's Will is as long as it is heavy with pathos. It is full of detailed instructions about who should get what, how the business should be divided up, how the capital should be dispersed and under what conditions to his eleven children and their families, how the younger children should be educated, how Robert and James were supposed to buy out David's share of Landale & Co., how Mary was to get an annuity for life unless she remarried. But all in vain. Robert managed to save St Mary's for his mother; his brother-in-law, George Wilson, generously bought all the furniture – valued at £380 – so the house would not be stripped bare. But everything else, the land, the property, the bleachfield up at Lochty Water, all was sold to pay off the creditors. The duellist, in the end, was defeated not by his banker but by his business.

The night before he duelled with Aaron Burr, Alexander Hamilton wrote out a Will in which, paradoxically, he set out why he believed it was wrong for him to fight the vice president of the United States. Intriguingly, Burr's high office was not an issue. Instead, Hamilton wrote: 'First, my religion and moral principles are strongly opposed to the practice of duelling, and it would ever give me pain to shed the blood of a fellow creature in a private combat forbidden by the laws. Secondly, my wife and children are extremely dear to me; and my life is of the utmost importance to them, in various views. Thirdly, I feel a sense of obligation towards my creditors, who, in case of accident to me, by the forced sale of my property, may be in some degree sufferers. I did not think myself at liberty, as a man of probity lightly to expose them to hazard. Fourthly, I am conscious of no ill-will to Colonel Burr distinct from political opposition, which, as I trust, has proceeded from pure and upright motives. Lastly, I shall hazard much and can possibly gain nothing by the issue of the interview.' He was right. The morning after he wrote those words, Hamilton ignored his own advice, took a boat over the Hudson river to New Jersey and was shot dead. Nothing could be more self-contradictory, hypocritical, schizophrenic even. Here was a man who ostensibly opposed duelling yet took part in several encounters, the last of which cost him his life. Yet similar divided emotions were felt by many other duellists who struggled with the dilemma. Their concern for family, fear of death, religious scruples, rational objections – they were all overcome by a sense of personal honour that obliged them to fight. Yet for such a strongly motivating concept, honour was something that meant a lot of different things to many people.

There was, at one end of the spectrum, a sense of honour that was an ideal, a genuine and real honour established by a mix of public reputation and personal sense of self-worth. This was the honour, as the old saw had it, that only a man could give to himself. It was about a man's self-control, his will, his ability to hold to his principles above daily desires, his respect for others. A duel to defend this kind of honour could be seen as a genuine combat, a noble act that was justifiable, meaningful, chivalrous even. The radical philosopher, Jeremy Bentham, believed that duelling corrected a real social evil: 'It entirely effaces a blot which an insult imprints upon the honour.' This kind of duel could be placed on a par with fighting to defend family, home or country. It was probably something that a man did once or twice in his life. This concept of honour was so valuable that a grievous insult upon it justified a challenge. Combat on these terms was over a genuine difference between two men. This was the kind of honour that could be challenged only by a gross slur on reputation, a serious accusation of impropriety; in other words, of dishonourable behaviour.

Yet at the other end of the spectrum, there was an artificial, paltry idea of honour, a lightweight social construct, a feeble concept easily threatened. This was the kind of honour that could be slighted by an accidental jostle in a pub or a trivial squabble. This was not honour, just a pale imitation, something that provoked duels that were both absurd and ridiculous. This was the honour of peer pressure, where men fought simply to follow custom and avoid public shame. In 1827, the night before he attended a duel, a New Yorker called WG Graham wrote in his Will: 'It is needless for me to say I heartily protest and despise this absurd mode of settling disputes. But what can a poor devil do except bow to the supremacy of custom?' The next morning he was shot dead. There was something rather pathetic about a duel to protect this kind of gossamer honour, where the combat was little more than a courtly ritual, albeit a lethal one. This was the kind of duelling honour that the historian Kevin McAleer disdained. 'It concealed a value vacuum,' he wrote. 'Destitute of noble values by which to live, duellists embraced a set of aristocratic guidelines for which to die: a code of honour. They proved all-too-human, less modern-day knights than adolescent schoolboys in the locker room snapping towels to exhibit some simple-minded and vaguely slapstick notions of masculinity.' This was the honour of the serial, almost professional duellist where the breach was simply a thin pretext to fight. This was the honour of the fanatical duellists, like the Irish gentry who used to 'hunt in the day, get drunk in the evening and fight the next morning'. The greatest exemplar of this was Robert George Fitzgerald, a pugnacious Irishman born in 1748 who fought some twenty-six duels in his violent and seemingly pointless life. Known as 'Fighting Fitzgerald', this merciless old Etonian fought to satisfy his temper, take his revenge, and fill in the hours between drinking and hunting. He was shameless in breaking the codes of duelling. There was nothing honourable about anything he did.

The fatal weakness of the duel as an institution was that it failed to distinguish between these two different concepts of honour. Writing in 1855, the American duelling historian Lorenzo Sabine had spotted the problem and differentiated between the lesser 'duel upon a mere question of honour' and the more important 'combat for positive wrong or deep injury'. Yet all the numerous duelling codes were silent on the subject. They set out in detail how the nature of the insult should determine the nature of the duel. But they never specified whether the nature of the insult should determine whether the duel took place in the first place. Antony Simpson said the codes never specified 'the exact circumstances that justified the issuing of a challenge'. The rules simply insisted that a gentleman was obliged to accept all challenges, however ridiculous they may be. Some insults were a genuine affront to a man's honour, so grievous they could not be overlooked. Others were absurd and should, and could, have been ignored. Yet the duel did not distinguish between the two insults; a slight was a slight, however trivial, and that provoked a challenge.

Historical generalisations are always a risk and inevitably challenged by individual cases. Yet on occasion it is useful to attempt some, not least to illustrate a wider point. Thus, after the reading of numerous accounts of duels, it is possible to conclude that when the duel was in its infancy, more of the combats were affairs of genuine honour than when the duel was dying out, when more of the encounters were prompted by less serious insults. In the early years, as the duel slowly replaced murderous assassinations or bloody affrays, the combats were seen by many as a way of regulating behaviour among men. The duels were there to resolve genuine, substantial differences where honour was at stake, something which reflected duelling's origins in judicial combat. But as the years went by, more of the duels were driven by the more artificial concept of honour. 'Here and there a man might be defending a genuine principle,' wrote the historian Victor Kiernan, 'but such exceptions were lost in the welter of meaningless scrimmages.' Ultimately, it was this that killed off duelling. For the further a duel moved away from resolving a genuine dispute, the more it was likely to fall into disrepute.

David Landale's duel with George Morgan reflected this shift. By the 1820s, more duels were driven by this artificial concept of honour than before. Thus it was considered absurd by David and his friends to duel over a business dispute. That kind of conflict was not covered by the now specious concept of honour that most duellists seemed to hold. Duellists fought now because people had looked at them in the wrong way or spoken out of turn, not because they had had a row with their bank manager. But once George struck David with an umbrella on the public street, all that changed. At once, they had gone back in time to a place where two gentlemen, who had a grievance of genuine substance and whose honour was at stake, must duel. The nature of the insult was vital. Thus David's duel went right back to the institution's origins. Like those who took part in trial by combat, David fought according to strict ritual and rules, believing profoundly that it was God and not skill that determined the outcome. And just like the knights in the days of chivalry, David fought with due ceremony another member of society's elite in a dispute designed to establish honour rather than victory or defeat.

This is the heart of the story of David Landale. His fatal encounter with George Morgan stood out simply because it was so unlike most other duels of the time. It was a duel based on a genuine dispute and was not a specious conflict. It was a duel between debutant duellists, not practised combatants. It was a duel in which the reputation and honour of two men were genuinely at stake. And above all, it stood out because it contained so many signs that duelling was on the way out: David's constant doubts about the propriety of fighting; his repeated search for approval among his friends; his inexperience as a duellist; Millie's reluctance to be a second; his and Milne's uncertainty about the rules; the apparent relaxation over time of those rules; George Morgan's reluctance to challenge; his ignorance about the law; the attempts by Dr Johnston's family to stop him attending the encounter; David

Landale's acknowledgement that success in the duel was not enough to restore his reputation and that instead he needed the trial and acquittal to restore his business credit; the public disapproval of the encounter.

These doubts, these uncertainties, they all reflected the wider social changes taking place in the first half of the nineteenth century that brought about the end of duelling – the middle-class opposition, the development of the courts, the popular hostility, the retreat of individualism. In the 1820s, Britain stood on the cusp of modernity and the decline of duelling illustrates a shifting society that was finally forced to confront, and eventually discard, a bloody tradition as it embraced the industrial, scientific and social advances of the era. As the historian Donna T Andrew wrote, there was 'a new vision of society based on reasonableness, Christianity and commerce, in which duelling ceased to be practised simply because it appeared incongruous and foolish'. In this context, the eventual rejection of duelling by Victorian society marked a gear change in history when Britain shed a little of its past so it could embrace the future, a moment when the ancient surrendered to the modern.

A fatal duel often led to bad blood. A single moment, a gentle touch on a trigger, could lead to generations of seething resentment that divided families and communities. For all the pretensions of honour, for all the ritual, a duel was at its core about two men trying, and often succeeding, in killing each other. The most ardent disciples of the *code duello* might forgive each other as they died in each other's arms. But their families and friends were less forgiving. So many times were wives left without a husband, children without a father, families without a living. That bred a resentment and acrimony that time rarely healed. George Morgan had neither wife nor children. But that did not stop his family feeling something more than ill will towards David Landale. 'The death of Mr Morgan caused much bitter feeling between the two families,' wrote the anony-mous correspondent 'C' in the *Kirkcaldy Advertiser* in 1907.

So it is all the more extraordinary what then happened. For in the spring of 1851, Alexander Morgan, nephew of the long-dead George Morgan, son of the surviving brother, David Morgan, fell in love with a young Kirkcaldy girl. The dour banker was thirty-four years old, he had a good profession, and he was ready to start a family. She was nineteen, the daughter of a respected local merchant, the fifth of seven sisters, a good catch who was ready for marriage. Yet her name was Ellen Landale and her father was the man who twenty-five years earlier had shot Alexander's uncle dead.

How Alexander and Ellen met, how they courted, we do not know. What is certain is that they were married by the Rev. John Alexander at the Free Church in Kirkcaldy on September 2 1851. There can be no doubt that this was an astonishing act of reconciliation between both families. The fact that Alexander proposed, the fact that Ellen accepted, both suggest that the match was accepted by the families. The records do not list the marriage witnesses but the ceremony would surely not have taken place were it not with the consent of the parents. David Landale might have been struck down by a stroke but he was still ten years from death and had not lost all his faculties. David Morgan, Alexander's father, was still very much alive.

The marriage between Alexander and Ellen flourished. They moved into the Morgan family home, a comfortable, decent sized house on Kirkcaldy's High Street. They hired a gaggle of house servants – the usual trinity of cook, housemaid and nursemaid – and set about raising a family. Over the next twenty years, they produced four daughters and five sons, the youngest of whom they even called George. In subsequent decades, the Landale and Morgan families were joined in business as well as love. For in the 1880s, three of Alexander and Ellen's sons – David, Alexander and Robert Morgan – travelled to Calcutta in India, three small additions to the diaspora of Scots spreading across the British Empire in search of excitement, adventure and work. Already out in Calcutta was Alexander Landale, David Landale's youngest son and Ellen's older brother. Together Alexander Landale and his three nephews set up a company of brokers called Landale & Morgan which traded in almost everything but specialised particularly in jute, which was sent back to Kirckcaldy for the town's linoleum business. According to some accounts, the firm survived until the 1950s. When Alexander Morgan retired in 1875, after more than thirty years in charge of the Bank of Scotland in Kirkcaldy, he and Ellen moved up the coast to spend their declining years in St Andrews. Aged eighty-five, Alexander finally died of bronchitis at exactly 8 p.m. on June 3 1902. As so often happened, Ellen herself died only a few months later, aged seventy-one. They are buried in the same grave in the shadow of the ruins of St Andrews cathedral looking out over the North Sea, just a few miles up the coast from where, a generation before, their father and uncle had duelled at dawn.

Acknowledgements

This book, like any other, would not exist were it not for the help of others. I would like to thank in particular the staff at the National Library of Scotland and the National Archives of Scotland; Alan Brotchie who pointed me in the direction of some important papers; Gavin Grant, Dallas Mechan and Katherine Shearer at Kirkcaldy Library; Helen Robertson and Kellyanne Campbell at the Fife Chamber of Commerce in Kirkcaldy; Joyce and Robin Baird of Cardenbarns Farm; Andrew Dowsey at the Fife Council Archive Centre; Joe Murphy at Perth Sheriff Court; Anne Mead for her enthusiasm and energy in keeping this story alive; Sian Yates, Rosemary Moodie and Seonaid McDonald for their diligence in digging around in the Bank of Scotland archives; the Viscount Ingleby for his help and permission to use his portraits of David Landale; Dr James Kelly of St Patrick's College, Dublin, for scouring the manuscript for idiocies; Richard Morgan for allowing me to benefit from his own work in this area; Professor Charles Munn of the Chartered Institute of Bankers in Scotland; Joyce Black; David Johnstone; Mike Catignani; Robert Morgan; David Russell; Charlie Pownall; Andrew Sparrow and Lauren Blair. Of course, any errors in what follows are mine and mine alone.

Some people deserve special thanks. Guy Walters must take full responsibility for encouraging me to stop talking and get writing. My agent, Tif Loehnis at Janklow & Nesbit, has my eternal gratitude for believing in *Duel* in the first place, arguing its case with such enthusiasm and having the patience to take a novice under her wing. And of course my huge thanks go to Jamie Byng, Andy Miller and everyone at Canongate for their unflagging support and commitment. My greatest debt, however, is to my wife and children who bore my absence, obsession and exhaustion with reserves of love and patience that I can only attempt to return.

James Landale,
London, April 2005

Sources

Primary sources

The Cockburn Papers

Cockburn, Lord. The case of David Landale. MSS. Advocates Library/National Library of Scotland. Ref: Adv.MSS.9.1.2

This is the biggest primary source for the book. The manuscript contains all the evidence gathered for David Landale's trial. His lawyer, Henry Cockburn, had the documents copied for his own records because of the legal precedent the case established in duelling law. The bulk of the manuscript is the witness evidence of twenty-nine individuals involved in the Landale/Morgan duel. They were interviewed immediately after the duel in a Scottish legal process known as precognition in which evidence is gathered by the authorities to determine whether or not there should be a trial. Their evidence amounts to 40,000 words of direct testimony. It is this that has allowed me to recreate the duel in such detail. Most of the dialogue in the book is direct speech as reported in the evidence. Some, however, is indirect speech that I have turned into direct speech by a) inserting quotation marks, b) replacing the word 'witness' with the name of the witness, and c) replacing a name or two with a pronoun. No other words were changed.

Those who gave evidence were:

Robert Stocks, Alexander Balfour, William Russell, David Birrell, Michael Barker, Provost Millar, James Fleming, Robert Inglis, Alexander Beveridge, James Aytoun, James Brown, William Tod, James Cumming, David Morgan, William Millie, Lt. William Milne, Dr Alexander Smith, Dr James Johnston, Gilbert Garner, John Mason, Robert Kirk, David Macrae, George Graham, George Aitken, Thomas Ronald, George Douglas Mitchell, William Henry, William Oliphant and Walter Fergus.

The Cockburn manuscript also includes:

1. A handwritten introduction by Henry Cockburn, including his description of David Landale's purchase of the pistols and Lord Gillies' attitude to the case.
2. A selection of the most important letters relating to the case. They include: David Landale's application for a cash credit and his complaint to the Bank of Scotland in Edinburgh; David Morgan and George Morgan's letters defending their conduct; the Bank of Scotland's response; and the flurried exchange of correspondence between David Landale and George Morgan in the run up to the duel.
3. The formal charge against David Landale.
4. A list of potential witnesses.
5. The brief formal statement of David Landale's defence.
6. Henry Cockburn's detailed written defence.
7. David Landale's detailed personal notes for his counsel.
8. A full report of Lord Gillies' ruling.

Legal documents

The second largest primary source is a collection of legal documents relating to the Landale/Morgan duel kept at the National Archives of Scotland in Edinburgh. These come in three groups:

1. Case papers, High Court of the Justiciary. Ref: JC 26/478. These comprise summons, petitions, lists of witnesses, lists of jurors, and key evidentiary documents.

2. Precognition documents, Lord Advocate's department. Ref: AD 14/26/368. These comprise the sketch of the duel site; petitions for arrest; and correspondence between the prosecuting authorities, including Adam Rolland, the crown agent, Will Douglas, the local justices' clerk, and Andrew Galloway, the sheriff depute for Fife.

3. North Circuit minute book entries. High Court of the Justiciary. Ref: JC 11/72. This comprises a brief but formal account of the trial.

Accounts of the trial of David Landale

Report of the trial of David Landale Esq. Before the circuit court of justiciary at Perth on Friday, 22 September 1826, second edition, Perth: R Morison

A Famous Fife Trial: The Kirkcaldy Duel Case, Cork, Purcell & Co., printers, 24 Patrick Street, 1893

Perthshire Courier, September 28 1826

Edinburgh Weekly Journal, September 27 1826

Edinburgh Evening Courant, September 25 1826

Morning Herald, London, September 27 1826

Scotsman, September 27 1826

The Times, September 28 1826

Newspaper articles

Edinburgh Evening Courant, August 24 1826 – early report of duel

The Scotsman, August 25 1826 – early report of duel

Edinburgh Weekly Journal, August 29 1826 – early report of duel

The Times, August 28 & 29 1826 – early reports of duel

Fifeshire Advertiser, October 5 1861 – David Landale's obituary

Fifeshire Citizen, September 24 1904 – the last duel in Fife

Fifeshire Advertiser, May 4 1907 – a narrative of the duel and trial

Fifeshire Advertiser, May 11 1907 – more correspondence, including letter by 'C'

Fifeshire Advertiser, May 18 1907 – more correspondence

Fifeshire Advertiser, May 25 1907 – copies of David Landale's letters to his land agent, John Anderson. These letters give detailed and first hand evidence of what David Landale was thinking and feeling during and after the trial

The Fife Free Press, June 7 1902 – Alexander Morgan's obituary

Findlay, Jessie Patrick. *The last duel fought in Fife*, local Fife newspaper, date uncertain, likely to be 1920s, two such articles, both held at Kirkcaldy Library

Fifeshire Advertiser, October 12 1940, 'The last duel fought in Scotland' by J Y Lockhart

General Register Office for Scotland, Edinburgh

1. Census returns: David Landale, 1851 & 1861; David Morgan, 1851; Alexander Gibson Morgan, 1851, 1861, 1871, 1881, 1891, 1901

2. Marriage certificates: David Landale & Isabella Spears, December 7 1819; David Landale & Mary Russell, March 19 1828; Alexander Gibson Morgan & Ellen Russell Landale, September 2 1851

3. Death certificates: David Landale, October 4 1861; Alexander Gibson Morgan, June 3 1901

Other sources

1. Minutes of meetings, Kirkcaldy Chamber of Commerce: July 18 1825; November 14 1826. Records held at the Fife Chamber of Commerce, Kirkcaldy.
2. Documents from Bank of Scotland archives: letters from the Bank of Scotland directors in Edinburgh to George and David Morgan. Ref: BS/1/32/11; background material on David, George and Alexander Gibson Morgan, compiled by archivists; copies of some of David Landale's bonds and cash accounts.
3. Wills: David Morgan, National Archive of Scotland, ref. SC20/50/24 pp. 1263–94; David Landale, National Archive of Scotland, ref. SC 20/50/33 pp. 1497–1520 and 1607–10.
4. Selected military documents relating to George Morgan, held at the National Archive at Kew, ref. WO 31/419, WO 31/363 and WO 31/344.
5. Map of Kirkcaldy, John Wood, Edinburgh, 1824. Reproduced by Caledonian Maps, Scotland, 1992.

Chronology of letters

January 23 1826 From David and George Morgan to George Sandy, Secretary to the Bank of Scotland, Edinburgh. Expresses their view that David Landale's security is good.

April 8 1826 From David Landale to William Caddell, Treasurer, Bank of Scotland. Argues his case for the cash credit.

April 25 1826 From David and George Morgan to David Landale. Their refusal to pay one of David's bills worth £1000.

June 5 (possibly 3) 1826 From Alexander Balfour to David Landale. Balfour's request to have his debt with Landale reduced.

June 23 1826 From David Landale to William Caddell, Treasurer of the Bank of Scotland, Edinburgh. Explaining why David withdrew his business from the bank.

June 27 1826 From David Morgan to David Landale. Invitation to dinner.

June 28 1826 From David Landale to David Morgan, declining invitation to dinner.

July 11 1826 From Archibald Bennet, Bank of Scotland, to David Morgan. Contains copy of Landale's letter of complaint and demands an explanation.

July 21 1826 From David Morgan to Archibald Bennet, Secretary to the Bank of Scotland. Defends himself against Landale's accusations.

July 31 1826 From Archibald Bennet to David and George Morgan. Demands how big Landale's overdraft is and how many of his bills are still outstanding.

August 2 1826 From George Sandy to David and George Morgan. Demands Landale update his insurance policies with the bank.

August 3 1826 From George Morgan to Archibald Bennet. Defends himself against Landale's charges.

August 8 1826 From Archibald Bennet to David and George Morgan. Demands full statement of Landale's debts with the bank.

August 9 1826 From George Sandy to David and George Morgan. Issues modest telling off for George Morgan but allows him to continue in office.

August 12 1826 From George Morgan to David Landale. Morgan's first demand for an apology from Landale.

August 12 1826 From David Landale to George Morgan. Landale's first reply to Morgan, insisting that he can substantiate his accusations.

August 12 1826 From George Morgan to David Landale. Says Landale's reply was evasive and points directly to those accusations he finds most offensive.

August 14 1826 From David Landale to George Morgan. Landale's second reply, insisting he has evidence from Robert Stocks, and informing Morgan that he will be out of Kirkcaldy for a few days. Morgan returns this reply without response.

August 22 1826 1 p.m. From David Landale to William Millie. Requests that Millie delivers challenge to George Morgan, and says he will go to Edinburgh to buy pistols.

August 22 1826 From David Landale to George Morgan. The challenge.

August 22 1826 From David Landale to John Anderson, setting his affairs in order and issuing instructions.

August 23 1826 From David Landale to John Anderson. In Glasgow. In the evening after the duel. Says he will write to legal authorities.

August 24 1826 From George Sandy to David Morgan. Acknowledges death of George Morgan.

August 24 1826 From Andrew Oliphant to Adam Rolland, crown agent. Explains circumstances of duel and attempts to arrest participants. Also hints at Morgan's unpopularity.

August 24 1826 From David Landale to John Anderson. In Glasgow. Says he will travel using an alias.

August 28 1826 From David Landale to John Anderson. In Keswick. Asks for arrangements to be made for him to get cash from the banks.

August 29 1826 From David Landale to John Anderson. In Keswick. Tells Anderson to stop worrying.

September 5 1826 From David Landale to John Anderson. Location unknown. Welcomes the support of his friends who are lobbying for him.

September 11 1826 From David Landale to John Anderson. In
Edinburgh. Seeks Cumming's evidence about Morgan's earlier
threat to David on the street.

September 20 1826 From David Landale to John Anderson. In
Edinburgh. Two days before the trial, asks for stomach powders
and warm shoes.

Secondary sources

Select bibliography:

Anon. *The British Code of Duel*, London, Knight and Lacey, 1824.
Republished by Richmond Publishing Co., 1971

Anon. *Guide to the City and County of Perth*, fourth edition. Perth,
R. Morison, 1824

Atkinson, John. *The British Duelling Pistol*, London, Bloomfield/Arms
and Armour Press, 1978

Atkinson, John. *Duelling Pistols and Some of the Affairs they Settled*,
London, Cassell, 1964

Baldick, Robert. *The Duel – A History of Duelling*, New York, Clarkson
Potter, 1965

Billaçois, François. *The Duel – its Rise and Fall in Early Modern France*,
trans. Trista Selous, London, Yale University Press, 1990

Bosquett, Abraham. *The Young Man of Honour's Vade-Mecum*, London,
1817

Bremner, David. *The Industries of Scotland*, Edinburgh, Adam and
Charles Black, 1869

Bryson, John. *Industries of Kirkcaldy and District*, reprinted from the
Fife News, Kirkcaldy, 1872

Buchan, George. *Remarks on the Late Trial of David Landale Esq. for the Killing of Mr Morgan in a Duel*, Edinburgh, John Lindsay & Co., 1826

Burleigh, JHS. *A Church History of Scotland*, London, Oxford University Press, 1960

Cameron, Alan. *Bank of Scotland 1695–1995 – a Very Singular Institution*, Edinburgh, Mainstream Publishing Co., 1995

Campbell, AJ. *Fife Shopkeepers and Traders, 1820–1870*, vol III, held at Kirkcaldy Library

Churchill, Winston. *A History of the English-Speaking Peoples*, vol IV, London, Cassell, 2003

Cockburn, Henry. *Memorials of his Time*, ed. Karl Miller, Chicago, University of Chicago Press, 1974

Cohen, Richard. *By the Sword*, London, Macmillan, 2002

Conrad, Joseph. *A Set of Six*, first published 1906, republished Pennsylvania, Wildside Press, 1995

De Massi, Coustard. *The History of Duelling in All Continents*, London, 1880

Douglas, William. *Duelling Days in the Army*, London, Ward & Downey, 1887

Durie, Alastair. *The Scottish Linen Industry in the 18th Century*, Edinburgh, John Donald, 1979

Fraser, George MacDonald. *Flashman*, London, HarperCollins, 1999

Frevert, Ute. *Men of Honour – a Social and Cultural History of the Duel*, Cambridge, Polity Press, 1995

Gregg, Pauline. *A Social and Economic History of Britain*, London, Harrap, 1973

Hague, William. *William Pitt the Younger*, London, HarperCollins, 2004

Halliday, Hugh. *Murder among Gentlemen: a History of Duelling in Canada*, Toronto, Robin Brass Studio, 1999

Hamilton, Joseph. *The Code of Honour as Approved by Several Gentlemen of Rank*, Dublin, 1824

Hamilton, Joseph. *The Only Approved Guide through all Stages of a Quarrel*, Dublin & Liverpool, 1829

Holland, Barbara. *Gentlemen's Blood – a History of Duelling from Swords at Dawn to Pistols at Dusk*, New York, Bloomsbury, 2003

Kelly, James. *'That Damn'd Thing Called Honour' – Duelling in Ireland 1570–1860*, Cork, Cork University Press, 1995

Kiernan, VG. *The Duel in European History – Honour and the Reign of Aristocracy*, Oxford. Oxford University Press, 1989

Lockhart, John. *Kirkcaldy 1838–1938 – a Century of Progress*, Edinburgh, the Allen Lithographic Co. Ltd, 1939

Maupassant, Guy de. *The Coward*, extract cited in *The History of Duelling* by Robert Baldick, p190–92

McAleer, Kevin. *Dueling: the Cult of Honor in Fin-de-siecle Germany*, Princeton, Princeton University Press, 1994

Millingen, John Gideon. *The History of Duelling*, two vols., London, Richard Bentley, 1841, republished Elibron Classics, 2004

O'Brian, Patrick. *HMS Surprise*, London, HarperCollins, 1996.

'Patriot, A Christian'. *Reflections on duelling*, Dublin, 1823

Pigot & Co. *New Commercial Directory of Scotland*, London, 1825/26

Pushkin, Alexander. *Eugene Onegin*, trans. James E Falen, Oxford, Oxford University Press, 1998

Raikes, Thomas. *The Journal of Thomas Raikes*, vols. 1 & 2, London, 1858

Rogers, Samuel. *Recollections of the Table Talk of Samuel Rogers*, London, The Richards Press Ltd, 1952

Rush, Philip. *The Book of Duels*, George Harrap & Co., 1964

Sabine, Lorenzo. *Notes of Duels and Duelling*, Boston, Crosby Nichols & Co., 1855.

Simpson Ross, Ian. *The Life of Adam Smith*, Oxford, Clarendon Press, 1995

Stanton, Lieutenant Samuel. *The Principles of Duelling*, London, 1790

Steinmetz, Andrew. *The Romance of Duelling in All Times and Countries*,

2 vols., London, 1868, republished by Richmond Publishing Co., 1971

Stevens, William Oliver. *Pistols at Ten Paces – the Story of the Code of Honor in America*, Boston, Houghton Mifflin Co, 1940

'Traveller, A'. *The Art of Duelling*, London, 1836, republished by Richmond Publishing Co., 1971

Truman, Major Ben C. *The Field of Honour, being a complete and comprehensive history of duelling in all countries*, New York, Fords, Howard and Hulpert, 1884

Waugh, Evelyn. *Officers and Gentlemen*, London, Penguin, 1955

West, Sir Algernon. *Recollections 1832–1836*, vol. 1, London, 1899

Wilson, John Lyde. *The Code of Honor or rules for the government of principals and seconds in duelling*, 1838

Journal/ Magazine Articles

Andrews, Donna T. *'The code of honor and its critics: the opposition to duelling in England, 1700–1850'*, *Social History 5*, No. 3, 1980

Holland, Barbara. *'Bang! Bang! You're Dead'*, *Smithsonian Magazine*, October 1997

MacNiven, Ian. *'Banker and Customer: a quarrel and its sequel'*, *Scottish Bankers*, vol. XLVII, No. 186, pp. 102–08, August 1955

Mead, Anne. *'Pistols at Dawn'*, *Scots Magazine*, August 1995

    'The Last Duel. A three-page account of the duel not published, author's private papers

    'An Affair of Honour', another account of the duel, not published, author's private papers

Morgan, Richard. *'George Morgan 1754–1829 and the origin of the Morgans in Kirkcaldy'*, private paper, March 2002

Morgan, Richard. *'David and George Morgan, Agents of the Bank of Scotland in Kirkcaldy'*, private paper, April 2004

Simpson, Antony. 'Dandelions on the Field of Honour: Duelling, the Middle Classes, and the Law in Nineteenth-Century England', Criminal Justice History, vol. 9, 1988

Index